The Occasional Meditations of Mary Rich, Countess of Warwick

MEDIEVAL AND RENAISSANCE
TEXTS AND STUDIES

VOLUME 363

The Occasional Meditations of Mary Rich, Countess of Warwick

Raymond A. Anselment

ACMRS
(Arizona Center for Medieval and Renaissance Studies)
Tempe, Arizona
2009

© Copyright 2009
Arizona Board of Regents for Arizona State University

Library of Congress Cataloging-in-Publication Data

Warwick, Mary Rich, Countess of, 1625-1678.
 The occasional meditations of Mary Rich, Countess of Warwick / [edited by] Raymond A. Anselment.
   p. cm. -- (Medieval and Renaissance texts and studies ; v. 363)
 Includes bibliographical references and index.
 ISBN 978-0-86698-411-9 (alk. paper)
 1. Warwick, Mary Rich, Countess of, 1625-1678. I. Anselment, Raymond A. II. Arizona Center for Medieval and Renaissance Studies. III. Title.
 DA447.W3W37 2009
 942.4'8706092--dc22
 [B]
                                                            2009039472

Front Cover:
The line engraving by Robert White is from the frontispiece in Anthony Walker's *Eureka, Eureka* (1678).

∞
This book is made to last.
It is set in Adobe Caslon Pro,
smyth-sewn and printed on acid-free paper
to library specifications.
Printed in the United States of America

For Sam Pickering

Contents

	Folio	Page
Preface		*xiii*
Introduction		1
Occasional Meditations		41
Upon desiring my docter to give me a potion	3r	41
Upon my takeing a great deale of paines to make a fire	7r	42
Upon a cage of canary birdes that hung up in my closet	11r	43
Upon walkeing a good longe walke in a garden to gather a rose	15r	44
Upon seeing the sun when I was walkeing	18r	45
Upon seeing a hog lye under an acorn tree	23r	47
Upon being in a great heate after walking	26r	47
Upon calling my little bitch that lay in my closett by the fire	27v	48
Upon seeing a piece of ice very harde in the morneing	30v	48
Upon seeing a fire burn very well	33v	49
Upon seeing a childe when she was wallkeing with me step into a dirty podull	36v	50
Upon my being in a great deale of company	38v	50
Upon seeing one take a great deale of paines to pump a little water	40r	51
Upon seeing a sieve brought and layde under a cock of water	41r	52
Upon seeing when the sun shined upon a diall	42r	52
Upon seeing an empty vessell brought to a fontane	42v	53
Upon seeing a very faire and bewtifull aple	44v	53
Upon a henes flying undauntedly at a kite that came to gett her chikenes	46v	54

Upon seeing a mother watch her childe	48v	54
Upon a very fine gonde [gown]	50v	55
Upon takeing a great deale of paines to take out a spot of ink	52r	55
Upon the diferent goeing out of two candulles	53v	56
Upon seeing a mouse in a plase wher I had sett a great many, seaverall littell, glasses of cordialles	57r	57
Upon lookeing in a lookeing glase in the morneing	59v	58
Upon goeing to walke in a very sereane and sunshine morneing	61v	59
Upon seeing a birde fly very high in the aire	64v	60
Upon a poore womanes deasireing me to give her somthinge to cure a consumption	66r	61
Upon lookeing in a prospective glasse	67v	62
Upon washing out with the helpe of a littell water a great deale of writing	68v	62
Upon being awalkeing and feeleing a few dropes of raine	69v	63
Upon sealeing a lettar	70v	64
Upon lookeing in a very falte [faultie] and flatringe glasse	70v	64
Upon layeng by som burnt endes of wode	72v	65
Upon ones payeng for a house but a littell fine	73v	65
Upon siting in my arbor in the Willdernes at Lees	74v	66
Upon stayeng betwene Chelsy and Lees	76r	67
Upon a begares beging of my Lady Robertes	76v	67
Upon lookeing out of my window at Chelsy	77v	68
Upon observeing the skies for som dayes togeather to promise raine	78v	69
Upon seeing a blind minestur in Chelsy pullpett	79v	70
At Durdones. Upon lookeing into a glasse bee hive	80v	71
Upon plokeing [plucking] a rose and putting it in my bosom	81v	72
Upon seeing a fagote that had a great many littell stikes in it	82v	72
Upon seeing a very devoute persone very meanely clad	84v	73
Upon ones takeing a great deale of paines in washing and scouring an olde pewtare diech [dish]	85v	73

Table of Contents ix

Upon seeing a great blase but instantly goe out	87v	74
Upon a Gloworme	88v	74
Upon observeing at table some with great dealight feed upon a dish that others naushate [nauseate]	89v	75
Upon a kindeled stick of fire being car'ed from one house to another to kindle there new fires	90v	76
Upon ones being reatired for their devotiones	91v	76
Upon laying the fire together	92v	77
Upon wallkeing in Chelsy garden	93v	78
Upon chuseing a patron [pattern] of a fine stofe [stuff]	95v	79
Upon a spot in my gonde [gown]	97v	80
Upon seeing my Lady Anne Baringtones picture	98v	80
Upon observeing a mower	99v	81
Upon observeing in a fielde of corne two eares	101r	81
Upon an aple tree that grew in the high way	102v	82
Upon being very much offended with one of my sarvantes for being dronke	104v	83
Upon my Lady Anne Baringtones childes weaneing	105v	83
Upon walking and being much delighted	107v	84
Upon a hen of my Lady Essex Richs	109r	85
Upon putting some linnets in to the same cage with a canary bird	110v	86
Upon seeing some grond that was dry have great cracks in it	111v	87
Upon observeing a sheepe to bite very close to the earth	112v	87
Upon seeing the sunn shine when it rained	113v	88
Upon coy duckes bringing in many with them	114v	89
Upon letting the fire in my chamber goe allmost quite out for want of care	116r	89
Upon seeing young aples before thay ware ripe lye dead under the tree	117r	90
Upon observeing a snail crepe constantly forward in the walke without turneing backe	118r	91

Upon observeing a snaile that where so ever it crept it left some slime	119r	91
Upon observeing a candle a little before it went out to give a more then ordinary light	120r	92
Upon the sudden putting out of a candle	121r	92
Upon being told that where the rich mines are the grounds about them are barren	122r	93
Upon observeing in the court yard many severall paths towardes the house	123r	94
Upon finding in my selfe a great backwardness to cast up my accountes	124r	94
Upon observeing after a great storme . . . fruit blown doun	126r	95
Upon eating my meate with out salt	127r	96
Upon observeing a mother before she layd her child to sleep kiss it	128r	97
Upon observeing that when a glass was very full it was apt to spill	129r	97
Upon hony combes	130r	98
Upon my haveing many yeares agoe a very dangereous fitt of siknes	131v	99
Upon the filere hedge that grew before the [great] parlor dore	134v	100
Upon a great and fruitfull aple tree that grew before the parlor doore	136r	101
Upon my forgettfullnes to wind upe my watch	137r	102
Upon viewing a map	137v	102
Upon the opinion of some that water that has bene onse heate afterwardes is colder	139r	104
Upon a childes falling into the dirt	139v	104
Upon two persones deportments	140v	105
Upon letting blood	142r	105
Upon ones stealing by a private way in to the house	143r	106
Upon observeing a childes being frited from what it likte	143r	106
Upon blowing of a fire to warme another	144r	107
Upon tasting some drops of citron water	145r	107
Upon seeing it very fair over head but finding it very dirty under feete	146r	108

Table of Contents   xi

Upon observeing . . . a stomakefull child	146v	109
Upon the quenes ballett	148r	110
Upon a birds being kept fast by being onely tyde by one leg	149r	110
Upon a birds when it flew doune being caughte in a snare	150r	111
Upon observeing that every place was the better where the sheep were folded	151r	112
Upon bending a young twig	152r	112
Upon a spoon full of strong orange water	152v	112
Upon my being exsidingly affected with . . . persones who ware in the plague time	154r	113
Upon a doctors cutting and scarifying his sike [sick] patient	155v	114
Upon the pitty I have had for som poore dwarfes I have seen	157v	115
Upon lookeing over a hedge in to a garden	158r	116
Upon the opinion that moules [moles] neaver have their eyes op'ned till just before their deathes	159r	116
Upon a day when the sunn appeared not	159v	117
Upon two fishes	160v	117
Upon a cabinet of my Lady Broghilles	162v	118
Upon a tree in atome [autumn]	163v	119
Upon walkeing in atome [autumn] amongst dead leaves	165v	120
Upon an old broken cabinett of my Lady Lakes	166v	120
Upon the sunns setting in a cloud	168v	121
Upon a piece of sullied gold	169v	122
Upon my haveing but very little windowes for some time in my closett	170v	123
Upon a candles being sett against a wall	171v	123
Upon smelling spice after it had been bruised	172v	123
Upon a birdes hopping from one bough to another and fixing noe where	173v	124
Upon lookeing in to the glass bee hive that is in the garden	174v	124
Upon goeing to visitt a friend	175v	125
Upon lookeing in to a barne	177r	126

Upon a damm that was made to stop water	178r	126
Upon this pasage in the life of Alexander the Great	178v	127
Upon observeing that my coach-horses when I was neare home went much faster	180r	128
Upon my friends begining a journy when the sunn was neare setting	180v	128
Upon observeing that some leaves continued a great deale longer upon the trees then others	182r	129
Upon a sparke of fire	183r	130
Upon an hour glass	184r	131
Upon the skye when it was full of bright stars	185r	131
Upon observeing that as sone as one of the birds that was in my cage began to sing the others that were in it began to doe so too	186r	132
Upon a bird that I have kept alive ten yeares in a cage	187r	132
Upon my Lord Grayes house at Eping	188r	133
Upon the cutting down of the Willderness	190r	134
Upon the Indians being fond of colord beades	192r	134
Upon observeing that a fire made with billets would not burne	192v	135
Upon a dispute with a friend	194r	136
Upon a little boyes reafuseing to lerne his catekism	196r	137
Upon wondering at an unthankefull persone	198v	138
Upon a physicians cureing a most desperate disease	200r	139
Upon a flower that opened it selfe towards the sun	201v	139
Upon a doors being opened to lett in a person of quality	203r	140
Upon drinkeing tea	204v	141
Upon my keapeing in a rome for som time a bird	206v	142
Upon my maides makeing the fire to blaze	209v	143
Upon giveing opium to stupify the person that takes it	211r	143
Upon a bucketts makeing a great noyse when it was lett doune the well	211v	144
Upon a frends giveing me a present	214r	144

Upon one that had offended me	215v	145
Upon seeing a person very patient under very smarting paines	217r	146
Upon leaves that fell from a tree in athome [autumn]	218r	147
Upon beeing in a storme	219r	147
Upon my Lord of Manchestors being at Lees	221r	148
Upon Tom Colemanes haveing sarved my lord for many yeares	221v	149
Upon observeing after a great storme some little sticks faln	223v	150
Upon a great mist that was abroad	225r	151
Upon a great housekeeper	226v	152
Upon seeing as sone as I waked in the morneing upon my beds testor just over my head a fine imbroydered crown	228r	153
Upon a stand in the parke	230r	154
Upon woundes that have been stanched	231r	155
Upon being with a persone that was in labor	232r	155
Upon my Lady Cranbornes haveing one side of hur strouke by the dead pallsy	233v	156
Upon a journy from Lees to Londone	237r	157
Upon the consideration of the different esteem that is put upon an estate onely for life and that which is an inheritance	238r	158
Upon the weeders sweeping	239r	158
Upon goeing to prayers	240v	159
Upon an ill tenante	242v	160
Upon some poore persones waiting without the gate	243v	160
Upon a fathers different caredge in the education of his children	244v	161
Upon a disease called the tarantula	246v	162
Upon my lookeing out of my window at Chellsy upon the Theames	249r	164
Upon workeing	250v	164
Upon a very dusty table that had a very fine carpett over it	252r	165
Upon childrenes being at play in the streetes and falling there afighting	253v	166
Upon drawing of a curtaine	255v	167

Upon deasireing a friend to preserve safe for me some pretious things	257v	168
Upon my often wakeing in a night	259v	168
Upon perswadeing one to take care not to loose their stomake to their meat	260v	169
Upon a persone that had great knowledge and very quick but unsaintifyed parts	262r	170
Upon seeing a silke worme spin	263v	171
Upon my dogs care when hee was a hunting not to loose me	267v	172
Upon a boy that was selldome obedient to his fathers comandes	269v	173

PUBLISHED OCCASIONAL MEDITATIONS

Upon a Damm made to stop the Water	175
Upon the … working of a Bee and a Spider	176
Of my Gardeners chusing fine young thriving Stocks to graft on	177
Upon the lighting many Candles at one	178

Textual Notes: Additions and Deletions	181
Biblical Quotations and Citations	199
Index	207

Preface

The British Library Department of Manuscripts granted permission to publish the occasional meditations of Mary Rich, Countess of Warwick, in its Additional Manuscripts collection. The research and writing of this edition benefited especially from the holdings of this library, the Homer Babbidge Library of the University of Connecticut and its resourceful Interlibrary Division, Yale's Sterling and Beinecke Libraries, and the Society of Genealogists in London.

Besides the early modern scholars cited in the documentation, the edition is indebted to the biblical knowledge of its copyeditor Leslie MacCoull. Ben Brockman shared his understanding of the Book of Common Prayer; and over pots of tea at the British Library, Fred Biggs helped weigh vexing questions of emendation. As she has so many times in the past, my wife Carol offered tactful and incisive comments that once again helped refine initial observations and their expression. I have also been very fortunate to have had several colleagues whose friendships have with time become even more meaningful; this book is dedicated to one of them.

Introduction

Anthony Walker's commemorative life of Mary Rich, Countess of Warwick, published in 1678, the year of her death, includes thirteen "Occasional Meditations upon Sundry Subjects."[1] Four of them are unique to this publication; the rest are among the 182 "Ocasionale Meditationes" the countess wrote in the last fifteen years of her life. While meditations are one of the "modes of piety" that were thought of as "feminine concerns," Rich's occasional meditations are a form of religious devotion that possibly no other contemporary woman developed as distinctly, if not extensively.[2] Many of the meditations written by women focus on scriptural passages or religious topics; others tend toward prayers and

---

[1] Anthony Walker, *Eureka, Eureka. The Virtuous Woman found Her Loss Bewailed, and Character Exemplified in a Sermon Preached at Felsted in Essex, April, 30, 1678* (London, 1678). The earliest of the 182 occasional meditations that have survived are dated 1663 and the last 1677; none is from the years 1664–1666, 1669, or 1674.

[2] Stressing "the practice of piety" in the female culture of the early modern period, Sara Mendelson and Patricia Crawford emphasize "that private godliness and public morality were labelled as feminine concerns, especially towards the end of the seventeenth century" (*Women in Early Modern England 1550–1720* [Oxford: Oxford University Press, 1998], 226). Recent scholarship on women's spirituality tends to focus on devotional poetry and diaries, stressing as well voice and gender; for example, Helen Wilcox, "'My Hart Is Full, My Soul Dos Ouer Flow': Women's Devotional Poetry in Seventeenth-Century England," in *Forging Connections: Women's Poetry from the Renaissance to Romanticism* (San Marino, CA: Huntington Library, 2002), 19–38, and the essays by her and others in collections such as *'This Double Voice': Gendered Writing in Early Modern England*, ed. Danielle Clarke and Elizabeth Clarke (Basingstoke: Macmillan Press Ltd, 2000), and *Write or Be Written: Early Modern Women Poets and Cultural Constraints*, ed. Barbara Smith and Ursula Appelt (Aldershot: Ashgate, 2001). See also below, n. 12. The feminine practice of meditation, however, has not been discussed extensively. In her edition of Elizabeth Egerton's "Loose Papers," Betty S. Travitsky does place Egerton's meditations in "the Protestant meditative tradition," especially 162–65 of *Subordination and Authorship in Early Modern England: The Case of Elizabeth Cavendish Egerton and Her "Loose Papers*," MRTS 208 (Tempe: ACMRS, 1999). Women writers receive no attention in Barbara Kiefer Lewalski's seminal chapter on the meditation in *Protestant Poetics and the Seventeenth-Century Religious Lyric* (Princeton: Princeton University Press, 1979), 147–78. Elaine Hobby considers some women meditators, none of whom writes occasional meditations, in *Virtue of Necessity: English Women's Writing 1649–88* (Ann Arbor:

thanksgivings related to events such as births, illness, and death.[3] In brief, spontaneous responses to daily life, Mary Rich discovers spiritual significance in the commonplace. This sustained body of devotion in the quarto folios of a British Library manuscript gives important dimension to the religious sensibility of an aristocratic woman praised as "the most Illustrious Pattern of Sincere Piety, and Solid Goodness this Age hath produced."[4]

Rich's occasional meditations are a distinctive part of a seventeenth-century tradition associated most significantly with the writing of Bishop Joseph Hall and developed by, among others, her brother Robert Boyle, the noted natural philosopher. Hall's three editions of *Occasional Meditations* (1630, 1631, 1633) and his earlier comments on the form in *The Art of Divine Meditation* (1606) delineate a practice he characterizes as "extemporal and occasioned by outward occurrences offered to the mind";[5] other commentaries further emphasize the sudden, quick, and brief nature of these reflections on the meaning of an event or experience.[6] The essence of the occasional meditation is in the words of Boyle "to

---

University of Michigan Press, 1989); as does Patricia Demers, *Women's Writing in English: Early Modern England* (Toronto: University of Toronto Press, 2005), 99–112.

[3] See, for example, Sarah Davy, *Heaven Realiz'd or The Holy Pleasure of daily intimate Communion with God* (n.p., 1670); An Collins, *Divine Songs and Meditacions*, ed. Sidney Gottlieb, MRTS 161 (Tempe: ACMRS, 1996); *Eliza's Babes: or The Virgin's Offering (1652)*, ed. L. E. Semler (Madison, NJ: Fairleigh Dickinson University Press, 2001); Alice Thornton, *The Autobiography of Mrs. Alice Thornton, of East Newton, Co. York*, ed. Charles Jackson, Publications of the Surtees Society 62 (Durham: Andrews and Co., 1875); Katherine Austen, "Book M," British Library Additional MS. 4454; Mary Carey, "Lady Carey's Meditations, & Poetry," Bodleian Library MS. Rawlins D. 1308; Elizabeth Egerton, Countess of Bridgewater, "Devotional Pieces," British Library MS. Egerton 607, with Travitsky, *Authorship*. Exceptions include several in the Bridgewater and Austen manuscripts as well as in *The Meditations of Lady Elizabeth Delaval Written Between 1662 and 1671*, ed. Douglas G. Greene, Publications of the Surtees Society 190 (Gateshead: Northumberland Press Limited, 1978). The occasional meditations included in *Lady Anne Halkett: Selected Self-Writings*, ed. Suzanne Trill (Ashgate: Aldershot, 2007) are also especially noteworthy. See also below, n. 11.

[4] Walker, *Eureka, Eureka*, title page.

[5] Joseph Hall, *The Art of Divine Meditation*, in *Bishop Joseph Hall and Protestant Meditation in Seventeenth-Century England*, ed. Frank Livingstone Huntley, MRTS 1 (Binghamton: Center for Medieval and Early Renaissance Studies, 1981), 72.

[6] Richard Rogers, *The Practice of Christianitie. Or, An Epitomie of seuen Treatises, penned and published in the yeere 1603* (London, 1618), 262–64; Thomas Taylor, *Meditations From The Creatures*, 3rd ed. (London, 1632); Richard Baxter, *The Saints Everlasting Rest*, 8th ed. (London, 1659), 700, and *A Christian Directory: Or, A Summ of Practical Theologie, and Cases of Conscience*, 2nd ed. (London, 1678), Book One, 257; Isaac Ambrose, *Media: the Middle Things*, 3rd ed., in *Prima, Media, & Ultima: The First, Middle, and Last Things; in Three Treatises* (London, 1657), 219–21; Thomas Watson, *A Christian On the Mount: Or, a teatise [sic] concerning meditation*, in *The Saints Delight* (London,

spiritualize all the Objects and Accidents that occur" to the devout soul. He recognizes, moreover, "not onely a Theological and a Moral, but also a Political, an Oeconomical, or even a Physical use."[7] The objects of creation and acts of providence are, in effect, limited only by the experience and sensitivity of the beholder. The 140 "expressions of... voluntary and sudden thought" Hall published in *Occasional Meditations* range from those inspired by a spider in his window and a bird flying into his room, to a harlot carted away and a coffin covered with flowers. Influenced by Hall's "sweet ejaculations," Lancelot Reynolds found "spirituall and holy use" even in the contents of a urinal and dust on a road.[8] John Flavel's *Husbandry Spiritualized* and Edward Bury's *The Husbandmans Companion*, on the other hand, limit their occasional meditations to the works of God encountered in "natures school," where moles ruining a garden and the gathering of a leek become instructive.[9] Some of the occasional meditative pieces reflect subjects of emblem literature such as snails, ants, and grasshoppers. Many do not move beyond observation and moral consideration, while others tend toward abstraction and prayer. All vary considerably in length. The goal of the occasional meditation, however, remains the same, "our particular observing and improving."[10]

Mary Rich's occasional meditations have a religious and personal immediacy that sets them apart from other works in this tradition. While her manuscript includes meditations on some of the same objects found in Hall's editions—reflections on, for example, a sundial, a glowworm, and a blind man, she avoids his emblematic and homiletic tendency. Rich does not limit herself to a narrow reading of nature or display the weighty learning of later writers. Her contributions to this genre are for the most part linked to the events of Essex and London life and

---

1657), 215–22; John Ball, *A Treatise of Divine Meditation* (London, 1660), 77–85; William Gearing, *The Mount of Holy Meditation: Or a Treatise Shewing the nature and kinds of Meditation*, 2nd ed. (London, 1662), 30–39; George Swinnock, *The Christian-Mans Calling: Or, A Treatise of Making Religion ones Business... The Third and last Part* (London, 1665), 372–90; Edmund Calamy, *The Art of Divine Meditation* (London, 1680), 6–28.

[7] Robert Boyle, "Discourse," in *Occasional Reflections upon Several Svbiects. Whereto is premis'd A Discourse About such kind of Thoughts* (London, 1665), 80, 24. All quotations are from *The Works of Robert Boyle*, ed. Michael Hunter and Edward B. Davis, 14 vols. (London: Pickering & Chatto, 1999–2000), 5:53, 30.

[8] Lancelot Reynolds, *Spiritvall Intervals, Or The Soules Exercise. In Certaine Meditations on sundry objects and occasions* (London, 1641), A7v, a1v.

[9] John Flavel, *Husbandry Spiritualized: Or, The Heavenly Use of Earthly Things* (London, 1669); Edward Bury, *The Husbandmans Companion: Containing One Hundred Occasional Meditations [sic] Reflections and Ejaculations, Especially Suited to Men of that Employment* (London, 1677).

[10] Nathanael Ranew, *Solitude Improved by Divine Meditation... First intended for a Person of Honour, and now published for general Use* (London, 1670), 142.

are occasioned by extemporal responses to her personal experience.[11] The pattern of Rich's meditations is disarmingly simple. They typically end with a prayer to God. The homely quality of her exercises reflects the immediacy of the occasion in a personal voice seldom heard in seventeenth-century occasional meditations. The many pieces she wrote and reread over a period of fifteen years are rich in detail, a significant expression of a deeply religious woman who achieved a distinct sense of self through her piety and writing. In their deceptive simplicity they complement the spirituality of seventeenth-century devotional poetry that also seeks "a personal voice, a subject position for the self from whose perspective the divine is viewed."[12] This first edition of the complete occasional meditations illustrates the achievement.

---

[11] Among the meditations written by women that might be considered occasional, several reflect the immediacy of daily life. See, for example, Egerton's "Vpon occasion of the vnwinding of a skean of Silke" (British Library MS. Egerton 607, 108v–109v), also Travitsky, *Authorship*, 196–97; Delaval's "Upon the sight off a very poor old man at chruch [sic] who was a Roman Catholick" and "Upon the haveing wormes in my gum's and the takeing of them out" (*The Meditations of Lady Elizabeth Delaval*, 76–79). Egerton never uses the term "occasional meditation"; and Margaret Ezell states that Delaval's interest is in "the conventions of romance, of fiction, not of spiritual meditation" ("Elizabeth Delaval's Spiritual Heroine: Thoughts on Redefining Manuscript Texts by Early Women Writers," *English Manuscript Studies 1100–1700* 3 [1992]: 216–37, here 235, 226). Austen does label some of her pieces, which deal mainly with issues in her life, meditations; some resemble the occasional, such as "Upon lending Mr C money" and "Upon my Jewel" ("Book M," 52v–53r, 74v–75v). The significant body of "Ocationall Meditations" and "Obseruations" Anne Halkett wrote are often concerned with important political and personal events that at times may outweigh and are more engaging than the reflections and resolutions. She does, however, acknowledge the influence of Hall and Boyle (Trill, ed., *Lady Anne Halkett*, xxvii and n. 57), and in her own fashion she too, like Rich, is intent upon turning the occasion to a spiritual advantage. "Goeing through the Greene" on a visit to her sick minister—and not any objects she encounters along the way—gives her the time "for many variety of reflections" (169); similarly the unwarranted libel against the minister later "putts mee in Mind" (178) as does "reflecting vpon what occured to mee yesterday" (190).

[12] Helen Wilcox, "'Whom the Lord with love affecteth': Gender and the Religious Poet, 1590–1633," in *'This Double Voice,'* 185–207, here 189. Gender as well as self-representation is increasingly and complexly a central concern, e.g., the other essays in *'This Double Voice,'* especially Elizabeth Clarke, "Ejaculation or Virgin Birth? The Gendering of the Religious Lyric in the Interregnum," 208–29, and those in *Write or Be Written*. Besides the growing number of editions that make available the writing of early modern women, less well-known manuscripts have received attention, especially as a result of the research done by scholars such as Elizabeth Clarke associated with the Perdita Project at Nottingham Trent University. The increasing interest is apparent in the anthology *Early Modern Women's Manuscript Poetry*, ed. Jill Seal Millman and Gillian Wright (Manchester: Manchester University Press, 2005), and the collections of essays, *Early*

I
"This excellent Ladies life"

The life of Mary Rich, Countess of Warwick (1624–1678), is set forth largely by herself in an autobiographical account she began in 1672 entitled "Some Specialties In the life of M Warwicke" and in a lengthy diary beginning 25 July 1666 and ending with the 24 November 1677 entry.[13] Both reflect the tradition of seventeenth-century spiritual remembrances described in the work John Beadle dedicated to her father-in-law Robert Rich, second Earl of Warwick, and his third wife, Eleanor. "It is good to keep an History, a Register, a Diary, an Annales," Beadle advocates, "not onely of the places in which we have lived, but of the mercies that have been bestowed on us, continued to us all our dayes."[14] Beadle encourages all to see in their daily lives the deliverances of a "gracious providence" and to "study seriously the vanity."[15] Mary Rich seems to have heeded the advice of the writer she knew personally,[16] echoing the phrase "gracious providence" and the word "vanity" in her reminiscences of divine benevolence and personal folly. Unlike the diary, however, in which "amongst other things" she recorded "the *dayly frame of her own heart* toward God,"[17] the autobiography is less spiritual and more secular. Together, the works form the basis of a biographical understanding of Mary Rich's self-representation.[18] The religious tenor of their genres and

---

Modern Women's Manuscript Writing: Selected Papers from the Trinity/Trent Colloquium, ed. Victoria E. Burke and Jonathan Gibson (Aldershot: Ashgate, 2004), and *Writings by Early Modern Women*, ed. Peter Beal and Margaret J. M. Ezell, special number of *English Manuscript Studies 1100–1700* 9 (2000).

[13] "Some Specialties In the life of M Warwicke," British Library Additional Manuscript 27357, will be cited in the text by folio number. The five diary manuscripts, British Library Additional Manuscripts 27351–27355, will be cited by the last digit in the manuscript and the folio number, separated by a virgule.

[14] John Beadle, *The Journal or Diary of a Thankful Christian* (London, 1656), 11. Isaac Ambrose had earlier cited the habit of the ancients and his own practice of keeping "Diaries or Day-books of their actions, and out of them to take an account of their lives" (*Media: the Middle Things*, 87). Michael Mascuch states that among "printed handbooks of Christian duty" this is the first "explicit mention" of keeping such written accounts (*Origins of the Individualist Self: Autobiography and Self-Identity in England, 1591–1791* [Stanford: Stanford University Press, 1996], 76).

[15] Beadle, *The Journal or Diary of a Thankful Christian*, 158, 118.

[16] On 7 September 1666 she visited the minister at Barnston. Charlotte Fell Smith states, without documentation, that Beadle's guide for journals and diaries "was one of Mary's favourite books" (*Mary Rich, Countess of Warwick [1625–1678]: Her Family & Friends* [New York: Longmans, Green, and Co, 1901], 201).

[17] Walker, *Eureka, Eureka*, 60.

[18] Each is central to the two significant discussions of the Countess of Warwick's life: Charlotte Fell Smith's *Mary Rich, Countess of Warwick* and Sara Heller Mendelson's

the immediacy of her words show the spirituality of a woman whose meditations answer John Beadle's exhortation to "Labour by faith to see and observe God in all things, . . . upon every spire of grasse, upon every drop of rain."[19]

The thirteenth of fifteen children, Mary was born in Youghal, Ireland on 11 November 1624 to Richard Boyle, first Earl of Cork (1566–1643), and his second wife, Catherine Fenton.[20] Mary remembered her father as "tender" and "Indulgent" (2v); his rise in Ireland from limited means to "one of the greatest men of fortune" (4/59r) she attributes to providence and to divine mercy. In her account Richard Boyle left England in 1588 with only twenty-seven pounds and without any prospect of family inheritance. Through God's favor he amassed an income of twenty thousand pounds a year and acquired the positions of Lord Treasurer and Lord Justice of Ireland (2r-v). History records his climb to wealth and power as that of an ambitious adventurer who exploited the opportunities Ireland of-

---

chapter on Rich in *The Mental World of Stuart Women: Three Studies* (Amherst: University of Massachusetts Press, 1987), 62–115. Both works single out especially the life. Fell Smith values "an accuracy of detail, and so much precision of dates as to make it an extremely valuable document" (159). Mendelson characterizes the life as "a sensitive recollection of the most significant secular incidents" (110). Mendelson has also written the entry on the author in the *Oxford Dictionary of National Biography*, ed. H. C. G. Matthew and Brian Harrison, 61 vols. (Oxford: Oxford University Press, 2004), 46:671–73. For an alternative and somewhat overstated reading of the life and its relationship to the diary—"the diary's trenchant attack on romance's delusive qualities and coercive power" (153)—see Ramona Wray, "[Re]constructing the Past: The Diametric Lives of Mary Rich," in *Betraying Our Selves: Forms of Self-Representation in Early Modern English Texts*, ed. Henk Dragstra et al. (Basingstoke: Macmillan Press Ltd, 2000), 148–65.

[19] Beadle, *The Journal or Diary of a Thankful Christian*, 66–67.

[20] The opening sentence of "Some Specialties" dates her birth "November the 8, 1625, at yohall in Ireland" (2r); her father remembers that his seventh daughter "was borne at yoghall on St Martyns day being the xjth daie of November 1624 and Thursdaie, about three of the clock, in the afternoon" (Richard Boyle, *The Lismore Papers Viz. Autobiographical Notes, Remembrances and Diaries of Sir Richard Boyle, First and 'Great' Earl of Cork*, First Series, 5 vols., ed. Alexander B. Grosart [London: Chiswick Press, 1886], 2:111). Sara Mendelson has found a reference to Mary in a document written in 1625 (*The Mental World of Stuart Women*, 64, 203 n. 7). An indenture signed 1 March 1624/5 ("in the yeare of o^r Lord God accordinge to the computaton of the Church of England 1624" [7r]) states that the earl will provide four thousand pounds for "the La: M. the 7th D. of the Ld E" and any subsequent daughters as a marriage portion (British Library Additional Manuscript 18023, 10v). The detailed recollection of Richard Boyle, including the sign of the zodiac and the names of the godparents, also favors the earlier date. 11 November 1624, St. Martin's day, was in fact a Thursday. Boyle adds, "the signe in Aries: her godfather Sir Charles Mc Chartie of Blarney Knight, and her godmother my sister the Lady Mary Smythe and my cozen An parsons als Lowther, the wife of garrald [=Gerard?] Lowther Esqr" (*The Lismore Papers*, 2:111–12).

fered someone willing to employ questionable means and able to marry well.[21] The second son of Roger and Joan Boyle, Richard Boyle used his connections with patrons, his authority as deputy escheator, and his marriages to the daughters of William Apsley and Sir Geoffrey Fenton to acquire extensive lands in the Irish province of Munster and a rent-roll that increased from four thousand pounds in 1613 to twenty thousand pounds annually by the late 1630s.[22] Boyle became Baron of Youghal in 1616 and Viscount Dungarvan and Earl of Cork in 1620, later settling for a time in the Dorsetshire manor of Stalbridge and attempting to establish himself among English society and its centers of power.[23] For much of his life, Mary would not be near him, having been sent when she was three years old to "be carefully and piously educated" (2v) in the household of Randall Cleyton.[24] Aside from her many regrets in the diary about a later disobedience, the relationship between father and daughter is known only through her autobiography and his "True Remembrances."

Both accounts emphasize Mary's independent nature and willful defiance of her father's wishes. When summoned in 1638 from Lady Anne Cleyton, the woman who had cared for her "as If she had bene an own mother to me" (2v), Mary soon went with her father to Stalbridge, where she met the next year James Hamilton, the son and heir of the first Viscount Clandeboye, James Hamilton, and his third wife, Jane Philipps. As he had for her older sisters, the Earl of Cork had arranged a marriage—this time to Hamilton—beneficial to the family fortunes; unlike her sisters, fourteen-year-old Mary refused to accept the match, "his persone being highly disagreeable to me" (4r). Despite her father's "very high

---

[21] Terence O. Ranger documents the rise of this successful "Irish adventurer" in "Richard Boyle and the Making of an Irish Fortune, 1588–1614," *Irish Historical Studies* 10 (1956–1957): 257–97. Other studies of Boyle's life include Dorothea Townshend, *The Life and Letters of the Great Earl of Cork* (New York: E. P. Dutton and Company, 1904); Nicholas Canny, *The Upstart Earl: A Study of the Social and Mental World of Richard Boyle first Earl of Cork 1566–1643* (Cambridge: Cambridge University Press, 1982).

[22] Ranger, "Richard Boyle and the Making of an Irish Fortune," 257, 262, 275; Canny, *The Upstart Earl*, 6, 154 n. 19.

[23] Boyle first occupied Stalbridge House, "the fifth largest manor house in Dorsetshire," in August 1638, though he purchased the estate in 1636 without having seen it (R. E. W. Maddison, *The Life of the Honourable Robert Boyle F.R.S.* [London: Taylor & Francis Ltd., 1969], 60, 57).

[24] Boyle placed his children at an early age in the care of others. Mary's brother Robert states in his autobiographical *An Account of Philaretus* that their father "had a perfect aversion for their Fondnesse, who use to breed their Children so nice & tenderly, that a hot <Sun>, or a good Showre of Raine as much <endangers them as> if they were made of Butter [or] of Sugar" (*An Account of Philaretus During his Minority*, ed. Michael Hunter, in *Robert Boyle by Himself and His Friends* [London: William Pickering, 1994], 3). Their mother Catherine died on 16 February 1629/30, when Mary would have been five years old (*The Lismore Papers*, 3:18).

displeasure" and, she notes, his attempts to pressure her "extreamely to it," she held to a proviso in the agreement that the marriage would take place only "If we lik'te when we saw one another" (3r). Over the next several months the earl failed to change his daughter's attitude.[25] Withholding a quarterly allowance of twenty-five pounds "for her disobedience in not marrying . . . as I seriously advized her" had no effect.[26]

Mary chose instead to marry for love, disregarding her father's will once again and incurring his great "displeasure" (9r). Her marriage to Charles Rich on 21 July 1641 was in her words the victory of passion over duty and reason: "he did Insensibly steale away my heart" (7v-8r). The second son of the second Earl of Warwick, Charles had none of the financial prospects Richard Boyle required. His deep disapproval failed, however, to lessen her resolve neither to marry Charles without parental consent nor to marry any other suitor. Though Mary Rich describes her response as a "resolute but Ill and horably disobediant answere" (13r, 14v), she remained equally certain at that time that she would be "much more hapy" with Rich's lesser income than she would "with the greatest with out him" (15r). Eventually reconciled, Mary once again displeased her father when she frustrated his plans for a large wedding and married in the Shepperton parish church of St Nicholas without telling her family.[27] Another reconciliation followed, but Mary and Charles Rich nevertheless began married life without much of their seven-thousand-pound marriage portion.[28] For the next sixteen years the Riches lived with Charles's family, often at their Essex estate.

Mary Rich saw this period as a turning point in her life. The second Earl of Warwick, Robert Rich, and his second wife, Susan Halliday, lived in the large country house that had been built by Richard Rich on the five hundred acres ac-

---

[25] She maintained "a very high aversnes . . . although my self and all [my] sons and daughters, the Lo. Barrymore, Arthure J[ones], and all other her beste frends did moste effectually entreat and persuade her thervnto, and I comaund t[oo]" (Boyle, *The Lismore Papers*, 5:116).

[26] Boyle, *The Lismore Papers*, 5:139.

[27] The parish register of St Nicholas, Shepperton, Middlesex, records that "Mr Charles Rich, second son to the Right Hon. Robert Earl of Warwick, and Lady Mary, daughter of the Right Hon. the Earl of Cork, married July 21, 1641" (Daniel Lysons, *An Historical Account of Those Parishes in the County of Middlesex, which Are Not Described in the Environs of London* [London: Cadell and Davies, 1800], 225).

[28] In the last entry of his diary, 29 September 1642, Richard Boyle lists among his debts, "I doe owe to my noble son in lawe, charles Riche, as the remainder of seaven thowsand pownds for my daughter, the Ladie Marye, his wives marriadg portion, much abowt three Thowsand pownds; the payment wherof I doe chardge my son, heir, and executor faithfully (with the beste expedicon he possibly can) iustly to paie and satisfie" (*The Lismore Papers*, 5:232).

quired in the sixteenth century with the dissolution of the monasteries.[29] Here Mary encountered the religious spirit the earl fostered in a household that entertained "many emenent and exselent Deavines" (16v) and welcomed ministers who sought the support denied them elsewhere.[30] When she later poured out her soul to God in formal meditation, Rich often praised the benevolent providence that guided her to a religious family "where I was incouraged in piety and where I had good meanes for my Soule" (3/155r). The five years the couple lived with the earl and his second wife and the eleven years spent in the company of his third wife, Eleanor, the widowed Countess of Sussex, were not, however, entirely years of prayer.

As Mary Rich settled into married life at Leighs and in London, a willful struggle with God replaced that with her father. The first years of her marriage were, according to her remembrance, years of vanity. More specifically, she later mourned the "low and sinfull estate" and "naturall estate" writers of journals and diaries admitted about their lives before their "age in Christ,"[31] a life she recalls of "mispending my preatious time in reading romances and in seeing and reading playes, and in dressing and adorneing my vile body and in lookeing in Glasses to sett my selfe out with the neaglekte of my immortall Soul" (2/256v). The fear that she would lose her only child, Charles, born on 28 September 1643, touched her deeply. Earlier the loss of her year-old daughter Elizabeth in the second year of marriage had "much affected" both parents, but when their four-year-old son

---

[29] Leighs was also spelled Lees, Leez, and Leeze. Located on the river Ter, Leighs Priory became a grand family seat: "It was all built of brick, and consisted of two Courts, an outer, and an inner one; the latter of which, towards the gardens, was faced of freestone, or stone-mortar." Pond-Park, the area surrounding the house, consisted of some 400 acres; a similar sized park lay beyond this, and a third "called Little or Littley Park" with a circumference of some four miles (Philip Morant, *The History and Antiquities of the County of Essex*, 2 vols. [London: T. Osborne, 1768], 2:101). Descriptions of the estate, its ruins, and subsequent twentieth-century restoration include: A. W. Clapham, "The Augustinian Priory of Little Leez and the Mansion of Leez Priory," *Essex Archaeological Society Transactions*, n.s. 13 (1915): 200–17; Charlotte Fell Smith, "Leez Priory, Essex, the Seat of Mr. M. E. Hughes-Hughes," *Country Life* 35, no. 900 (4 April, 1914): 486–93; Herbert Gardner Burghclere et al., *An Inventory of the Historical Monuments in Essex*, 4 vols. (London: His Majesty's Stationery Office, 1916–1923), 2:158–61; Huon Mallalieu, "Delicious Leez," *Country Life* 183, no. 34 (24 August 1989): 77.

[30] Clarendon observes that the Earl of Warwick was "looked upon as the greatest patron of the puritans," "opening his doors, and making his house the rendezvous of all the silenced ministers," and "spending a good part of his estate" (Edward Hyde, first Earl of Clarendon, *The History of the Rebellion and Civil Wars in England*, ed. William Warburton, 7 vols. [Oxford: Oxford University Press, 1849], 1:256, 2:598). See also Barbara Donagan, "The Clerical Patronage of Robert Rich, Second Earl of Warwick, 1619–1642," *Proceedings of the American Philosophical Society* 120 (1976): 388–419.

[31] Beadle, *The Journal or Diary of a Thankful Christian*, 156, 152, 48.

became gravely ill, the mother apparently suffered a spiritual crisis. Certain that the boy's illness was punishment for her backsliding, Mary Rich promised in prayer to "become a new Creature" (19v) if his life were spared. When young Charles regained his health, she began to fulfill the bargain by returning from London to Leighs.

The account of the newfound spiritual fulfillment Rich attributes to "converting grace" follows the format John Beadle advocates in *The Journal or Diary of a Thankful Christian*: "Let every man keep a strict account of his effectuall calling, and of his age in Christ; and (if it may be) set down the time when, the place where, and the person by whom he was converted."[32] "Gracious providence" brought the ministry of Anthony Walker, the Earl of Warwick's household chaplain, who became for her "a kind of a spirituall father" (22r). Through the goodness of God, Rich writes, and with Walker's guidance, she saw the emptiness of secular London life; his encouragement and that of her sister Katherine Jones, Viscountess Ranelagh, helped her develop a spiritual joy. The Bible and religious works replaced "Idlle bookes," and a new preoccupation with "reading[,] meditation and prayur" (24r) structured a daily life noteworthy for its zealousness. Concern about her salvation led Rich to the wooden dell beyond the garden walls and stone bridge over the river Ter known as the Wilderness, where throughout the remainder of her life, whenever possible, she spent long hours in meditative retreat. She no longer sought former company, preferring to associate with "holy and strikte deavines." "I was," Rich confesses, "so much changed to my selfe that I hardly knew my selfe" (25r).

The nature of this spiritual transformation eludes denominational labels. The conversion episode in Mary Rich's autobiography stresses that earlier she had been "stedfastly set against being a Puritan" (23r). The Earl of Warwick's parliamentary sympathies and support of dissenting ministers suggest that she subsequently embraced the beliefs that characterize her as a Puritan.[33] The minister, Anthony Walker, who played so significant a role in her conversion had remained, however, within the established church. In the biography that complements his sermon on the death of the Countess of Warwick, Walker affirms that the woman he knew for many years "*regularly, devoutly*, observed all the orders of the Church of *England*, in its Liturgy and publick Service, which she failed not to attend twice a day with exemplary Reverence."[34] His further statements about her mistrust of "Ritual Observances," refusal to wear any cosmetics ("neither paint nor patch"), and reluctance to waste time in recreational games

---

[32] Beadle, *The Journal or Diary of a Thankful Christian*, 48.

[33] See, for example, Lawrence Stone's characterization in *The Family, Sex and Marriage in England 1500–1800* (New York: Harper & Row, 1977), 210–11.

[34] Walker, *Eureka, Eureka*, 72–73. Mendelson characterizes Mary as both "a good Puritan" and "a conforming Anglican" who "displayed a latitudinarian fellowship with the local clergy of almost all denominations" (*The Mental World of Stuart Women*, 84, 85).

might suggest a puritanical disposition,[35] though the ministers with whom she associated were remarkably diverse. These included the Archbishop of Canterbury, Gilbert Sheldon, and the bishop of London, Henfrey Henchman, as well as many Nonconformists such as Henry Wilkinson and Martin Holbech. Authors of favorite books encompass a range of theological positions from that of the Latitudinarian Simon Patrick to that of the Puritan John Janeway. Besides the numerous preachers at Leighs, Rich notes among those in London, Edward Stillingfleet and Gilbert Burnet. More than most, the dissenting divine Richard Baxter played an important part in her spiritual life. Mary Rich heard and summarized some of his sermons, owned a number of his works, and read his often-published *The Saints Everlasting Rest*.[36] Baxter was also a frequent visitor whose religious conversations Rich valued highly. While she recorded Stillingfleet's caution against the belief "that the Covenante of Grace was an unconditionle covenante as If nothing ware to be done by us in order to our salvation" (4/113r), another sermon by Thomas Woodrooffe she summarizes stressed the "holy calling not according to our workes but according unto his own purpose and grace" (5/146v). At the core of her devotion remained the conviction that salvation was possible only through Christ and faith, not her own righteousness. She hoped and at times believed that her name was chosen from among thousands and written in the Book of Life (1/28v; 2/102r, 116r). In a secluded and inward world, Rich contemplated this mercy and faith, but the course of her next years drew her away from an absolute commitment to pious devotion.

The deaths of Mary's father-in-law and his first son, Robert, altered her life significantly. In recording the Earl of Warwick's death on 19 April 1658, Rich mourned the loss of the kind, amiable man who had become her father. Warwick's death also marked the end of the sixteen married years that she claims "I constantly lived with him" (28r). Much of this time Charles Rich and his wife presumably fulfilled the social obligations of a second son and undistinguished member of parliament, but the autobiography reveals little about these years. When the Earl of Warwick died, the title and the Essex estates went to his first son, Robert, and the life at Leighs that had meant so much to Mary Rich ended. A year later, 30 May 1659, Robert died without a male heir, leaving the title and possession of Leighs to Charles, who became the fourth Earl of Warwick. With the death came the responsibility of raising her brother-in-law's three daughters, Anne, Mary, and Essex. Rich insists that she never wanted to become Countess of Warwick, having married for love and not position. She accepted the unanticipated inheritance "with much disturbance and feare least by have-

---

[35] Walker, *Eureka, Eureka*, 73, 58. In *The Restoration Church of England, 1646–1689* (New Haven: Yale University Press, 1991), John Spurr observes, "The private piety of the Restoration elite often contained (or perhaps retained) more than a hint of the plain puritanical devotions of an earlier generation of godly gentry" (367).

[36] Between 1650 and 1688 twelve editions were published.

ing a more plentifull estate I might be drawne to love the Glory of the world too well" (29r-v). Rich returned to Leighs, she avers, "with a deasigne to indeaver to glorefy God what I could" (29v).

The Essex estate and its Wilderness solitude offered limited refuge from the London life she lived as the Countess of Warwick and a member of the Boyle family. Mary Rich depicts herself as a woman drawn against her will into the circles of prominence and power. Within a year of assuming his title, her husband had been among those chosen to approach Charles II about the restoration of the monarchy. He was also now a member of the House of Lords, though he did not play an important part in government.[37] The Riches maintained residences in London, including a rented place in Chelsea, where she entertained guests such as Lord Chancellor Edward Hyde, first Earl of Clarendon. Mary dined as well at Whitehall with her deceased sister-in-law Anne's husband, the Lord Chamberlain Edward Montagu, second Earl of Manchester.[38] She writes that she was also well received at court and often visited Charles II's wife, Queen Catherine. The relationship with the future monarch's first wife, Anne Hyde, Duchess of York, seems to have been quite close.[39] Rich's commentary on this world of power and its many social duties reflects her care to avoid becoming consumed by them. After dining with the lord chamberlain and waiting on the queen and duchess, she assured herself that retirement and divine worship were all the more desirable than the bejeweled court splendor (1/127r, 160r). After a Whitehall feast in the Banqueting House, she wrote that the trumpets reminded her of heavenly ones, prompting thoughts about the vanity of glory (1/78v-79r). News while dining at Clarendon House that the king had demanded the seals of Chancellor Hyde's office led to similar musing about uncertain glory (1/112r), which later became "a loude sarmon" against trust in fortune (1/134v).

Even without the distractions and obligations that disturbed her religious devotions, Mary Rich struggled with profound family crises. Four years after Charles inherited the Warwick title, the Riches' son, Charles, became gravely ill with smallpox at their residence in Lincoln's Inn Field. Mary sent his wife, Anne, home to her father, her nieces back to Leighs, and her husband to Lady Ranelagh's. Alone she cared for her twenty-year-old son until he died on 16 May

---

[37] He was one of six peers from the House of Lords who along with twelve members of Commons presented "the humble invitation and supplication of the parliament, that his majesty would be pleased to return, and take the government of the kingdom into his hands" (Clarendon, *The History of the Rebellion*, 6:259–60).

[38] Anne, the second wife of the earl, had died in 1642; their daughter Anne married Robert Rich, second Earl of Holland and fifth Earl of Warwick (Ian J. Gentles, "Edward Montagu, second earl of Manchester," in *ODNB*, 38:702–8).

[39] The Boyle and Hyde families were linked by marriage. Anne, the oldest daughter of Edward Hyde, first Earl of Clarendon, was the sister of Laurence Hyde, who was married to Henrietta Boyle, the daughter of Mary Rich's brother Richard, first Earl of Burlington.

1664. At the news her husband "Cryed out so terably that his cry was herd a great way" (31v). The bereaved mother herself attempted to relieve her grief with the conventional religious solace that Charles had died well, "makeing so good and sober an end" (31r). She struggled with the guilt common to grieving by accepting his death as just punishment for her transgressions, and she tried to lessen the pain of her loss with the hope that God intended some benefit in her suffering. But the anguish is apparent: "I loved him at a rate (that If my heart do not deceave me) I could with all the willingnes in the world have dyde ether for him, or with him, (If God had seene it fitt)" (31v). After her son's death, Mary sought the waters of Epsom and Tonbridge to relieve the physical pain of heartache and had her husband sell the house in Lincoln's Inn Field. She could never bear to reenter it. Annual commemorations on the day of Charles's death reveal that for years she could not ease the sense that her sins had caused his death.

The failure to have another child compounded both loss and guilt. In a disclosure quite remarkable for a seventeenth-century wife, Mary Rich attributes her infertility to divine punishment for a sin earlier in her marriage. She had decided against a larger family when, after the birth of two children, she feared the loss of her attractiveness. Her husband added the further worry that additional children would burden the limited estate of a second son. When the Riches hoped that at the age of thirty-eight she could bear another child, Mary believed sin and not age was the reason they failed. God made their suffering incurable because they had earlier tried to circumvent his will. Her only consolation was the faith that God would provide in an eternal dwelling "a name bettar then that of Sonnes and Daughters" (34v). The "dreadfull" affliction of Charles's death became for Rich also a "saintefide" affliction "that I might take up with God alone for my happynes" (1/86r).

The protracted infirmity and death of her husband intensified the personal and spiritual conflict that drew her closer to God. Bouts of ague and affliction from the stone were not as debilitating as the attacks of gout that left her husband Charles unable to use his limbs, feed himself, or turn without help in his bed (35r). An October 1664 letter from Charles Lyttelton in the Hatton correspondence attests to the crippling debilitation that caused "such a weakenesse in his limbes" that Charles lies "continually tormented" and "never stirrs but on crutches when he is at the best ease."[40] Sleepless nights of constant attendance at Charles's bedside, Mary Rich writes, sapped her energy, distracted her from prayer, and prevented her going to church. The months and years of care, especially when her husband "wolde not sofur me to be long from my attendance

---

[40] *Correspondence of the Family of Hatton*, ed. Edward Maunde Thompson, Camden Society, n.s. 22 (London: Camden Society, 1878), 40. A 5 March 1666 letter to Robert Boyle mentions the relief Charles Rich found from the stroking of Valentine Greatrakes, "the Stroker" (*The Correspondence of Robert Boyle, 1636–1691*, ed. Michael Hunter et al., 6 vols. [London: Pickering & Chatto, 2001], 3:86).

upon him" (1/104v), appear to have taken their toll emotionally and physically. "Violent" reprimanding of her nieces and severe headaches followed confrontations with her husband. As Charles's condition worsened and his ill temper grew, Rich's references to her melancholy spirit also increased. His "bittar and provokeing expressions," she reports, occurred suddenly and inexplicably. The language continues much the same: her husband "without any cause given by me fell into a great and sudden passion" (1/177r). On one occasion the failure of workmen to complete repairs on Warwick House led to violent cursing; on another, he reacted passionately to news of his brother Hatton's grave sickness. The frustration and despondency from crippling pain and long periods of confinement were obvious as well to Anthony Walker. His epistle prefaced to the sermon preached at the fourth Earl of Warwick's funeral tactfully alludes to the "other effects" the countess suffered when the afflictions of gout became so unbearable that her husband "was sometimes less kind to you and others, than his Natural Temper."[41] Mary Rich did not accept his behavior easily. She admitted the folly of often falling into dispute with her husband and the difficulty of curbing her temper. A particularly contentious argument over an unknown issue reveals the extent of the discord and her strong-willed yet vulnerable nature: "I was confident I was in the right, but he in the dispute growing violently pationate I still inconsideratly held on the dispute, which made him in his passion breake forth and c[urse] most bitterly" (2/184r). That night in asking God's forgiveness Mary Rich resolved to avoid further conflict. The next day she broke her resolution in another passionate disagreement over "lawfull and nessessary busines." She often struggled to contain herself, leaving her husband's presence when she feared she would retort or uttering rejoinders when none could hear.

Rich says she endured his unpredictable moods with greater patience; however, she could never remain silent in matters of salvation. Often her one-sided and long discourses about the need to control passion, avoid swearing, and accept God's will end with the tag "God was pleased to make him with patience heare me" (1/119r) or "he seemed affected" (2/26r), though she is forced to admit that her husband was not always pleased to listen to her. He reacted vehemently to an after-dinner lecture about the care of his soul, was equally upset about her encouragement to attend church services, and forbade further talk about repentance or his "everlasting Concernment" (3/59r). When "in very great passion" this bitter, incapacitated man would hear no more about the need to cease his outbursts against God, she adds, "I Instantly held my tongue, but it was a grief to me" (3/133v). Her numerous prayers and admonitions testify to a deep worry about his spiritual well-being. Though Mary Rich seems unsympathetic and unduly judgmental when she bemoans her husband's unwillingness to suffer "with

---

[41] Anthony Walker, *Leez Lachrymans. Sive Comitis Warwici Justa: A Sermon, Delivered at the Funeral of the Right Honourable Charles, Earl of Warwick, Baron Rich of Leez* (London, 1673), A2v.

that submission to Godes will as I thought he ought to doe" (2/10r), more often her husband's suffering "much affected" her heart (1/293r) and prompted tearful prayers asking God to show him mercy and forgiveness. As Charles worsened, his wife increasingly mourned his sins, weeping for his offenses and praying for his repentance.

The worry about her husband's health and soul once again drew Mary Rich closer to God. In more despondent moments when she concluded, "It was much bettar for me to dye then to live," the contemplation of heaven was "reviving and comfortable" (2/99r). God also raised her depressed spirits with "soule ravishing Comfort" (3/137v). The desire to be "absent from the body that I might be present with the Lord" (3/143v) and the longing to be dissolved with the biblical bridegroom reflect the consoling faith of the Song of Solomon that "I was my belovedes, and my beloved was mine" (2/50v). The tendency to refer to both Charles and God as her lord underscores the turn from her husband toward divine love. Oppressed and troubled by "great unkindness" and "what I sett my heart too much upon" (3/113r; 3/56v), Rich renewed her commitment to God and assured herself of "hapyness in the Creator" (3/56v). Though concern about Charles's soul never lessened, the burden of tending to a suffering and intemperate husband eased with the hope that after the crosses she had endured "from what I loved best" her Lord "would make me to take up with him above for my felicity" (3/188r).

The final months and the last days of Charles's life were an emotional period of such intense conflict that it appears more than ever to have frightened and depressed his wife, who grieved for his deteriorating health and pleaded for his salvation. Charles's outbursts against both God and his wife became from her point of view more passionate and embittered than she could ever recall. He forbade his wife to speak about salvation and attacked her in the presence of others. Incessant, even haranguing spiritual counsel must have exacerbated the bitterness of long suffering, prolonged pain, and fear of imminent death. Mary's growing references to melancholy underline her own depressed spirit. Also revealing is her statement two weeks before her husband's death that she would soon be "freed" from her afflictions, a statement she then emended "by my death" (3/203r). The end of his life in her account is unusually graphic, yet for her it is paradoxically terrifying and consoling. Neither the best medical attention nor her prayers prevented the rattle in his throat and loss of speech, the lapse of reason and inability to recognize others, and the convulsions that so horribly distorted his face.[42] Four days before his death, in her account, God restored her husband's reason, and he attended patiently to his wife. "This day," she reassured herself, "my Lord sayd many kind things to me and sayd he wold make me amends" (3/210r). Though her emaciated, enfeebled husband never completely regained his facul-

---

[42] In a marginal comment on the 12 August diary entry, William Woodrooffe wrote, "I saw him ab^t ye stables; . . . he look'd like Death" (3/206r).

ties, Mary Rich states that hours before his death on 24 August 1673 he heard her cries to lift his heart toward God and replied, "so I doe, so I doe, and called upon me to pray for him" (3/214v). His death within hours left his wife bereft. She took solace in the belief that he had died well and in the "inward comfort that I had done my duty to him" (3/215v).

In the grief-stricken days following her husband's death, Rich prayed that God would "keepe my heart close to him in my widow condition" and that he would "make upe this deare relation . . . by being unto me all in all" (3/216v, 222r). Several weeks later she found consolation in the love of her maker to whom she had "espoused" her soul and from whom "nothing could separate" (3/224r, 224v). The acceptance of Christ as her new spouse follows the Pauline counsel in the epistle to Timothy, which encourages widows to trust in God and continue "in supplications and prayers night and day" (1 Timothy 5:5). A well-established tradition in the seventeenth century advocated that the widow should "learne to cast her whole loue and deuotion on him," emulating the pious devotion of the biblical Anna, Judith, and Naomi.[43] For Rich this commitment was unreserved. Two years after her husband died she vowed again to give her heart completely to God, this time in a cryptic statement about the folly of trusting those from whom she had expected happiness and comfort. When Mary observed the anniversary of her husband's death, a day of fast, prayer, and meditation, absent are any tender memories. Instead, she regretted having caused him to offend God in their disputes, and she was sorry that the estates in her control had not been a better means of divine glory (4/52r-v; 5/177r-v). Each of the two anniversaries Rich describes was an occasion for humbling herself, a sinful creature who deserved to suffer the loss of her husband. The litany of sins rehearsed in meditative solitude is part of a familiar exercise. When on the second anniversary her thoughts turned to her husband's sickness and death, she noted only that the recollection filled her with admiration for God, who is the focus of the anniversaries.

The anxiety and desire to be close to God also became a focus of her widowhood. In the solitude of the Wilderness and a garden in Chelsea, Rich increasingly lamented her lack of zealous commitment to the glory of God, her failure to improve the talents she has been given, and her waste of precious time. Rich also followed the spiritual directive in *The Journal or Diary of a Thankful Christian* to "Look often into this Journall, and read it over," using the diary she kept not only to recall gifts of divine mercy but to realize how far she had wandered from her former spirituality.[44] Though Rich regrets the folly and vanity of her

---

[43] T. E. [Thomas Edgar(?)], *The Lawes Resolvtions of Womens Rights: Or, The Lawes Provision for Woemen* (London, 1632), 232. See, in particular, Raymond A. Anselment, "Katherine Austen and the Widow's Might," *Journal for Early Modern Cultural Studies* 5 (2005): 5–25, here 13.

[44] Beadle, *Journal or Diary of a Thankful Christian*, 102. Beadle also advises, "be thankfull for all Gods mercies; otherwise, why do you keep such a Journall?" (140).

youth, she also recalls fondly the period after her conversion and its sense of divine fulfillment. A new and emphatic attention to backsliding accentuates the spiritual sloth, dullness, and barrenness now part of her frequent litany of sins. The emphasis on unworthiness, though seemingly formulaic, is perhaps also part of the spiritual self-examination and humility common in contemporary treatises on repentance.[45] Divine discourses in this solitude reflect the delight and solace, comfort and communion, of "the sweet refreshing hours I had formerly injoyed" (4/42r, 80v, 123r, 136v, 179v).

Mary Rich's inclination toward retreat did not mean that she could not engage the secular world. The Earl of Warwick's will had given the estates for life to his wife, an act that she attributes to God and providence. Before Rich assumed the legal responsibilities enjoined by her role as executrix, she completed negotiations for the marriages of her nieces Mary and Essex. When against all her advice Essex broke off a match, her upset aunt, perhaps recalling her own, resolved to let the young woman determine her own good. The countess continued, however, to vet prospective suitors until Essex agreed to accept one that met her aunt's approval. Rich's persistence and skill are also apparent in negotiating her husband's trusts, fulfilling the stipulations of his will, and discharging his debts. With the help of a relative, both houses of parliament authorized a bill for sale of lands to clear the earl's debts (4/84r).[46] Rich also sought the advice of Lord Chief Justice Matthew Hale about the legal right to family livings and relied often upon the legal and financial counsel of another relation, Francis Boteler. When on 16 October 1676 Rich had fulfilled her last duties as executrix, she thanked God that she had discharged her obligations without "any dispute" and that she could now devote the rest of her time to divine service (5/25r-v).

In her final years social discourse provided another expression of a life devoted to piety and charity. Besides many conversations with ministers who were visitors at Leighs and in London, Rich had "Christian conference" with a number of family members and neighboring acquaintances. Other than the attempts

---

[45] Francis Fuller, *A Treatise of Faith and Repentance* (London, 1685), 88–89; Christopher Blackwood, *A Treatise Concerning Repentance, Wherein also, The Doctrine of Restitution Is handled at large* (London, 1653), 5–6. See also the self-abasement of Elizabeth, Viscountess Mordaunt, *The Private Diarie of Elizabeth, Viscountess Mordaunt* (Duncairn, 1856), 121.

[46] On 12 November 1675 Rich observed in the House of Lords the progress of a bill first read in Commons on 26 October "to enable a Sale of Lands for Payment of the Debts and Performance of the Trusts of *Charles* late Earl of *Warwick*, deceased" (4/84r; *Journals of the House of Commons*, 9:363). On 9 November the bill was brought to the House of Lords, reported out of committee on the twelfth, passed without amendment on the seventeenth, and received royal assent on the twenty-second (*Journals of the House of Lords, Beginning Anno Vicesimo-septimo Caroli Secundi, 1675*, 12:14, 20, 25, 34; see also Fell Smith, *Mary Rich, Countess of Warwick*, 294).

to console Lady Essex at the death of her mother-in-law, Elizabeth Finch, and to reconcile Sir Richard Everard and his son Richard, the nature of such conference remains uncertain. Seventeenth-century commentaries on the "fruitful edifying Speech," "mutual exhortings and comfortings," and "heavenly discourse" essential to Christian conference suggest an obligation to praise God and communicate the fulfillment of a holy life.[47] Rich's communion with others presumably imparted the warmth she felt in prayer and meditation, thereby kindling "flames of holy love" within herself. "When we blow the fire to warm another," Baxter emphasizes in his directions for Christian conference, "both the exercise, and the fire warm our selves."[48]

Discourse and conference are implicitly part of Rich's understanding of charity. Her summary of a sermon by Baxter defines charity as "dayly doeing good In those stationes G had plaste us in" (4/110r). Another sermon by George Gifford, which she summarized, describes the obligation to be generous in aiding the needy and the "desire to make our relations and friendes good" (4/98v). The help Mary Rich extended to ministers, families in distress, widows, orphans, and neighboring poor is among the "considerable acts of charity" that afforded her pleasure and satisfaction. Anthony Walker reckons she gave away a third of her own wealth: "as her love to God was the soul of her Religion, so the exuberancy of her charity towards those who needed her abundant liberality, was the conspicuous Crown which beautified all her sweetness, and goodness towards Men."[49] Rich also practiced charity in other ways. She encouraged her niece Mary St John "to make a good use of Godes afflicting hand" (4/12r) after her child died, sharing her experiences of divine support. Rich comforted and counseled the husband of Frances Everard and an Atwood sister for their losses, exhorted sick neighbors to repent and embrace God, and moved an injured man to tears and a promise to live a better life. Among those Rich tried to reform, including a nephew, were a number of servants, whom she reproved for their transgressions and exhorted to seek God's mercy. Occasionally she had the satisfaction of noting that they seemed affected, even moved to tears, and that others, including neighbors, came to her for guidance. One of the last entries in the diary, nevertheless, includes among her shortcomings the failure to use well the estate God had given, "which I might have imployed more of In doeing good to my fellow Christianes" (5/216v).

While the severity of the self-judgment is characteristic of Mary Rich's previous religious exercises in self-reproach, the humility and sense of incompleteness may also reflect a growing awareness of her impending death. The loss of

---

[47] Baxter, "Special Directions for Christian Conference, Exhortation, and Reproof," in *A Christian Directory*, Book Four, 83–88; Robert Leighton, *A Practical Commentary upon the First Epistle General of St. Peter* (London, 1694), 412–13.

[48] Baxter, *A Christian Directory*, Book Four, 84.

[49] Walker, *Eureka, Eureka*, 99, 97.

others often prompted Rich to reflect on her own death, thoughts very common in the last months of her husband's illness; but the tendency in widowhood to dwell on this subject seems more immediate and personal. Rich returned to the past in birthday meditations, spent hours rereading the diary, emphasized her backsliding, and underscored her unworthiness. Together with the noticeable insistence upon the vanity of unsatisfying life, these and other meditative hours on the Last Judgment and the joys of heaven give new urgency to her "cry to G to be found In him not haveing my own righteousnes but his, and that I might now lay hold upon eternal life" (5/123v). The contemplation of eternity does not, however, dwell on the fear of hell. In the hope of future glory, she prayed instead that she would be prepared for death. Mary Rich, Countess of Warwick, died at Leighs on 12 April 1678 as she sat in a chair at prayer with one of her attending ministers; she was buried on April 30 at the Felsted church, Holy Cross.[50]

The "Virtuous Woman" Anthony Walker celebrates in the life he enlarged from the Felsted sermon eulogizes the Countess of Warwick as an unrivalled "example of *Heroick Virtue*, of *Generous Piety*, of *sincere, humble, unaffected, serious, fruitful Religion*."[51] Anne Woodrooffe, another close friend, mourns the eclipse of this "shining light." "Never did I meet with any that had so much piety accompanied with so much Sweetness of Nature, *in Her lips was ye law of kindness*."[52] Both Walker and Woodrooffe recall from personal experience a compassionate, charitable woman who spent hours in meditative solitude. Walker's long work in particular further testifies to the religious devotion evident in the many prayers, Scripture readings, sermons, Sabbath and communion services integral to her life. His personal memories also corroborate the sense Rich conveys of herself in the autobiography and diary of someone who strove to become "*complete in Christ*, all of a piece,"[53] despite the afflictions and attractions of the world.

---

[50] Walker, *Eureka, Eureka*, 116–17. The Leighs estate went to Robert Montagu, third Earl of Manchester (bap. 1634-d. 1683), the son of Charles Rich's oldest sister, Anne. The Essex holding was sold in the eighteenth century to the Duke of Buckingham. His half-brother in turn sold it to the governors of Guy's Hospital, who had the mansion razed, leaving only the gatehouse and minor buildings (see above, n. 29). Robert Rich, the son of Henry Rich, first Earl of Holland, gained Warwick House along with the title Earl of Warwick. "The Heirs, or Representatives," of Charles Rich's sisters Anne, Frances, and Lucy and his nieces Anne Barrington, Mary St John, and Essex Finch got the bulk of the estate (Morant, *The History and Antiquities Of the County of Essex*, 2:102–3).

[51] Walker, *Eureka, Eureka*, 41.

[52] William Woodrooffe, "A Copy of what my good Mother wrote upon ye Death of Lady Warwick," British Library Additional Manuscript 27357, 42r (alluding to Proverbs 31:26). Anne was the wife of Thomas Woodrooffe, the chaplain of Mary and Charles Rich.

[53] Walker, *Eureka, Eureka*, 69.

II

"Concerning Meditation Extemporal"

The quartos entitled "Ocasionale Meditationes made by M Warwicke" are the distinctive contribution of Mary Rich to a genre identified in the seventeenth century with Bishop Joseph Hall and explored in the works of three authors she knew personally. Rich probably had seen at the very least one of the several editions of Hall's *Occasional Meditations*, and she was well acquainted with Nathanael Ranew, Richard Baxter, and Robert Boyle. Ranew, the former minister at Felsted, was the recipient of a lifetime stipend from the second Earl of Warwick and was among the clergy welcomed at the nearby Leighs estate. There he undoubtedly discussed the nature of meditation with the earl's daughter-in-law Mary, who was the "Person of Honour" for whom he wrote the lengthy discourse published in 1670 as *Solitude Improved by Divine Meditation*. Rich often met as well with the Nonconformist divine Richard Baxter, whose conversations and sermons she valued. Among the works of Baxter she read, the fourth part of *The Saints Everlasting Rest* is an important Protestant work on meditation.[54] And she was often in the company of her brother Robert and would have been familiar with the "Discourse Touching Occasional Meditations" in his 1665 publication *Occasional Reflections Upon Several Svbiects*. Boyle acknowledges the importance of Joseph Hall's *Occasional Meditations* and the bishop's earlier comments on the form in *The Art of Divine Meditation*. He proposes, however, further consideration of the nature and usefulness of reflective thinking.[55] Boyle's significant commentary on the occasional meditation and those he himself wrote over a number of years are an important contribution to the occasional pieces that he claims "considerable Persons have been of late induc'd" to write, though none of these is named.[56] Mary Rich would have had many opportunities to discuss firsthand the nature and practice of an increasingly well-established form.

Occasional meditations are by their nature dependent upon the tradition of meditation in general. Contemporary commentaries, including Ranew's, point out that the Psalms call meditation a form of prayer, a collocation seen in the

---

[54] Lewalski, *Protestant Poetics*, 166. In *The Poetry of Meditation: A Study in English Religious Literature of the Seventeenth Century*, rev. ed. (New Haven: Yale University Press, 1962), Louis L. Martz considers this work "the greatest of all the native English treatises on meditation" (332), a judgment John Booty echoes in "Joseph Hall, *The Arte of Divine Meditation*, and Anglican Spirituality," in *The Roots of the Modern Christian Tradition*, intro. Jean Leclercq and ed. Ellen Rozanne Elder, *The Spirituality of Western Christendom* 2 (Kalamazoo, MI: Cistercian Publications Inc., 1984), 202.

[55] Boyle, "Preface," *Occasional Reflections*, 5:16–17.

[56] Boyle, "Preface," *Occasional Reflections*, 5:20.

same Hebrew word for both prayer and meditation.[57] Among religious duties, meditating is often listed after reading the Scriptures and before praying.[58] For Bishop Hall and later commentators the essence of meditation is discourse: "The heart must speak to God that God may speak to it."[59] The "*deep and earnest musing*" and the "searchings and ponderings" that engage the understanding, memory, and will are thought of as inseparable from colloquy.[60] "By Meditation," Richard Sibbes observes, "the soule prieth into the soule, and with a reciprocall judgement, examineth her selfe, and every faculty thereof."[61] In Richard Baxter's summary, the successful meditation moves from "Truths received and remembered, into warm affection, raised resolution, and holy and upright conversation."[62] Toward this end, James Ussher advises in a manual for meditation, which Mary Rich may have read, that meditators need not worry about the language: "look what thy heart speaks to this point."[63] Outpouring of the heart is an expression of the Holy Ghost and a manifestation of grace. "Meditation is the tongue of the soul, and the language of our spirit."[64] It is the heart's pleading with God that ends in rest only after the meditator has "pleaded thy *heart* from *Earth* to *Heaven*; from conversing below, to a walking with God."[65]

Bishop Hall's 1606 treatise on the art of meditation, which he defines as "nothing else but a bending of the mind upon some spiritual object, through divers

---

[57] Ranew, *Solitude Improved by Divine Meditation*, 17, 128; Gearing, *The Mount of Holy Meditation*, 6; William Bridge, *Christ and the Covenant, the Work and Way of Meditation* (London, 1667), 422–23; Calamy, *The Art of Divine Meditation*, 3.

[58] The biblical figure most commonly cited as a model is David; Christ's mother, Mary, who pondered in her heart the significance of her son (Luke 2:19), and Enoch, who was thought to meditate as he walked with God (Genesis 5:24), are also singled out, as are Isaac, the first to have meditated (Genesis 24:63), Solomon, and Joshua. See, among others, Hall, *The Art of Divine Meditation*, 73, 80, 82; Ranew, *Solitude Improved by Divine Meditation*, 28, 82; Bury, *The Husbandmans Companion*, A3v.

[59] Hall, *The Art of Divine Meditation*, 85.

[60] Ambrose, *Media: the Middle Things*, 216; Ranew, *Solitude Improved by Divine Meditation*, 100.

[61] Richard Sibbes, *Divine Meditations and Holy Contemplations* (London, 1638), A5v-6r.

[62] Baxter, *The Saints Everlasting Rest*, 696.

[63] James Ussher, *A Method for Meditation: Or, A Manuall of Divine Duties, fit for every Christians Practice* (London, 1651), 35–36. The Irish primate was, according to Gilbert Burnet, "very particularly the Friend of the whole Family" ("A Sermon at the Funeral of the Honourable Robert Boyle," in *Robert Boyle by Himself and His Friends*, ed. Hunter, 47).

[64] Jeremy Taylor, "Of Meditation," in *The Whole Works of the Right Rev. Jeremy Taylor, D.D.*, ed. Reginald Heber and rev. Charles Page Eden, 10 vols. (London: Longman et al., 1848–1865), 2:143.

[65] Baxter, *The Saints Everlasting Rest*, 776.

forms of discourse," distinguishes two kinds. The meditative conversation "must needs be either extemporal and occasioned by outward occurrences offered to the mind; or deliberate and wrought out of our own heart."[66] Others labeled the two categories extemporal, occasional, ejaculatory, or sudden and set, solemn, or deliberate.[67] Form, duration, and place are essential to the distinction. Solemn meditations deliberate at length upon set subjects that are often biblical and theological, the "matters in divinity" which in Hall's list include Christ's passion and redeeming love, sin and election, and the four last things—death, judgment, heaven, and hell.[68] Solemn meditation tends to follow a formal pattern of analysis and application, striving to move the heart or affections in devotion. Occasional meditations are shorter and more spontaneous. Richard Baxter points out they differ from deliberate meditations as "short ejaculation" and discourse do from "set prayer" and sermons.[69] Boyle and Ranew see them as "short Flights Heaven-wards" and the soul's quick darting to heaven.[70] Occasional meditations are also free from the constraints of time and place that limit deliberate meditations. Isaac and David, among other biblical figures, offer precedents for solemn meditating either in the morning or the evening; and most commentators state their preference for the best time, though they leave the choice of hours to the individual as long as a set period of meditation is observed daily. Fields, gardens, chambers, or other solitary places of retirement are also requisite. There meditators can emulate Isaac, who walked while he meditated; Christ, who withdrew into a garden; or David, who preferred the isolation of his room.[71] The other form of meditation is by its nature simply extemporal; it is, in the words of some commentaries, a parenthesis in the midst of daily business, a moment when the mind is moved to thoughts about God.[72]

---

[66] Hall, *The Art of Divine Meditation*, 72.

[67] For example, Rogers, *The Practice of Christianitie*, 262, 264–65; Ambrose, *Media: the Middle Things*, 216–17; Watson, *A Christian On the Mount*, 215, 222; Ball, *A Treatise of Divine Meditation*, 77; Thomas Gouge, *Christian Directions Shewing How to walk with GOD All the Day long* (London, 1661), 37–38; Gearing, *The Mount of Holy Meditation*, 30, 39; Calamy, *The Art of Divine Meditation*, 6.

[68] Hall, *The Art of Divine Meditation*, 84.

[69] Baxter, *The Saints Everlasting Rest*, 700; *A Christian Directory*, Book One, 257.

[70] Boyle, "Discourse," 5:25; Ranew, *Solitude Improved by Divine Meditation*, 9. Ranew also emphasizes the soul's and heart's mounting through the wings of meditation toward heaven (51) as does, among others, Richard Rogers, *Seaven Treatises Containing such direction as Is Gathered ovt of the Holie Scriptvres* (London, 1604), 258.

[71] Genesis 24:63, John 18:1, Psalm 63:6. Hall, *The Art of Divine Meditation*, 77, 80, 81, 82; Ussher, *A Method for Meditation*, 28–29, 44; Ranew, *Solitude Improved by Divine Meditation*, 98, 126, 342–43; Rogers, *The Practice of Christianitie*, 279–80; Baxter, *The Saints Everlasting Rest*, 707; Ambrose, *Media: the Middle Things*, 217–18.

[72] Baxter, *The Saints Everlasting Rest*, 700; Calamy, *The Art of Divine Meditation*, 18; Thomas White, *A Method and Instructions for the Art of Divine Meditation, with Instances of the several Kindes of Solemne Meditation*, 2nd ed. (London, 1672), 14.

No subject is too slight and all objects are useful; the words and works of God, the course of providence and daily life, and the commonplaces of individual experience are all suited to the "quick *interposings* of good and holy thoughts."[73] Though Robert Boyle specifically includes reflections on the political world and the fate of governments, he enthusiastically declares that for the occasional meditator "the whole World would be a Pulpit, every Creature turn a Preacher, and almost every Accident suggest an Use of Instruction, Reproof, or Exhortation."[74] At the same time, he and others heed Hall's caution about "farfetched" meditations that strain the relationship between circumstance and application. The occasion must give rise to the theme and not be itself the focus.[75] The distinction between the ant and the bee is fundamental: the ant is a gatherer and the bee a transformer. The industrious bee that turns the sweetness from various flowers into nourishing honey becomes in contemporary works symbolic of the meditator who transforms the figurative flowers of existence into a "Celestial sweetness."[76] Meditations can, Boyle believes, turn nature into a teacher of ethics and divinity.[77]

The rules governing this transformation are inexact. Bishop Hall offers no guidelines, pointing out the diversity of both the occasions and the responses. Later writers are similarly reluctant to propose a single method. The premium is on substance rather than expression. Edward Bury dismisses those who might criticize his meditations by arguing that they were written to improve the lives of others, "not to make them speak better." Thomas White advocates in his instructions a plain, easily understood style.[78] Each of these writers follows the lead of Mary Rich's brother Robert Boyle, who contends that piety rather than wit should be the goal of extemporaneous expression.[79] Written meditations, of course, by their nature were not spontaneous; Rich spent entire mornings or afternoons writing them and sometimes revised her first thoughts. Even then, for most writers the simplicity in emblematic expression leads to a moralistic, if not a spiritual, conclusion.

The opportunity to "dress" the soul in the mirror of experience is for many the art of seeing, turning the "Eye of Reason" both inward and upward. Also common among metaphors is Jacob's ladder, which at the bottom rests on earth

---

[73] Baxter, *The Saints Everlasting Rest*, 700–1; Ranew, *Solitude Improved by Divine Meditation*, 142–43, 205.

[74] Boyle, "Discourse," 5:53.

[75] Hall, *The Art of Divine Meditation*, 74; Boyle, "Discourse," 5:30.

[76] Boyle, "Discourse," 5:28, and Ranew, *Solitude Improved by Divine Meditation*, 29; also Bury, *The Husbandmans Companion*, A3r; White, *A Method and Instructions for the Art of Divine Meditation*, 78–79; Taylor, *Meditations From The Creatures*, 24.

[77] Boyle, "Discourse," 5:28.

[78] Bury, *The Husbandmans Companion*, A1r; White, *A Method and Instructions for the Art of Divine Meditation*, 45.

[79] Boyle, "Discourse," 5:31.

and at the top touches heaven. "When we Meditate with the Mind," Ranew contends, the affections and heart are themselves warmed, kindled, and inflamed: "as the Head acts, the Heart glows."[80] Mary Rich's occasional meditations, however, are better characterized by the "way of Thinking" her brother Robert advocates, a mode that distinguishes occasional from formal meditations. Diary entries about lengthy spiritual exercises in the solitude of her Wilderness retreat or in the privacy of her closet briefly recount visions, for example, of the Church Triumphant when God carried her to the vistas of heaven or when contemplation of the Last Judgment put her in "an extrordnary awakened frame" (4/69r). These and other formal meditative experiences often consumed Rich with "ravishing" thoughts and joys, moved her to unrestrained tears of yearning for divine love, and left her heart "much transported." In her occasional meditations, Rich reflects piously on many experiences that touch her less emotionally. Reflective rather than affective, they reveal the goal of meditative thinking her brother advocates: to spiritualize experience, to see "That *all things work together for good to them that love God* (Rom. 8.28)."[81]

Mary Rich's responses to her son Charles's death further show the difference between her formal and occasional meditative practice. On the anniversary of her son's death, 16 May, she fasted, prayed, formally meditated, and performed other acts of devotion and charity. The account of the 1668 observance, for example, refers to "large meditationes" on Charles's sickness and final hours. Pondering his death and her joy at his contrition for his sins moved her heart to praise God for the solace of her son's final reconciliation. Thoughts of her own death followed as she asked God to prepare her also for her final hours and enable her to offer a contrite heart. Before she retired to her room, where she reread her son's funeral sermon, Rich states she also pleaded for the merciful salvation of her husband's soul (1/188r-v). In other meditative commemorations she accepts the justice of God's taking an only son as punishment for her transgressions. With tearful self-castigation and with litanies of sin, Rich sought the humility and shame of a penitent mourner. By the last of these soul-humbling days she struggled with the realization that hers was still a stony heart even though twice during the day God moved her to sighs and tears as she condemned herself and bemoaned not only her sins but those of the nation.

Unlike the strong emotions of these formal commemorations, Mary Rich's single occasional meditation on Charles's death is reflective and instructive, prompted by her husband's orders to prune back the Wilderness. Despite her pleas to leave untouched "this sweet place" of solitude she had enjoyed for over twenty years, the work went ahead. In the meditation the loss of this retreat parallels the loss of her son: although Rich had begged God to spare the twenty-year-old who had grown to her "unspeakable satisfaction," her divine Lord cut him down in

---

[80] Ranew, *Solitude Improved by Divine Meditation*, 49, 50.
[81] Boyle, "Discourse," 5:52, 53.

death so that he might have new life. From this consolation Rich turns again to God for help in avoiding unseemly attachments in a mutable world. Her prayers beseech God to give her comfort in the faith that her son will flourish anew in heaven and to help her remember that she will join him soon. There is on Mary Rich's part no speculation or suspicion about her husband's motives for cutting the Wilderness and none of the soul-searching and tearful self-criticism characteristic of the formal meditations' emphasis on sin and failure.

In their creative turn of mind the occasional meditations draw religious conclusions that tend toward statements of purpose and resolution. The series on the making or maintaining of a fire illustrates the essential difference from the more formal exercises. The neglected fire in her chamber rekindled with a piece of wood, when turned to "spiritual advantage" (below, 90), reminds Rich of her failure to keep the dying fire of divine love burning through "short ejaculations" to heaven. She prays that God will "sanctify" her meditation, making her more receptive to heavenly warmth, and that he will cause the fire in her heart to burn more intensely. Where her brother Robert's reflection on the difficulties of making a fire verges on abstract discourse about the relationship between lesser and necessary religious practices as well as different degrees of affections,[82] Mary sees in fire the essence of her spirituality. The flame that blazes only after much blowing is a metaphor for devotion inflamed by meditation from sparks covered in the embers of her corruption (below, 42). The fire symbolizes the devout soul she strives to embody. Burnt sticks used to kindle fires and flames that blaze without the help of bellows figuratively describe means of meditative discourse and fulfillment (below, 65, 77). The warming that comes from the effort of blowing on a slow fire to warm someone in the room and the sight of a maid blowing sparks into a flame are emblematic of the devotion and love reborn through conference with others (below, 107, 143). Likewise the burning stick brought to kindle a fire in another house (below, 76) recalls that the presence of a religious person inspires devotion in others. Rich does not experience in any of these meditations the transcendent love symbolized by the figurative fires. Rather she implores God to inflame this heavenly fire in her heart through the kindling of meditation and prayer, and she beseeches him to make her a means of inflaming the hearts of others.

Though the occasional meditations focus on the yearning rather than on the realization, they have a unique vividness. With the exception of those by her brother Robert, many of the published meditations are occasional only to the extent that they are based upon sight, hearing, or report; the context is usually little more than a statement of time or place. Rich's occasional meditations tend to reflect her experiences rather than a series of objects often common to emblem books. Some meditations are based on specific people and places familiar to the

---

[82] Boyle, "Reflection II. Upon his making of a Fire," in *Occasional Reflections*, 5:85.

diary; others seem very much a part of her daily life. She sees the beggar who cries out with joy upon receiving a small sum of money outside the gate of her husband's cousin Letitia Robartes. She watches the boat on the Thames from her window at Chelsea and considers the cabinet of her sister-in-law, Lady Broghill. Meditations occasioned by the poor woman who comes to Mary Rich, hoping for a cure for her consumption, or by the dazzling display at the queen's ballet weave a texture of immediate life. The caged canaries come to her attention when her servant feeds them; the ice she stamps on in the morning melts during the day. The descriptions of nature as she walks in her woodland retreat particularly reflect the unusual spontaneity of her associative process. Rich's encounter with the snail, an emblem common to the period, is typical.[83] Her contemplation of its slow progress when she comes upon the snail twice during her walk emerges naturally from her world.

Traditional and untraditional meditative objects such as the lark or the glow-worm, the empty vessel by the fountain, the sieve placed under the pump's spout, and the pump itself seem images from actual experience and reveal a heightened awareness of detail. Threatening weather during a morning walk prompts meditation on the radiance of God's countenance shining suddenly in a vale of tears. Rich describes at considerable length her reluctance to continue in the darkening gloom for fear of getting caught in the rain and her reactions to the dazzling sun that appeared momentarily, disappeared, and then reappeared. She then relates in equal detail the journey of her "disconsolate soule." When on another morning the light from the fire in her chamber shining through the curtains drawn about her bed illuminates the crown embroidered on the canopy, her thoughts turn to awakening after death and the hope of a heavenly crown. Throughout, the occasional meditations convey the vividness of daily life. The dog that ignores her calls, content to lie by the fire until she leaves the room, runs about the house searching for her and jumps with happiness when it has found its mistress. A hen raised by her niece Essex later returns each day to lay an egg and receives a new straw-lined nest, not as reward but as encouragement to lay more. A mouse scurrying about threatens to knock over and break delicate cordial glasses until caught in a trap, the cheese still held in its mouth. The daughter of her niece Anne Barrington reacts fretfully to the bitter substance placed during weaning on the nurse's breast, unquieted by even the most enticing of foods.

Images of children and their behavior typify Mary Rich's singular sensitivity to detail and language. The child that falls in the dirt and cries to his parents resembles the children of God who plead to be washed in the fountain of Judah and the blood of Christ. In her yearning for God's fatherly love, Rich develops

---

[83] See Hall, "XXIX Upon the Sight of Two Snails," in *Occasional Meditations*, 139; Bury, "Med. 71 Upon a snail," in *The Husbandmans Companion*, 333–37; and the emblematic significance of the snail, for example, in Randolph L. Wadsworth, Jr., "On 'The Snayl' by Richard Lovelace," *Modern Language Review* 65 (1970): 750–60.

the child-parent relationship fundamental to Christianity. Though the spiritual meaning is paramount, she does not sacrifice the literal for the figurative. The irritable child in Bishop Hall's meditation is in hers the "stomakefull child" whose refusal to admit his fault and beg his father's pardon after being whipped provokes the irate parent to beat him even more severely (below, 109).[84] The "untorde childe" who deliberately walks in a puddle she could have easily sidestepped provokes her irritation. Boys who lose track of time, fail to return to their studies, and begin to fight with each other need a father's severe reprimand to send them back to their lessons. When parents bring her their little boy who refuses to learn his catechism, Mary Rich becomes a stern, forbidding woman who fares no better with the active, stubborn child. Only the sound of thunder brings him running. Between the frightening claps, the boy quickly returns to his play; and when assured that God has finished thundering, he simply runs away.

The delightful vignette of the severe mistress and her reluctant pupil has a personal, almost ironic dimension. During one of the stays at her Chelsea residence, Rich heard a sermon preached by a blind minister. The diary entry for 6 July 1667 notes that afterwards she "had much good discourse" (1/101v) with him and expected the nieces in her charge to repeat the sermon's principal points. The brief meditation on this encounter later adds that she overcame her surprised and troubled response to his appearance in the pulpit and realized in conversing with him that he was both pious and happy (below, 70). Such personal revelation appears neither in the diary nor in two earlier seventeenth-century meditations on blindness. The sight of a blind man cautiously making his way prompts Joseph Hall to reflect that blindness has forced the man to trust in the guidance of others; Lancelot Reynolds observes that the idleness of a blind man increases his misery since it disposes him to vice. Both meditations focus on the spiritual significance: Hall asks God to save him from spiritual blindness, and Reynolds beseeches God to remove the film from his eyes so that he may see divine mercy and weep tears of contrition.[85] Rich develops this theme by drawing a distinction between outward and inward blindness, but she places herself in the discourse. Pity for the minister's blindness proves sentimental and self-indulgent; gratitude for her sight teaches that she may be more blind than he. Rather than abject self-abasement common in the diary, Rich's tone is closer to the wryness of her response to her physician when ill: "being asked by him how I then felte my selfe, I answered, ill, and began to make moveing complaintes of my distempered and pained body. Which made him then conclude I began to mend" (below, 99–100).

A personal voice is also unmistakable in the few meditations about her husband. Aside from that occasioned by the cutting of her Wilderness retreat, none refers explicitly to their relationship; nor do any consider his death. Her husband

---

[84] Hall, "XCVIII Upon a Child Crying," in *Occasional Meditations*, 176–77.
[85] Hall, "LVII Upon the Sight of a Blind Man," in *Occasional Meditations*, 152; Reynolds, "XXVIII. Upon a blinde idle man," in *Spiritvall Intervals*, 107–8.

is, however, undoubtedly the subject of the 1673 meditation "Upon a dispute with a friend." Hurt and grief are palpable in its description of "cruell and despitefull wordes, he speakeing like the pierceing of a sorde [sword] and saying all he could that he fansed would displease and disoblidge me" (below, 136). Strikingly similar is the description of her husband's tirade in a 27 July 1673 dispute: "he then broke out of a soden to speake like the pierceing of a sword to me" (3/198r). The diary records that the confrontation left Mary Rich despondent, and in the next days she asked God for patience and consulted trustworthy intimates for advice. In "heart-humbling meditation" she sought comfort in answering evil with good and bore this "otherwise insupportable burthen" by beseeching God to transform her suffering into sorrow for her sins. God is also, not surprisingly, the source of solace in the meditation upon "this pious lady" forced to limit her devotions by her husband's demands. Similar entries in the diary suggest that she is the unidentified lady, one who resolves to choose suitable times of devotion that will allow her to "pay my duty to my husband" (below, 77). Each of these meditations is perhaps an attempt to distance as well as conceal painful domestic struggles. Specific references to Charles are absent possibly because Mary Rich quite simply had no need to reconsider all she set forth at length in the diary. The same may be said of her husband's death, though her response to the bleeding of a stanched wound might well be about the grief that re-emerges "by veiwing new persones or nearely related persones to him whose removall from me by death has so often made me against all my resolutiones breake forth in to disquieting patiomes" (below, 155).[86]

In the pious affirmations of these and other occasional pieces, both voice and context personalize the religious experience. Reactions to the plague show the distinctiveness. In Bishop Hall's meditation "Upon the Red Cross on a Door" the sign of the pestilence reminds him of the blood the Israelites sprinkled on their lintels, ensigns brought into battle, and the cross of Christ. The tag at the end of a series of witty inversions concludes with the hope that God will withdraw his divine vengeance.[87] Elizabeth Delaval's meditation on the London plague of 1665 is less rhetorical though still impersonal. "Wo is me; how can a Christian now refraine from sheding plenty of tear's day by day."[88] Mary Rich, on the other hand, moves beyond the sign and the door to ponder the fate of the wives and mothers quarantined within, shunned by their neighbors and left alone

---

[86] The quartos of both the occasional meditations and the diary are missing for 1674, the period in which she may have dealt more immediately with her grief. Those for 1675 include the brief recognition that death taking "from me my husband hast made me, as it ware, halfe dead" (157).

[87] Hall, *Occasional Meditations*, 161.

[88] Delaval, "Meditations writ upon the continuance of the plague," in *The Meditations of Lady Elizabeth Delaval*, 91–92. See also Katherine Austen's response to "these multitudes of people y^t are took away dayly," "Book M," 87r-88r.

with dead husbands and children. When her thoughts turn to a consideration of those who must live with spiritually dead husbands or children, the specific reference to "my relations" is thinly veiled (below, 113–14). Compassion and empathy also distinguish her reaction to "som poore dwarfes." Hall's response to the sight of a dwarf is limited to the didactic as he ruminates upon spiritual stature.[89] Rich's reaction is first pity and then self-recognition. Her meditation too ends with Matthew 6:27, but she recognizes her own failure "to have grown in grace and to have added one cubitt" (below, 115). Another meditation on the whetting of a scythe similarly adds a unique personal note. Hall begins his meditation by comparing recreation to the sharpening of a scythe, develops the necessity of sharpness in laboring, and concludes, "I would so interchange that I neither be dull with work nor idle and wanton with recreation."[90] After an encounter with mowers while walking in her garden, Rich writes that their whetting of a scythe reminds her of the need for "lawfull recreationes" suited to her temperament. She beseeches God, however, never to allow her to use these recreations except when she finds "an absolute necessity" to complete with renewed vigor her spiritual labors. Rich would be "so good a housewife of my time" (below, 81) that not a precious moment would be wasted unduly in recreation.

As God's handmaiden, Mary Rich knows that her duty entails more than the charity she describes in the diary. The occasional meditations implore God to make her an instrument of his glory through her life and conversation, a source of the light that continues to pervade her language and faith. She aims to be like the glowworm and in the midst of her darkest moments inspire others with a Christian fortitude and grace. With a cheerful heart and a serene mind, Rich would show the goodness of her heavenly father and draw others to similar service, to enkindle fire in the hearts of the unregenerate. The meditation on the small flame brought to a neighbor's house reflects the Christian conference central to her spiritual life: "by often speakeing all good of thee and of thy wayes" (below, 76) Rich strives to return souls to God. A thoughtful meditation on the windows in her closet shows considerable tolerance, however, for those who fail to see the spiritual light with her clarity and ends with the plea to be a means of imparting her faith to them (below, 123). Among the subjects of the last occasional meditations is the desire to be illuminated in mind and heart with the celestial fire that will move others to burn with the fire of "trew zeale" for God's glory.

Many of the meditations also extol the spiritual value derived from the example and conversation of others. Fire commonly illustrates the distinction between welcome and distracting company. Flames that burn only as long as the sticks remain together are fires of devotion fueled through religious discourse with "thy saintes here upon earth" (below, 50). Her maid's blowing a fire into a blaze suggests the Christian conference that melts the frozen heart (below, 143).

---

[89] Hall, "CXXXVII Upon the Sight of a Dwarf," in *Occasional Meditations*, 196.
[90] Hall, "CXXXI Upon the Whetting of a Scythe," in *Occasional Meditations*, 193.

The warmth and vitality of holy conversations matter more to Mary Rich than social class: shavings and chips kindle billets of wood into flames, and "lower and meaner parts" are at times preferable to "more raised and refined ones" (below, 135). On several occasions Rich contrasts worthy guests with unwelcome company. The candle that leaves a smudge on the wall is reminiscent of superficial talk that intensifies the desire for holy conversation with God-fearing companions. The chatter of the glib and flattering resembles the flawed mirror that distorts her image; the good and honest create a true reflection of her need for spiritual nourishment (below, 64). Rich draws a similar illustration from the linnets she placed in a cage with her canary (below, 86). The birds who imitate the canary parallel the influence of company, leading Rich to decry the profane and derisive language of undesirable companions and to delight in the beneficial discourse of pious acquaintances.

Those who are welcome share the faith and joy of the spiritually reborn. The unregenerate, Rich contends, are caught up in immediate pleasure. Like the natives of the new world smitten by trinkets and colored beads, they give away too much—pearls of inestimable worth—for tinsel trappings (below, 134–35). For them the Sabbath and the duties of the Lord are burdensome. Blind to their sinfulness, they are pharisaical in their haughty pride. The spiritually reborn, in contrast, know that they are unworthy of God's mercy, and they willingly accept his ordinances and joyfully serve him. Where others are driven by fear, they are drawn by love. The distinction is basic to seventeenth-century definitions of legal and evangelical repentance.[91] The comfort of the gospels and "the melting considerations of Gods great free and disinterested love" bring sorrow and repentance (below, 99). Those who never move beyond the letter of the law and the fear of punishment are not truly contrite, Rich concludes, because they do not mourn the dishonoring of God. The tears they may shed are not the penitential tears of the "more happy Christianes" (below, 65). The meditations further distinguish between evangelical disciples and professors of religion, those devoted to religious formalities and gestures belied by the emptiness of their hearts. The meditation on a storm-torn tree includes among these superficial believers the professed who accept without understanding. When tried by affliction, they prove to be little more than twigs and branches shaken by the winds. They fall to the ground, while disciples who have been tried by experience and have endured the tempests of the devil stand firmly rooted in their faith.

Other analogies from both the domestic landscape of her life and the Bible emphasize experience as fundamental to evangelical discipleship. A gaze inside a barn and a recollection from Matthew about the wheat and the chaff move Mary Rich to consider the pious few who live among the sinful throngs. Her caution

---

[91] William Perkins, *Two Treatises. The first, Of the Nature and Practice of Repentance* (London, 1632), 62–86; Blackwood, *A Treatise Concerning Repentance*, 4; Thomas Watson, *The Doctrine of Repentance, Useful for these Times* (London, 1668), 5–6.

against "censureing all to be chaffe" (below, 126) and her resolve to find the few grains of wheat imply a generous, tolerant spirit evident as well in the meditation upon the paths that cross the courtyard to the house. She admits the possibility of many pathways to heaven and entreats God to strengthen her resolve to love Christians who differ "in the lessar thinges of religion" (below, 94). For Rich the "fundamentales" are a steadfast commitment to the apostolic doctrines and to the truth embodied in Christ. Those who walk in the Lord's way, who attempt to live holy and spiritual lives, will ultimately come together in heavenly glory even though their paths may diverge. In a meditation on a friend's sunset journey, Rich cautions herself not to be like the self-righteous Pharisee and not to ignore the beam in her own eye as she censures the mote in others'. Thoughts on the responsibility of educating those in her charge affirm the wisdom of allowing them some liberty to discover for themselves what she has already experienced. They may thereby more fully embrace the essential truths when they are "experimentally able to say with that great and wise experimenter of the world" (below, 143) that the glittering attractions of the world are indeed vain.

Christian disciples, in her view, are bound by love and faith to God. The small boat she sees from her Chelsea window stays afloat in the tossing waves of the Thames because it is tied to a larger one. Similarly the "faith unto salvation" that keeps her safe in the midst of life's tempests "is not in my holdeing thee but in thy holdeing me" (below, 69). The meditations link love and good works, but they recognize that the dedication of a faithful servant in God's service is dependent on the greater power of divine love. In striving to use her talents for the good of fellow Christians, Rich has in mind her variation of Proverbs: "they that water shall be water'd of the Lord" (below, 94). Her addition of the three words "of the Lord" is especially pointed. She herself cannot fulfill the hope that she will be received into heaven. Religious service remains for her a source of temporal happiness; the eternal reward depends solely on the mercy of Christ (below, 125). The heavenly crown Rich envisions from the sight of her embroidered bed canopy is "a reward of free grace, not of meritt" (below, 154). From the cabinet of her memory she draws upon the assurance of the sacred word and the mercies she has experienced.

Through the prospective glass of faith Mary Rich also envisions the distant heaven toward which she journeys. Often she compares this sight, as she does in the diary, to the "heavenly Cannane" Moses saw from Mount Nebo, noting "I have on this side Jordan tasted some grapes of the land of promise" (below, 79). Signs of the pilgrimage heavenward are bountifully evident. The weather and lodging between Leighs and London suggest the troubles endured on the path to heaven. From an overheard conversation between two workmen rolling a stone walk, Rich thinks about the labor necessary to avoid the wide path to hell and to reach heaven's straight and narrow gates. In the creeping of a snail she perceives the wisdom of plodding steadily toward the heavenly Jerusalem, dependent upon God's guidance. "Troblesome dirty steps" (below, 108) are inevitable, but Rich is certain the sun of righteousness illuminates that path, helping those with the eyes of faith to "tread nimbly" through the dirt. Divine grace and the comfort of Scripture are the bright stars that keep Rich from staggering and wavering (below, 131). Though she would "run nimbly" to God, ultimately she depends upon him to move the "feet" of her soul (below, 90). From him she begs both a "filiall, child like feare" and the "allureing" mercies that will prevent wandering (below, 138). The God Rich praises as the good Samaritan is for her the God who carried Moses up the mountain. As the meditations more and more address her journey's end, the hope is for a similar view that will "make me goe and not be weary, and run and not faint" (below, 128).

An abiding hope throughout the occasional meditations is a good death. The preoccupation in the diary with the deaths of others and the ways in which Mary Rich's son and husband faced their final days has a counterpart in the desire to do well "a worke I neaver did" (below, 93, 130). Rich returns to the imagery of light and time as she ponders her final moments. The watch candle that sputters loudly in its basin of water as it goes out illustrates the final moments of a sinner caught up in worldly pleasures. The anguish of his tormented conscience is in marked contrast to the cheerful composure of the pious Christian, who resembles the candle that expires without a noise (below, 56). Another candle that flares brightly as it burns out recalls those who become greater "heavenly and spirituall" luminaries the nearer they are to death (below, 92). The candle suddenly extinguished is, in the subsequent meditation, a reminder that only a breath separates life from eternity (below, 92–93). In this and other meditations Rich pleads with God for the willingness to embrace death and for the assurance that the name of Mary Rich appears in the Book of Life. She concedes, however, that a good death may not always be the measure of a good life. A bright sun setting behind a cloud recalls the deaths of exemplary Christians who confounded the expectations of others and passed away with little discernible triumph. Her conclusion that it is better to judge people by their "forepast lives" rather than by their deaths (below, 122) is also the theme of a meditation on an hourglass, its final grains of sand inseparable from all that flowed before.

Accordingly the theme of many occasional meditations is a steadfast and inspiring life. The ideal is embodied in the glowworm that shines most brightly on the darkest of nights. Here and elsewhere patience is foremost in the "darke night of affliction" (below, 75). Rich asks God for the fortitude not only to accept "chearfully" the bitter cup but to inspire others with the supporting strength of grace. By her conduct and her "good workes" she would thereby illuminate his glory. The "perfect subjektion" (below, 155) enabling her to contain grief and sorrows lies in a God-given self-possession sustained by the profession of faith. The sight of a patient's ability to endure the excruciating pain of the surgeon's knife is instructive. Fortitude is "God allmightes opium" (below, 146) in enduring affliction. Mary Rich seeks to be another Simon and shoulder her cross. Conscious that she has lost much of the physical beauty she once tried to preserve, she turns to the spiritual beauty of meekness, calmness, and, above all, patience.

The desire "not onely to speake thy praises but all so to live thy praises" (below, 44) assumes special importance in a life devoted to God. The heliotrope instructs Rich to open her heart to the divine sun, which infuses her with its "warmeing, cherishing beames," and to turn toward the source of mercy in unending praise (below, 140). She learns as well from the gratitude of a beggar the importance of thankfulness, an additional grace (below, 68). Unlike the woman in the gospel of Luke who kept her head bowed to the ground, Rich longs to be a Hannah transformed by prayer and a David committed to praise (below, 152). She would be another Elijah, elevated in praise of her many bountiful mercies (below, 144–45). Mindful of the psalmist's invitation to join in the celebration of the Lord, Rich relies upon divine help: "lett me begin my hosannas on earth that I may by them be fitted to gine [join] with that heavenly host in singing halaluihas for ever" (below, 132).

In the meditations, moments of discourse and communion are a means of fitting their author for that heavenly choir. Mary Rich notes in the diary that when she reread them the meditations themselves were occasions for further appreciation of God's mercy and love. In essence they embody "Heavenly Mindedness," the "disposition to make pious Reflections upon almost every Occurrence, and oftentimes without particularly designing it."[92] Not all these occurrences, it has been suggested, are original. Rich incorporates material from sermons. Her distinction between legal and evangelical repentance drawn from an analogy of a needle and thread comes directly from a sermon by Henry Wilkinson she heard at Leighs on 4 September 1677 (5/182v). Another sermon by George Gifford in London is the source of the observation that crimson finery worn so proudly is dyed with the blood of fish (4/93r). Whatever the origin, Rich transforms the images and ideas into personal religious experiences, the significance of which emerges from a fertile, analogical sensibility. The sealing of a letter, cracks in the dried ground, and decoy ducks prove lessons developed from metaphors, comparisons, and relationships. The diversity of the subjects and the similarity of intent are a testimony of a profound and eloquent faith.

The best gloss on the achievement of these occasional meditations may well be her brother Robert's belief that such meditations should "cherish piety" rather than "express wit"; they should "help to make the *man* good, whether or no they make his *style* be thought so."[93] Mary Rich's meditative practice, however, is not

---

[92] Boyle, "Discourse," 5:52. In a different context of an occasional meditation, Rich asks for "the grace of heavenly mindedness" (92). A common seventeenth-century phrase, it is also linked with meditation. "Heavenly thoughts or Meditations," Baxter writes, "are much of the exercise of Heavenly mindedness" (*The Duty of Heavenly Meditation* [London, 1671], 7); see also Swinnock, *The Christian-Mans Calling*, 454–55.

[93] Boyle, "Discourse," 5:31.

the "loose and Desultory way of writing" her brother approves. The sentences in her meditations have little or no punctuation and are seldom combined into the semblance of paragraphs, but the effect is not one of haste or carelessness. The meditations convey the spontaneity of extemporaneous expression. Observation, application, and apostrophe form their simple rhythms; biblical language adds complexity to their texture; and homely images from household and landscape create vivid immediacy. The difference between Mary Rich and William Spurstowe in their meditations on the drawing of well water is instructive. The bucket and wheel for Spurstowe are the basis of a long and abstract lesson on the distinction between the bucket of faith and the wheel of reason.[94] For Rich the bucket that clatters against the sides of the well as it descends but makes no noise when pulled up full is a brief and concrete analogy showing the experience of those who first lack mercy and then find it. "But when thay are so filled, thay doe not with a loude voyse reaturne glory to God but are silent" (below, 144). An everyday chore yields a simple, unforced, and satisfying parallel. Her meditations may not be learned and didactic and may rely upon moralistic tags, but their concrete detail, vivid analogies, and homely comparisons set them apart from those in other seventeenth-century collections.

A "devout Reflector" who can "spiritualize all the Objects and Accidents,"[95] Mary Rich expresses an early modern sensibility that is both secular and spiritual. She senses the eagerness of Lord Manchester to assess the estate he will inherit and notes the shrewdness of Lady Lake, who hid her gold in a broken-down cabinet. Compassionate and tolerant of many, Rich is cold-hearted toward her "inconsiderate sarvant" Tom Coleman, dismissed after twenty years of service without an anticipated annuity (below, 149), and unsympathetic toward a sick tenant who had not paid his rent. The assumptions of social class confirm that she is an aristocratic woman of the seventeenth century. Yet experience and observation, she never forgets, are "usefull to mind me" or make her "mindfull" of her own limitations and desires, whether a remissness in meeting obligations to her Lord or a longing for a heavenly inheritance. Uncomplicated and straightforward, the language is rich in imagery, bringing to life not only her spirituality but her daily life at Leighs and in London. In transforming the ordinary into the spiritually meaningful, Mary Rich, Countess of Warwick, embodied in her many occasional meditations the religious devotion of a woman who strove to make her life one with God.

---

[94] William Spurstowe, "Meditation XXXIX. Vpon the Bucket and the Wheel," in *The Spiritual Chymist: Or, Six Decads* [sic] *Of Divine Meditations On several Subjects* (London, 1666), 87–90.

[95] The essence, for Boyle, of the occasional meditation ("Discourse," 5:42, 53).

Provenance

The initial fate of the holograph occasional meditations is uncertain, though they may have been in the possession of Anthony Walker, who had been a chaplain to the Rich family and was among her closest spiritual advisors. Thirteen of the meditations were published along with Walker's 1678 life of Mary Rich, "Printed for Nathanael Ranew, at the King's Arms in S. Paul's Church-Yard." Ranew, the son of the minister who had dedicated his treatise on meditation to the Countess of Warwick, was the bookseller for whom the work was printed. Conceivably Anthony Walker was the editor, perhaps at the request of Lady Ranelagh and Robert Boyle, who had encouraged him to expand and publish the life of their sister contained in his funeral sermon. Walker quotes from a missing quarto of the diary an extensive passage Rich wrote two weeks before her death, so he may have held or at least had access to her writing. The manuscripts then came into the possession of the Woodrooffes, the family of the Riches' chaplain Thomas Woodrooffe, who died in 1689.

Among the annotations in the diary is William Woodrooffe's statement that Walker's son-in-law, John Cox, had "promis'd" in an August 1698 letter "to my Brother T. Woodrooffe" that he would send him soon "these papers, & ye Rest" (4/1r). Cox had been married to the Walkers' only surviving daughter, Margaret, who had died in childbirth, and he seems to have had in his possession some, though not all, of the manuscripts. William Woodrooffe already had in his possession Rich's autobiography, to which he added on the blank end folios the notation "West Hanningfield," where he was then rector, and "A Copy of what my good Mother wrote upon ye Death of Lady Warwick" dated 21 March 1691/2.[96] The annotations in the occasional meditations further indicate that he was responsible for the notations and much of the emendation.[97] William Woodrooffe may have excerpted part of the diary and some of the occasional meditations in

---

[96] British Library Additional Manuscript 27357, 41r. Anne Woodrooffe wrote the original.

[97] A marginal comment for the diary entry 8 August 1671, for example, adds "this Aftn. I (wth Br. Tho) came to Leez, in order to my going to Charter-H. School" (2/212r). William earlier notes that he was admitted to the school through the influence of John Robartes, later the first Earl of Radnor (2/129r). Another annotation for the 19 September 1675 diary entry adds "ab^t. this time I went from Jesus Coll. to Leez" (4/67r), the college to which William had, in fact, matriculated the year before. Sara Mendelson states in the entry on Rich in the *Oxford Dictionary of National Biography* that the "diaries and occasional meditations" of the countess "were preserved and annotated by her household chaplain, Thomas Woodroffe" (*ODNB*, 46:672); see also T. Crofton Croker, *Autobiography of Mary Countess of Warwick*, Percy Society (London: Richards, 1848), viii. Mary E. Palgrave, *Mary Rich Countess of Warwick (1625–1678)* (London: J. M. Dent & Co., 1901), suggests that the son Thomas was the annotator (211–12); Charlotte Fell Smith, however, attributes them to his brother William (*Mary Rich, Countess of Warwick*, 168, 172–73).

a transcription apparently intended to be published, though by then some of the original manuscripts were missing. Later some of the meditations referred to by title disappeared.[98] A series of dates and annotations he jotted in the text of the occasional meditations indicates that he had and was rereading the quartos until just before his death in 1732.[99] His brother Thomas had died twenty years before without marrying, and the manuscripts went to William's daughter Anne.

The provenance of the manuscripts can then be partly traced from a letter Nathaniel George Woodrooffe wrote 7 February 1848 to Thomas Crofton Croker, who was preparing an edition of the countess's autobiography for the Percy Society.[100] Woodrooffe had given Francis Foster Barham, an established author, editor, and translator, the right to publish a manuscript containing transcribed excerpts from the diary in the 1847 volume of the Religious Tract Society.[101] He wrote to Croker that he had obtained the manuscript from William Herringham, the joint executor along with Thomas Woodrooffe of the estates of Anne Gurdon, the daughter of the annotator William Woodrooffe, and George Andrewes, William's nephew.[102] Nathaniel Woodrooffe's letter adds that Herringham had retained the rest of the countess's papers, which he sold to a Suffolk bookseller named Lorking before he died in 1819; they were then, as far as Woodrooffe knew, sold to another bookseller. In the preface to the 1848 Percy Society edition, *The Autobiography of Mary Countess of Warwick*, Croker notes that

---

[98] Nine meditations are listed by title under the heading "Occasional Meditations 1677" (8/108r-109r), none of which appears among those in the British Library manuscript.

[99] The dates 1725, 1726–1727, 1728, and 1731 on 2r and some annotations written after 1725 (e.g., 2/217r, 255r) suggest William Woodrooffe reread or at least looked again at the occasional meditations and diary.

[100] Croker includes part of the letter he received from Nathaniel George Woodrooffe (*Autobiography*, viii-ix); this letter as well as Croker's earlier letter to Woodrooffe is in Additional Manuscript 27351, 2r-7r.

[101] Mary Rich, *Memoir of Lady Warwick: Also Her Diary, from A.D. 1666 to 1672, Now First Published. To which are Added, Extracts from Her Other Writings*, ed. Francis Barham (London: The Religious Tract Society, 1847). Barham states the manuscript "is headed 'An Abridgment of the Lady Warwick's Diary', and is here printed *verbatim*" (xii); it is not the same abridgment found in Additional Manuscript 27358. His edition includes large sections of the life taken from Walker's commemoration, *Eureka, Eureka*, as well as the occasional meditations and scriptural reflections included at the end of Walker's work.

[102] Additional Manuscript 27351, 4v-5r; also in Croker, *Autobiography*, ix. Thomas Woodrooffe was William's grandson, the son of John Woodrooffe. The other executor, William Herringham, was married to William's granddaughter Anne, sister of the co-executor Thomas. See "The Pedigree of the Family of Woodrooffe," in Selina Mary Woodrooffe, *Pedigree of Woodrooffe, with Memorials and Notes* (London: Mitchell and Hughes, 1878), n.p., and reproduced in *Miscellanea Genealogica et Heraldica*, n.s., 3 (n.d.): 65–69.

he had seen "thirty or forty small quarto books or 'diary papers'" written by the countess for sale at the New Bond Street establishment of T. and W. Boone.[103] On 12 May 1866 the British Museum purchased from another London bookseller, H. G. Bohn, for five guineas the manuscripts of the original life, the diary, and the occasional meditations, as well an excerpted transcription of the diary and meditations. The library bound the quartos together in the five volumes of the diary and individual volumes of the other three works.[104]

The Manuscript

The following edition contains the 182 occasional meditations in Additional Manuscript 27356 and four that are unique to the 1678 publication. These holograph meditations written from 1663 to 1677 are in a series of quartos 149 mm. wide and 206 mm. high. The hand varies somewhat throughout the years as the writing becomes more or less compact. Paragraphing and punctuation are minimal, conveying a sense of their extemporal flow, though some signs of the author's revision are apparent. Rich indicates in the diary that she read and reread both her diary and meditations, quite possibly making then some of the changes that are stylistic as well as substantive. The manuscripts of both the meditations and diary also have a number of spelling emendations. Unlike the manuscript autobiography, which often leaves the spelling untouched, the other manuscripts reflect alterations beyond those of deleting the uninflected letter "e" at the ends of words, omitting this letter in the plural and possessive "es," or changing "ea" to "e" in such words as "deagree" or "deany." Some of these deletions and spelling corrections are undoubtedly those of William Woodrooffe. At times the color of the ink in a series of emendations is the same as adjacent notations, and often he will print the correct spelling above the word. But on other occasions the emendator's ink is the same color as the original ink, letters are altered or added within words, and erasures are unmistakable — raising questions about the author of the changes. It seems doubtful then that Rich made all the emendations, and there is no assurance that Woodrooffe did not alter the meditations in subsequent readings or that he is the only person who might have revised the original manuscript. Still, many of the textual changes are unquestionably hers.

Editorial Principles

The inability to determine the origin of all these emendations and the inconsistency among them underlie the editorial decision to preserve a sense of Rich's spelling that is faithful to her distinctive writing and the emendations, if not the text's orthography. She is herself a questionable speller, who sometimes spells a

---

[103] Croker, *Autobiography*, x.
[104] C. J. Wright, Head of Manuscripts, the British Library.

word differently in the same sentence; emendations are at best also inconsistent. A few such as "frend/friend," "besiech/beseech," and "bene/been" are made with considerable regularity: "e" is commonly changed to "i," for example, in "famely/family," "devide/divide," and "possebly/possibly"; "u" and "i" are typically added in "wold," "troble," and "ordnary"; "ale" is altered to "all" in "fale/fall," "smale/small." Others seem more a matter of happenstance. Some meditations appear heavily emended; others are left untouched. The alteration or addition of letters within words, moreover, is often difficult to differentiate from the original; and at times an insertion or alteration corrects part of a word, ignoring other corrections that might be warranted. Fortunately none of the changes of questionable orthography and authorship affects the meaning of the text, and all the revisions for style, clarity, and emphasis seem those of the meditations' author.

The edited text is therefore a compromise between the original and emended versions of the manuscript; it does not imply that the spelling is always that of Rich. Changes are retained in the edition when they seem to follow a semblance of principle apparent in her loose orthography or if they lead to greater clarity. Erasures that appear to be Rich's; words that are occasionally spelled conventionally in the meditations, autobiography, or diary; and changes that are made in these works with considerable consistency justify the alterations. Thus the emendations of "shipe" and "shepe" to "sheep," "receave" to "receive," or "maister" to "master" reflect Rich's spelling at times elsewhere, while the alteration of "reserection/resurrection," "salles/sallies," and "sublunare/sublundary" follows the pattern in her other works, whoever the emendator may be. Changes within words that may or may not have been hers are also kept when they further clarify the word. Rich's ear led her originally to spell "creep," "street," and "feet" as "cripe," "strite," and "fite"; and the possibility of similar confusion also arises with the absence of "c" in words such as "thike" (thick) and "baike" (back). Similarly her tendency to use "ich" interchangeably with "ish" and "ea" rather than "e" can be misleading without accepting the changes in "fich/fish," "perich/perish," "fleach/flesh" and "realich/relish." Though clarity of meaning is not as pressing in revisions that double the consonants—most commonly "f," "l," and "s," they are retained along with the tendency to delete the final "e." Among other spelling changes that may not be hers, especially notable is the omission of "s" in such words as "exstinct" and "exsalt" as well as the alteration of "s" and "k" to "c," for example, in "exselent" and "protektion." The edition does not, however, attempt to regularize the admittedly inconsistent spelling.

While a sense of the original spelling is at best approximated, the editorial methods follow established principles. Capitalization has been modernized, as have the letters "i" and "j," "u" and "v"; elided words are separated and contractions as well as superscripts expanded. Where Rich breaks words, those separated at the ends of lines are joined when they reflect her spelling; syllabic breaks within the lines are retained as variants in her spelling when the spacing and meaning are apparent. To avoid unnecessary ambiguity "to/too/two, of/off, on/

one/own," and "their/ther" have been silently emended; "ar/are" and occasionally "a/o" are similarly altered along with the occasional transposition or omission. Punctuation has also been modernized for further clarity, though sentences with minimal stops challenge modern punctuation and grammatical syntax. The parentheses and possessives are original to the manuscript; apostrophes, hyphens, and quotation marks are also unchanged. Any paragraphing is Rich's. Alterations and additions she made in revision are noted in the textual apparatus. Words in square brackets are those William Woodrooffe, for the most part, added above the line to clarify or correct spellings; words bracketed in < > indicate the probable original that has been blurred or partially torn away. Throughout, the foremost concern has been to reinforce meaning without unduly compromising the original spirit of the text.

Documentation

References to Rich's diary, Additional Manuscripts 27351–27355, are cited in the text with the last digit in the manuscript and the folio number, separated by a virgule. All biblical citations and quotations are from the King James Version, the translation she read. Biographical information identified as *ODNB* is from the printed text of the *Oxford Dictionary of National Biography*, ed. H. C. G. Matthew and Brian Harrison, 61 vols. (Oxford: Oxford University Press, 2004), and includes the author of the relevant entry along with the published volume number and pagination. No specific documentation is provided for definitions from the *Oxford English Dictionary*, which is acknowledged in each instance as *OED*. All other references, including standard works such as *Alumni Oxonienses*, are fully documented in the initial citation.

Occasional Meditations

[1r] 1st 1663.

[2r] Ocasionale Meditationes 1663 M Warwicke

[3r] *Upon desiring my docter to give me a potion,*[1] *though I knew it wolde be very unpleasant and wolde make me very sike*

How realy am I convinsed of the unpleasantnes of this potion, and how sarten [certain] am I that it will make me deadly sike, and yet how earnest am I in petitioning the docter to give it me because I know it is neasesary for my health and that it will purge away those ill humores that else wolde bride [breed] that which wolde cause, it may be, some desperate siknes, the feare of which makes me so deasireous of this potion that I [4r] nether stick at the unpleasantnes of the taste nor at the sickness it will ocasione. And why then, O brutish persone that I am, doe I not as earnestly petition thee, my God, who art the great physitian of my soule,[2] to purge me of my spirituall distemperes, which are much more dangerous then those of my body? And why am not I willing to take a potion of thy prescribing, though it may taste bitter, when I know that it is wholesome for me? O thou, my great physitian that seest what purge I have neade of to purge me of my sines, prescribe it to me; and though it be ever so bitar in the takeing doune, yet [5r] the cup which my heavenly father has mingled for me I will drinke.[3] O doe thou purge away all my sines; leave not a hoof behinde,[4] but purely purge away

---

[1] William Woodrooffe (hereafter WW) notes, "I suppose Dr Swallow" (3r).

[2] A common, patristically derived characterization of Christ's ministry, "Physician of Souls," and not a specific Gospel passage: "Christ came to be a *Physician* to sick souls"; "his Church is an Hospital, and he the Physician of Souls" (John Flavel, *The Method of Grace, In bringing home the Eternal Redemption* [London, 1681], 216; Richard Baxter, *Reliquiæ Baxterianæ* [London, 1696], Part III, 40). See also *Certaine Sermons or Homilies Appointed to be Read in Churches In the Time of Queen Elizabeth I (1547-1571)*, facsimile of 1623 edition, intro. Mary Ellen Rickey and Thomas B. Stroup (Gainesville: Scholars' Facsimiles & Reprints, 1968), part two, 269.

[3] John 18:11; see also the 14 October 1672 diary entry (3/73r).

[4] Hoof: "fragment or particle" (*OED*).

all my drosse.[5] And if thou seest that the unpleasant taste of affliction is neasisary for me, doe not spare giveing me that bitar pill (to the fleach) so it may be condusife to the saveing my imortal soule. And make me really beleeve that though noe afliction for the preasent is joyus but grievous, yet that afterwardes it workes the peaseable frutes of riteousnes to those that are exsersised ther in. And seeing I can be content for my vile body — which [6r] is but a house of clay[6] and which, though it is often repared, must at last turne to dust and be meat for wormes to feed upon[7] — to take nauseateing purges, O make me as much more deasireous of phisike to cleanse and purge my soule as that is more excellent then my body. O my God! here is thy patiante (sike of sinn) humbly petitioning thee to purge and to cleanse me from all filthenes of flesh and spirit that I may now perfect holynes in the feare of thee, my God.

[7r] *Upon my takeing a great deale of paines to make a fire and blowing it a long time before I could make it blase*

How many blastes have I bestode upon this sullen fire, and how great an exsersise of my patiance has it given me, and how much paines have I taken by turneing the stikes and making use of my skill in laying them together so hallow that thay might make a blase before I could make them doe any thing but lye and smother but not flame. And yet I was resolved [8r] that the difeculty should not discourage me but make me blow the harder; and at last I had this rewarde for my patiance, that the fire did flame as cleare as I did deasire it showld and was the gronde of this ocasionale meditation: that if I could take so much paines and waite so long to make the fire blase onely because it was pleasant and chearfull to me to beholde it, why showld I not much rather take paines and waite by meditation to blow up those sparkes of devotion that lay raked up under the emberes of my coruptiones. O Lord, I most humbly besiech thee, saintefy this meditation to me [9r] and make me find, as holy David did, while I am museing, the fire to burne.[8] And if when I have sequestered my selfe from the croude of the world and say'd to all my other worldly affaires, stay here while I goe yonder and worship and then I will come to you againe,[9] if I doe not upon this retireing of my selfe preasently finde the fire of devotion to flame, lett me not presently returne to the world; but lett me by the difficulty I find take more paines by prayer and

---

[5] Isaiah 1:25.

[6] Job 4:19; originally in the manuscript "vilde": older or dialect form of vile (*OED*). Rich may recall the "Burial of the Dead" and "who shall change our vile bodie, that it may be like unto his glorious body," in *The Book of Common Prayer . . . Together with the Psalter or Psalms of David* (Cambridge, 1663), I4r.

[7] Cf. Job 24:20, "the worm shall feed sweetly on him."

[8] Psalm 39:3.

[9] Recalling Matthew 26:36: "Sit ye here, while I go and pray yonder."

meditation upon thy pretious promises and, by thinkeing upon free grace [10r] and thy unmerited mersyes towardes me, stir up the grace of God that is in me, and stir up my selfe to lay hold upon God, and bring my sacrifice—though I canot command fire, and say, here is the sacrifise.[10] But Lord! doe thou command fire from heaven. Lett me spread my sayles for heaven; and though I cannot comand a winde to blow me thither, yet lett me looke towardes it. And then, O Lord, I doe beseech thee, doe thou command a gale from heaven to wafte me thither. O, doe thou blow these sparkes in to a flame [11r] and lett me by prayer and meditation not onely find the fire to glow and burne but to sett my heart in a flame of love to thee, my God.

Upon a cage of canary birdes that hung up in my closet, and when my servant had fed them, presently singing very sweetly

[12r] With how great delight have I observed these pretty birds while my sarvant was cleansing their cage and filling their little veselles with water and seades; who to show their gratitude to him, as sone as he had suplide their wantes, sing so sweetly as if thay meant not onely to reaturne him their retributiones for their provision but as if thay designed to make me change my opinion that nightingales deaserved the croune for singing above any other burdes.[11] But shure this observation showld not onely dealight me but instroukte me, too, by learneing from these pritty, gratefull creatures gratitude to that God that has not [13r] onely fed me but cloathed me all my life long, and that not with a littell water onely and a few seeds but with all the quintessense of the earth and with all the variety of creatures which his bounty has furnished this lowar world with for the use of the poore inhabetantes of it. O Lord, I most humbly beseech thee, seeing thou hast instructed me out of thy sacred word that praise is a tribute thou expectest from thy creatures by telling me that who so offereth it glorifies thee,[12] O make me be much in this spirituall duty and lett all that is with in me blese thee;[13] and make me, as I receave all from thee, so chearfully to return my praises [14r] to thee; and lett me not be more bruteish then these irrational littell creatures who are instantly and chearfully thankfull for the provision by which their lives are sustained, though he that handes it to them is but thy instrument and, as it

---

[10] Fires from heaven consume the sacrifices of both David and Solomon (1 Chronicles 21:26, 2 Chronicles 7:1).

[11] John Flavel acknowledges the beautiful song of the nightingale in his meditation "Upon the singing of a Nightingale," in *Husbandry Spiritualized: Or, The Heavenly Use of Earthly Things* (London, 1669), 233-37. In Aesop's fables the ass thought the cuckoo superior to the nightingale in singing ("Fab. CCCCXIV. An Ass made a Judge of Musick," in Roger L'Estrange, *Fables, of Aesop* [London, 1692], 390-91).

[12] Psalm 50:23.

[13] Cf. Psalm 103:1.

ware, thy stewarde to dispose of those provisiones thou hast provided for their preservation. And, O Lord, I most humbly beseech thee, lett me learn this lesson allso: to be thankfull as in the first place to thee, the founetaine from whom all my mersyes flow,[14] so to those streames by which thy goodnes is convayed to me by thy infeariur creatures. Lord, make me not onely to speake thy praises but all so to live thy praises.

[15r] *Upon walkeing a good longe walke in a garden to gather a rose; and being much pleased with the swetnes of it; and presently, when it began to wither, fling it away*

How longe a walke have I fetcht to gather this beautifull rose; and yet as sone as I smelte it, how fully did I thinke my paines rewarded by the fragrancy of the smell and the refrechment I received from it; and yet as sone as it began to wither, I heedlesly flung it away with out considering that if I had ploukte the leaves and [16r] kepte them by me thay wolde have bene usefull to me all the winter after by perfumeing any thinge I layded them by. Yet this inconsideratenes of mine in flinging this rose away is an ocasion to bring to my mind a much worse fault that I am often guilty of in relation to sermones, to heare which I am often content to take a great deale of paines to come to the house of God. And when from the mouth of one of his ministers I heare an exselent sermon, I am strangely pleased with the eloquense of it as I was with the beauty of the rose; but when he comes to the aplication, the sweet and spirituall part of it, that dos strangely refreach and cheare me, [17r] and I goe out from the house of God with great delight and refrechment. And when by meditation I have for a while indeavered to be filled with the swetnes of it, I preasently reaturne to worldly company, who with frothy, vaine discourse wither those blosomes of grace which ware so lately blown. And then when my affectiones are withered, I presently fling it out of my minde, not considering that if I had with Mary layde it up and pondered it on my heart,[15] it wolde have bene not onely usefull to my selfe afterwardes but I might have perfumed otherse by the fragrancy of it. O Lord, I besiech thee, lett this ocasionale [17v] meditation be so sett home and santefided to me[16] that I may for the time

---

[14] A commonplace in the seventeenth century, this description of God also occurs in Augustine's *Confessions* (Book VI, chapter 16), a work Rich notes on 29 September 1668 she was reading (1/242r). The phrase is related to descriptions of God as the fountain of living water and life (Jeremiah 17:13, Joel 3:18, Psalm 36:9, Proverbs 14:27, John 4:10-14, and Revelation 7:17).

[15] Luke 2:19.

[16] Sanctify: "To make holy," "To apply to such holy and divine use as God appointed" (Thomas Wilson, *A Complete Christian Dictionary*, 6th ed. [London, 1655], 567). Subsequent spellings commonly emphasize saintly, recalling 1 Corinthians 1:2—"them that are sanctified in Christ Jesus, called to be saints." See also Romans 15:16.

to com be not onely a hearur of the worde but a doeur of it.[17] Lett it not be onely like a nosegay which I may smell too for a littell while and then fling it away, but lett me chew the cud,[18] and lett it have an abideing good upon me that it may be good seed sowne in good gronde and may bring forth frute in my life and conversation,[19] that it may be the saver [savour] of life unto life and not the savor of death unto death.[20]

[18r] *Upon seeing the sun when I was walkeing of a soden shine out very bright, and presently a blake cloude interpose betwikste me and it that I could for som time hardely deaserne* [discern] *it*

How strange and sodenly was I surprised with joy to see in my walkeing in a darke, gloomie morneing (when I aprehended I showld be fain to retire home for feare of being wett by a showre which I expected wolde instantly fall) to see the sun so gloriously shine out that I was [19r] not able to keepe my selfe from gaseing so earnestly upon it that it had so dasled my eyes that to recover my sight againe I was fane for some littell time to winke. Which whilst I was doeing, a darke cloude so interposed betwixst me and that glorious creature that when I againe opened my eyes to gase upon that object I was before so delighted with, the cloude had so quite covered it that it was allmost imposible for me to deaserne any of it. But resolveing to watch for ites appeareing againe, I did at last deserne a littell of that light I was before so strangely dasled with; and in a littell times waiting, [20r] I had the satisfaction to see it shine as bright as it did at first and by it was lighted to this meditation: that what I did this morning observe was not alltogeather an unfitt comparison for a child of Godes condition in

---

[17] James 1:22.

[18] After hearing the minister preach the word, Richard Baxter advises in *A Christian Directory: Or, A Summ of Practical Theologie, and Cases of Conscience*, 2nd ed. (London, 1678), "*Chew the Cud, and call up all when you come home in secret, and by Meditation Preach it over to your selves. If it were coldly delivered by the Preacher, do you consider of the great weight of the matter, and Preach it more earnestly over to your own hearts*" (Book Two, 87). Edward Bury likens meditation to "the chewing of the cud, that turns all to nourishment" (*The Husbandmans Companion: Containing One Hundred Occasional Meditations* [sic] *Reflections and Ejaculations, Especially Suited to Men of that Employment* [London, 1677], a4r). See also William Gearing, *The Mount of Holy Meditation: Or a Treatise Shewing the nature and kinds of Meditation*, 2nd ed. (London, 1662), 45-46; Thomas Watson, *A Christian On the Mount: Or, a teatise* [sic] *concerning meditation*, in *The Saints Delight* (London, 1657), 59-60.

[19] Rich has in mind the parable of the sower and those "that heareth the word, and understandeth it; which also beareth fruit, and bringeth forth, some a hundredfold, some sixty, some thirty" (Matthew 13:23).

[20] 2 Corinthians 2:16.

this vale of teares.[21] Who when thay have bene walkeing in darkness, and have seene noe light, and have in their doubting condition bene ready to passe a sad dome [doom] upon themselves and say that in stead of haveing the light of Gods countenance shine upon them[22] thay expected nothing but uttar darkenes, yet God has sodenly, when thay lest expected it, lett the sun of riteousnes apeare so gloriously to them with healeing in his [21r] winges[23] that they have bene both pleased and, as it ware, dasled with that glorious sight which seemed a glimse of heaven on earth. But presently a cloude has over-shadode that glorious sunn. God has with drawne those comfortes to show them that those ware the soules swetmeates, not their constant fare, and that the darke cloude of their sines had interposed betwene that glorious sunn and them. But yet when that poore disconsolate soule has still gased towards heaven and patiently expected the apeareing of that glorious light, thay have discerned a littell glimering of Godes countenance [22r] and, by constant praying and waiting, have at last bene able to beholde the sunn of riteousnes[24] shine forth as bright as ever. O Lord, I humbly beseech thee, lett this meditation be instrouktive to me and make me, when by reason of my sines, which seperate betwene me and my God and hide the light of his countenance from shineing forth upon me,[25] I see a black cloude interposed, lett me not presently leave off lookeing up. But though for my sines I walke in darkenes and see noe light,[26] yet lett me still gase towards thee and then at last fullfill that promise that the Lord whom I seeke will sodenly com into his temple.[27] Lord, doe thou againe restore to me the light of thy countenance.

---

[21] A common phrase in the seventeenth century, its likely origin is the valley of Baca (Psalm 84:6), which in the Septuagint translates "the valley of weeping" (*The Anchor Bible Dictionary*, ed. David Noel Freedman, 6 vols. [New York: Doubleday, 1992], 1:566). The journey to Sion or heaven, commentators observe, leads through "the Valley of Baca the Valley of tears" (Thomas Hall, *A Practical and Polemical Commentary Or, Exposition upon The Third and Fourth Chapters of the latter Epistle of Saint Paul to Timothy* [London, 1658], 217). A secondary meaning for Baca, mulberry trees, denotes the aridity and sterility of this valley. See, among various interpretations, Jean Calvin, *The Psalmes of Dauid and others. With M. Iohn Caluins Commentaries*, trans. Arthur Golding (London 1571), part two, 35r-v; Thomas Shepard, *The Parable of the Ten Virgins Opened & Applied: Being the Substance of divers Sermons on Matth. 25.I, —13* (London, 1660), 153. On 3 February 1670 Rich contemplated heaven while "in this bocan this place of teares" (2/49v).

[22] Psalms 4:6, 89:15.
[23] Malachi 4:2.
[24] Malachi 4:2.
[25] Psalms 4:6, 89:15, 90:8.
[26] John 12:35, Isaiah 50:10.
[27] Malachi 3:1.

[23r] *Upon seeing a hog lye under an acorn tree and eate the acorns but never looke up from the ground to the tree from which they fell*

With what amasement and deatestation have I bene observeing this brutish creature who, whilst he is feading himselfe, still lookes doune to the gronde and onely makes use of his mouth, not his eyes, to looke up to the tree from which he is fed. And yet whilst I am censureing this brutish action, I am but censureing my own ofense, who may say with the psalmist, I was as a beast before thee.[28] For not [24r] unresemblingly have I dealt with thee, my God, for I have bene like the woman spoken of in the Gospell who was bowed down to the ground.[29] I have filde my selfe with the fatness of the earth but not looked up to that great housekeeper whose providence provided these good things for me. And when I have received abundantly from thee and have had a Benjamins mess by thy bountifull hand disht out to me,[30] I have bene ready to forgett to looke up to the giver of that plenty. But, O Lord, I beseech thee, make me when I have eaten and am full then to blesse thee and to acknowledge that it is the Lord that has fed me all my life long.

[25r] Ocasionale Meditationes 1663 M Warwicke

[26r] *Upon being in a great heate after walking and then for feare of catching colde putting on another scarfe*

How great a heate have I by my walkeing put my selfe into, and yet my feare of catching colde makes me put on another skarfe and keape out of the aire for feare of being presently chill and takeing some dangereous cold. O my soul, why showld I not more indeaver to preaserve the heate I gett at ordinances?[31] And when I have bene throughly warmed in duty, why doe I not by my meditation strive to continue that heate [27r] by keapeing my selfe warme with inflameing, warmeing considerationes and for some time sequestring my selfe and, as it were, keeping my selfe out[32] of the aire of chilling worldly company, remembering that it is much more easy to keep heate when by the duty I have attained it than to attaine it when my affectiones are quite cold? O Lord! make me, therefore, when through thy mercy towardes me I have got my affectiones hott, to preserve that warmeth that so it may in some measure be like the fire upon the alltar that never went out.[33]

---

[28] Psalm 73:22.
[29] Luke 13:11.
[30] Genesis 43:34.
[31] Ordained or prescribed religious and ceremonial practices; the sacraments, especially the Eucharist. "Any commandement of God appointed as a path for us to walk in." "Gods Decrees are his Ordinances, though unwritten," and "Gods written Precepts are his Ordinances" (Thomas Wilson, *A Complete Christian Dictionary*, 453-54).
[32] Rich wrote "lose" above "out," a variant of "loose."
[33] Leviticus 6:13.

[27v] *Upon calling my little bitch that lay in my closett by the fire; and when she would not come to me, goeing away; and she presently lookeing in all the romes [rooms] for me; and when she had found me, leapeing and fawning upon me*

[28r] How often have I called this little bitch; and though she lookes towardes me to show me she heares me, yet she will not stir from before the fire where she is layde, too much pleased with ease to be by my calling disturbed from it. And yet as sone as I had withdrawn my selfe from her by goeing into another room, she presently leaves the ease she was before so fonde of to follow me. And when she could not finde me in the rooms I used to frequent, she instantly searches all the house over till at last she fonde me. Which when she had done, she exprest so great joy at it by her leapeing upon me and fawning that if she could [29r] have spoken, she could by her wordes hardely have expreste her selfe more kindely to me. This observation I have made upon my little bitches caredge [carriage] towardes me makes me with detestation reflecte upon my own and, as Pharoes buttlar did, call my own fault to my rememberance this day;[34] for not unresemblingly have I dealt with thee, O my God, who hast many times called me. And yet when I have been at my ease, I have bene so lazy as to be loth to rise and with the spouse in the Canticles to make excuses by saying, I have put off my close [clothes]; how shall I put them on againe?[35] But when thou hast hid thy selfe from me, I have been presently so sensible of thy absense that [30r] I have run from ordinance to ordinance to finde thee;[36] and when thou hast mersyfully appeared to me againe so as I have bene able to say, I have seene the Lord; he has appeared unto Mary,[37] O what an extasy have I bene in, and what a transport of joy was I in at thy manifesting thy selfe againe unto me. O Lord, I beseech thee, the next time thou callest me lett me presently run unto thee that I may not have cause any more to make that sad complainte: that I sought him whom my soule loves; I sought him, but I could not finde him.[38]

[30v] *Upon seeing a piece of ice very harde in the morneing; and though I indeavered to breake it, yet I could not; but as sone as the sunn shined upon it was presently turned to water*

[31r] How hard was this water frose this morneing; for though I stamped harde upon it to breake it, yet I was able onely to make some little cracks in it but not to breake it. But now I see the sunn has by its shineing upon it quite melted and dissolved it in to water. Methinkes this may not unfitly be compared to the law and the Gospell worke upon the heart. The law, when it findes the heart hard frosen

---

[34] Genesis 41:9.
[35] Song of Solomon 5:3.
[36] See above, n. 31.
[37] John 20:11-18, Mark 16:9.
[38] Song of Solomon 3:1.

and stony, strikes at it to melte it and to breake it, by pronouncing the curses that God has threatned against those that continue not in all that is written in the booke of the law to doe it.[39] And though these threatninges may make some little impressiones, yet till [32r] the sunn-shine of the Gospell comes, it continues a hard stony heart;[40] but when that message of glad tideinges is once proclaimed the great mercy of God in giveing his onely son to take away the curse of the law by being made a curse for us,[41] and that he is so mersifull as to freely offer Christ to all that will upon his termes accept him to be their lord and saviour, and that he is the free gift of God, and that he has layde the chastisement of our peace upon his shoulders, and that by his stripes we are healded,[42] this does instantly dissolve the frosen hard heart and turnes it all into water, dissolves it in to teares of godly sorrow that it was so long harde against so mersifull a father. O Lord! I beseech thee, [33r] lett thy mersyes melte my harde, stony heart. O Lord, lett thy mercyes make me give up my self, my whole self, a liveing sacrifice unto thee, which is but my reasonable servise.[43]

[33v] *Upon seeing a fire burn very well but as sone as I had separated the sticks a little way asunder instantly to goe out*

[34r] How well did this fire burne when I first came into my closett; but when I had by the helpe of the tongs layde the sticks asunder, the fire went soe presently out that I was surprised at it and by this observation was more convinced of the neaseasety [necessity] and usefullness of the communion of saintes.[44] Who while thay are kept together and are discourseing of the matters of religion, and relateing to one another the mersyes of God towardes them, and telling their own experiences of the inward workeing of God upon their soules, and declareing, as David did, what God had done for their soules and how sweet and pleasant a thing it was to walke closely with God,[45] and by their mutuall discourses considering [35r] one another to provoke unto love and to good workes, their heartes did, as it were, burn with in them.[46] But as soon as thay ware separated asunder, that fire of devotion

---

[39] Galatians 3:10.
[40] Ezekiel 11:19, 36:26.
[41] Luke 1:19, 8:1.
[42] Isaiah 53:5.
[43] Romans 12:1. See also the Holy Communion prayer, "present unto thee, O Lord, our selves, our souls and bodies to be a reasonable, holy, and lively sacrifice unto thee," in *The Book of Common Prayer*, F1v.
[44] The "communion of saints" is a phrase from the Creed in *The Book of Common Prayer*, A3r; compare as well 2 Corinthians 6:14.
[45] Possibly an echo of Psalm 55:14, "We took sweet counsel together, / and walked unto the house of God in company."
[46] Luke 24:32.

that lately they felt warme them so inwardely that it did burne with in them was so exstinguished as to their present sens of it that thay have bene both surprised and troubled at it for feare it was not onely out for the present but quite extinct. O Lord, I beseech thee, lett this occasionale meditation be for the future so instructive to me that I may, as much as I am able and when I have opportunity, keap company with thy saintes here upon earth, being from my own experience convinced that is the best way to preserve the fire of devotion from goeing out [36r] and to warme my heart when it is colde. O lett me, when it is so, bring it into the company of an inflamed one that I may find it as the deade childe whom the prophet, by bringing his liveing body to it, was revived and warmed.[47]

[36v] *Upon seeing a childe when she was wallkeing with me step into a dirty podull when she might by lookeing to her way have avoyded it*[48]

[37r] How exstreamely ainegery [angry] was I with this untorde [untoward] childe who rather chuses to walke in the dirt and to step in to a dirty puddell then to take the paines to looke to her way and avoyde being smired [smear'd] with dirt by goeing in the cleane way and stepping over the dirty. And yet how many are there that will gine [join] with me in condemning this childes heedelesness that are with me also guillty of a much greater fault, who for want of considering my way often step in to the dirty pudell of sinn when I am walking in my journy to heaven, and goe out of the cleane path God has ordained me[49] and to besmire [besmear] my selfe all over with the filth of sinn, and rather chuse to wallow in [38r] that defileing way then in the cleane and sweet way that leades to heaven. O Lord! make me for the time to come, now I perceive the great danger that is in stepping into the dirt for the defileing of my selfe and how sartenly [certainly] I shall be spotted if I doe not step aside from that besmearing thing which will, if I touch it, cleave to me, step over it and by taking heed to my way chuse the cleane and avoyde that sinn, which if touchte will sartenly [certainly] blacken my soule.

[38v] *Upon my being in a great deale of company, and being by a friende secretly beckened to retire alone with her, and presently obaying that somones* [summons][50]

[39r] How sone did I take notice of that silent and undiscerned beck (to all the rest of the compeny) that my friend gave me to withdraw my selfe from the croude of

---

[47] Elisha revived the son of a wealthy Shunammite woman by putting "his mouth upon his mouth, and his eyes upon his eyes, and his hands upon his hands" (2 Kings 4:32-37).

[48] For another instance of a child's willful soiling of shoes see Thomas Fuller, "Mixt Contemplation III.," in *Good Thoughts in Bad Times. Together with Good Thoughts in Worse Times* (London, 1659), part one, 68-69.

[49] God's "way" is the "plain path" of Psalm 27:11.

[50] WW: "I take this Friend to be her Sister Ranelaugh" (38v).

company I was ingaged in, and with what chearefullness did I presently obay that summones to come to be alone with her that I might have a free and undisturbed converse with her, and how sweet and satisfactory was that entertainement to me. Not unresemblingly deales my gratious God with me. Many times when he sees me inconsiderately ingage my selfe into the insnareing croudes of the world, he does by the secret and undiscerned motions of his blessed spirit (to all but my selfe), as it were, by the constraining and sanctifying motiones of it becken me [39v] to reatire that I may have an uninterrupted comunion with him. And when I have instantly obayed that secret becke, O, what sweet refreshing howres have I then injoyed in that neare and intimate converse betwene God and my poore soule. I have then been able to acte my soule upon God and to receive in the influence of the goodnesse and mercy of God againe into my soule. I have injoyed fellowshipe with the father and with his son, Jesus Christ, and I have been so far from missing the croude I lefte that I have by prayer and meditation asoshated [associated] my spirit unto such pleaseing company that I have rather thought I have had a body too much [40r] with me than founde a wante of any. O Lord! I most humbly beseech thee, lett the former sweetness I have found in being alone with thee, my God, make me observe and take notice of the least motion and whisper of the spirit and obay the first moveinges of it that so I may taste those consolationes of God that are not small.

Upon seeing one take a great deale of paines to pump a little water, and one instantly coming and with great ease turne a cock and the water instantly flowing out

[40v] How attentively have I observd the paines this poore creature takes to pump a little water; and yet as sone as another had turned a cauke [cock], which was but an easy worke, the water flow'd with ease and in great plenty. Which made me presently reflect and think what I had observed was like the paines I many times take with my own heart to pompe out the teares of godly sorrow and yet cannot make those waters flow; but when the spirit comes to my assistance, it presently helpes my infirmityes and by turneing, as it ware, the cock makes it so easy to weepe over my sines that tears presently flow foreth. And I am then by the assistance of the spirit able to say, as David did, rivers of wateres runn [41r] doune myne eyes and, as Saint Peter did, to weep bitterly.[51] O Lord, I humbly beseech thee, lett this teach me in all my adresses to thee not to rely too much upon my own strength, remembering that without thee I can doe nothing,[52] but to humbly petition thee for the assistance of thy holy spirit to help my infirmityes and inable me to offer up a spirituall sacrifise acceptable unto thee, my God, through Jesus Christ.

---

[51] Psalm 119:136; Matthew 26:75, Mark 14:72, and Luke 22:62.
[52] John 15:5.

Upon seeing a sieve brought and layde under a cock of water when it was very dirty and car'ed away very cleane waichte [washt], *though because of ites numerous out-lettes it could retaine noe water in it*

[41v] I have observed this sives being brought and sett under a cock of water to be waichte [wash'd], and that not without need, for it was dirty all over. And though because of ites numerous outlettes it retained no water, yet I observed it was cared [carry'd] away washt quite pure from all ites former dirt. Which observation made me presently in my thoughtes compare what I lately saw to a poore, durty, polluted soule that is brought to the house of God and there sett under the droppinges of the ordinances[53] to be washt and cleansed from its former filth; and there has it may be sarmon upon sarmon dropt upon his poluted soule; and yet though he heares so many, by reason of the [42r] weakness of his memory he canot retaine any. Yet he goes away from the ordinance washt and purify'd by Godes word, which has a purifying, cleanseing vertue.[54]

Upon seeing when the sun shined upon a diall great croudes run to it; but as sone as the sunn was withdraune, all the former compeny goe from it and take noe more notice of it[55]

[42v] What a croud of people did I lately observe run and presse towardes the sunn diall while the sunn shined upon it; but as sone as it was withdraune, all the compeny was so, too, from so much as lookeing towardes it or regardeing it. Methinkes this may fitly be compared to the generality of the world who while the sunnshine of prosperety shines upon them thay have multetudes of followares and all presse towardes them; but if their prosperety be clouded and dos not shine forth so conspikeously [conspicuously] as formerly, thay presently reatire and walke by them as disdainfully and unregardlesly as if thay had neaver before run towardes them.

---

[53] See above, n. 31.

[54] Rich deleted the rest of the sentence: "and is able to clense a manes wayes by takeing heade ther unto and is as fire to purefy and consume all the drasse" (42r).

[55] Other meditations on sundials include, Joseph Hall, "II Upon the Sight of a Dial," in *Occasional Meditations (1633)*, in *Bishop Joseph Hall and Protestant Meditation in Seventeenth-Century England*, ed. Frank Livingstone Huntley, MRTS 1 (Binghamton: Center for Medieval and Early Renaissance Studies, 1981), 124; William Spurstowe, "Meditation XXXVI. Vpon the motion of the Sun on the Dyall" and "Meditation XXXVII. Vpon a Sun-Dyal and a Clock," in *The Spiritual Chymist: Or, Six Decads [sic] of Divine Meditations On several Subjects* (London, 1666), 79-84; Robert Boyle, "Discourse XV. Upon the Magnetical Needle of a Sun-Dyal," in *Occasional Reflections upon Several Svbiects. Whereto is premis'd A Discourse About such kind of Thoughts* (London, 1665), part two, 95-105. All quotations are from *The Works of Robert Boyle*, ed. Michael Hunter and Edward B. Davis, 14 vols. (London: Pickering & Chatto, 1999-2000), 5:131-34.

Occasional Meditations 53

Upon seeing an empty vessell brought to a fontane and instantly filde full

[43r] How sodenly is this vesell filld, though when it lately was brought to the fountane it had not so much as one drop of water in it. O my soule, methinkes what I have now seene should be instrouctive to thee and make thee instantly run to that fountain of mersy who is able in an instant to fill thy empty soule.[56] O Lord, I bring an empty soule to a full Christ; O poure into me of the oyle of grace freely.[57] O Lord, I know thou arte able to fill all the empty veselles that are brought to thee, for thou art an unexasteable [unexhaustible] fountaine; in thee are layde up all the treasures of grace.[58] O lett me out of thy fullnes [43v] receive grace for grace.[59] O Lord, I know thou arte not a sealed fountane;[60] O, therfore, flow into me and send me away brim-full of grace.[61]

[44r] Ocasenall Meditationes 1663 M Warwicke

[44v] *Upon seeing a very faire and bewtifull aple, but when I had cutt it finding it roten at the heart*

[45r] How beawtefull and lovely an aple dos this appeare to my eye, and how dos the gawde [gaudie] and curious out-side atract my sight to gase dealightfully upon it, and how desireous am I to taist it, to try wither the inside will prove as dealisious to my taist when I have eaten it as the rine dos to my sight now I have viewd it. But I had noe sonar pared off that dealicate enameled rine and cut the aple to taist it, but I fonde it quite rotten at the harte and fit for nothinge but to be thrown away and to put me in minde how fitly it might be compared to an hypocrite whose out side, like a painted sepullcar, apeares bewtifull but with in is full of nothing but rotenes and [46r] uncleanes.[62] And yet when he has put on his counterfeit garment, he has so well adorned it with painted apeareing, dissembled graces that he has by the beholdares bene taken for that which he was

---

[56] God, the fountain of living water and life (Jeremiah 17:13, Joel 3:18, Psalm 36:9, Proverbs 14:27, John 4:10-14, and Revelation 7:17); see also above, n. 14.

[57] The five wise virgins in Matthew 25:1-13 are sometimes seen to meet the bridegroom with the oil of grace and not the lamp of profession: Francis Roberts, *The True Way to the Tree of Life* (London, 1673), 61; John Mason, *The Midnight-cry. A Sermon Preached On the Parable of the Ten Virgins* (London, 1692), 16.

[58] Recalling perhaps Colossians 2:3: "in whom are hid all the treasures of wisdom and knowledge."

[59] John 1:16.

[60] In Song of Solomon the spouse is an enclosed garden, "a spring shut up, a fountain sealed" (4:12). Elsewhere God is the fountain "opened to the house of David" (Zechariah 13:1) and the living fountain or "the fountain of life" (Jeremiah 17:13, Joel 3:18, Psalm 36:9, Proverbs 14:27, John 4:10-14, and Revelation 7:17). See also above, n. 14.

[61] Cf. John 1:16.

[62] Matthew 23:27.

but onely the conterfeit of. But yet when times of triall have come, he has then made some discoveries that has showde he was rotten and unsonde at the hearte. O Lord! I humbly beseech thee, thou that deasirest and lovest trueth in the inwarde partes[63] purge out of me all the leaven of hipocrise,[64] and lett me not be carefull onely to seame holy and negligent of being so, but give me trueth in the inwarde partes, and lett religion be prinsepally seated in my heart, and make my heart sonde [sound] in thy [46v] statutes that I may not be ashamed.

Upon a henes flying undauntedly at a kite that came to gett her chikenes from her and then covering them under her winges to secure them

[47r] How dareing and undaunted a corage has this poore hen expreste in her atemptes to seacure her littell brode from being snachte from her, and how wisely has she taken care by gathering them under her winges to keepe them safe least if thay showld stragull [straggle] from her the kite might take some of them. But by her covering them from his sight, those poore, littell, harmeles creatures who ware much too weake to be seacured by their own strength are yet very safe being kepte under the winges of the hen. O my soule, this sight ought to be a use of comforte to thee and to strinthen [strengthen] thy weake faith, who many times upon the [48r] amaseing and terrifying consideration of thy own weakenesse and disability to secure thy selfe from the roreing lyones bolde atemptes to snatch thee away[65] art ready not onely to tremble but to think thou shalt one day perish by him. But, O Lord, lett me now consider that though I am weake, yet stronger is he that is with me than he that is against me[66] and that the lyon of the tribe of Juda[67] is able courageously to seacure me from all the bolde sallies of Satan to devoure me. And, therfore, make me run under the winges of thy protection;[68] and as a hen gatheres her chikenes under her winges, so doe thou cover me and seacure me.[69]

[48v] *Upon seeing a mother watch her childe; and though she lett it goe in plane way, yet when it came neare any stair or stumbling block, take it in her armes and lifte it over*

[49r] How pleaseingly have I observed the care this tender mother takes by her watchfull eye to preaserve her childe from falling; and though she lettes it goe alone in plane and safe way, yet as sone as it comes neare a stone or a stepe that

---

[63] Psalm 51:6.
[64] Rich's definition of the unleavened in 1 Corinthians 5:7.
[65] 1 Peter 5:8.
[66] Matthew 12:30 and cf. Romans 8:31.
[67] Revelation 5:5.
[68] The "shadow" or "cover" in Psalms 17:8, 36:7, 57:1, 61:4, 63:7, 91:4.
[69] Matthew 23:37, Luke 13:34.

may indanger it by stumblinge at it to catch a fall, she presently to prevent ites harme takes it in her armes to helpe and lifte it over that difficulty. Thus deales my tender and watchfull heavenly father with me in my journy towards heaven; who when I meete with difecultyes too great for me to overcome and that the divell layes stumbling blocks in my way which wolde sartenly [certainly] make [50r] me fall, my mersifull heavenly father takes me in his armes, and liftes me over, and so keepes me from those snares and trapes that are so cuningly and insnareingly layde to make me fall. O Lord, I humbly beseech thee, keepe me from all the snares that my grand enemy layes in my way to heaven by takeing me up in the everlasting armes of thy mersy and carrying me over them.[70]

[50v] *Upon a very fine gonde [gown], but haveing a great spot in it which was more deaserneable because it was of so brite and vivid a color*

[51r] How beawtifull a garment is this, and how vivid is the colar [colour] of it; but how planely is the spot in it deaserneable, and how much more is it taken notice of in this bright colour then it wolde have bene in a les fine gown. The thinge I was considering upon it was how well this spot might be compared to the faileinges of Godes children, which are more conspicuous and apparent to the eyes of the world because their beautifull garment of grace did more atracte the eyes of all to gaze upon them, espesally of the wicked, to discover their spotes, not to hide them but to deride them for them, not takeing notice of their own splashes but rather seeing the mote in their brotherse eye then the beame in their own.[71] [52r] Their sines, being of a much worse nature and a blaker dye then the sines of Godes own peculiar people, yet are neither so much talked of or taken notice of because thay are all over too much besmired to have one spot minded. O Lord, I humbly beseech thee, keepe me from haveing my garmentes spotted with the flesh; and though I have many infirmityes and a sinn that dos so easely besett me, yet keepe back thy sarvant from presumptuous sines[72] and lett me have noe spot which is not the spot of a childe.

Upon takeing a great deale of paines to take out a spot of ink out of a white paper, but yet some sullie still remaineing

[52v] How much paines have I taken to take out this spot; and yet though I have by the helpe of the knife taken away the blakenes, yet all the robing [rubbing] I can doe will not so quite take away the spot but that somthinge will remaine that discoveres it was once ther. Which makes me in my thoughtes compare this blot

---

[70] Recalling 2 Timothy 2:26 and 1 Timothy 3:7 ("the snare of the devil") and the "everlasting arms" of God's refuge (Deuteronomy 33:27).
[71] Matthew 7:3. Splashes: spattered, soiled, muddied (*OED*).
[72] Psalm 19:13.

in the white paper to that in ones reputation; which when it has bene once blurde by the volgures [vulgars] voyce, though ever so much paines has bene taken to remove and quite take out the spote, yet all has bene unefectuall; for though possibly some thinge of the untrew reporte has bene silensed, yet it has still lefte som blur and so much sullie that it neaver was quite removed.

[53v] *Upon the diferent goeing out of two candulles, a watch one that was sett in a basen of water makeing a very great noyse before it went out*[73] *and another goeing out so that I could hardely heare it*

[54r] How strange a noyse did this candell make before it did goe out. It was great anufe to make me take notes of it and wonder to see the diference betwene that and another that went out so silently that I could hardely heare it. Which made me instantly in my thoughtes compare what I had lately observed to the diferent goeinges of Christianes out of this world. Som brawny and obdurate sinnar who wold neather by the worde of God be drawne to consider of his latter end nor by the searious admonitiones of minestures or Christian friends be disswaded from his wiked life, but was resolved to live at such a rate as if he had made a covenante with death and at hell ware at an agrement,[74] and to indolge himselfe in all for[55r]bidne pathes, and to entertaine any thinge that aproachte him under the name of a deaversion that might keepe him from thinkeing of the evell day and of that death that still made his aproaches to him, though undeaserned or disregarded by him; but when God has sent his sargnt [sergeant] death to strike him upon the backe and bid him apeare before that God whom he so much despised, and that he was throune upon his bed of siknes where all his pleasures have lefte him, and that he heares the sentance of his death pronounsed by the mouth of his docter and feels what he sayes confirmed by the great paines he inwardely feeles, then he begines to send forth hideous and afrighting skreames prosideing [proceeding] from the [56r] tormentes of his trobled conchens [conscience] upon the sense of his fore-past life and his being now with in the prospecte of eternety, into which he presently lanches with this terrible and afriting noyse. Where as the pious Christian that has learnt out of Godes worde that he is but dust and that unto dust he must sone againe reaturne[75] has made it his bisnes, with holy Job, all the dayes of his apoynted time to waite till his great change dos

---

[73] Watch candle: a candle kept lit throughout the night or a candle with marks measuring the passing of time. A candle set in water could serve as a reminder not to allow the watch candle to extinguish itself or as a means to mark time. The warning "Let not your watch-candle go out" is common; see, for example, Edmund Calamy et al., *An Exact Collection of Farewel Sermons* (London, 1662), 43; Thomas Watson, *A Pastors Love Expressed to a Loving People* (London, 1662), 10.

[74] Isaiah 28:15.

[75] Genesis 3:19.

come;⁷⁶ and being prepared for death by the preparation of a good life and being somunde [summond] by death to departe this life, has not onely taken his death patiently but chearefully; and with calmenes and serenity, with out any noyse but cries for mersy has given upe his soule in to [56v] the handes of that God that he has so faithfully served in his life. O Lord, I beseech thee, grante that I may so improve the small remainedur of my time here upon earth in prepareing for my future state that death may not surprise me before I am fitted for my great change, but grante that I may so spend my moment heare that when I come to dye I may have nothinge ellse to doe but to dye and with confidence and with chearfullnes to resigne my soule into thy handes as into the handes of a faithfull creator and a most mersyfull redeamor.

*[57r] Upon seeing a mouse in a plase wher I had sett a great many, seaverall littell, glasses of cordialles, and for feare of his doeing harme amonge them, setting upe a mouse trape and bateing it very well, and by it instantly caching the mouse whilst the baite was in his moueth*⁷⁷

[58r] How fearefull was I that this mouse, haveing crepte amonge so many pretious littell glases of cordialles, showld doe harme; to prevent which mischife, I instantly caused a trape to be sett upe ther and had it baited with the strongest chise [cheese] I could gett. By which powrefull bait the mouse was sone allured to taste it. But it had noe sonar got ites teeth into the chese, but before it had swalowde it, the trape fell doune and keachte it by the necke. And thus dead, with ites tieth in the chise, was it by my sarvant for the odnes of the maner of ites being taken brought me to see. Which [58v] instantly made me consider how aptly this might be compared to the grande enemy of mankindes traps,⁷⁸ which he continually is baiteing with the most alureing and tempting bates to entrape there in poore deluded mortalles who are too apte to be intaingled ther in and boldely som times to venture upon forbiden frute because it appeares beautifull to the eye, not considering that the biterest pilles are gilded over,⁷⁹ and so rashly adventures to tast the seduseing baite, but is many times so punished for that presumption that before thay have had so much as a through taist of that pleasure thay so thursted after, the trape has so [59r] fast keachte them that it has instantly proved their ruine. Thus God dos som times punich the breach of his comandes with soden death. Thus the Israties [Israelites]

---

⁷⁶ Job 14:14.
⁷⁷ Quite different is Lancelot Reynolds's reaction, "XXI. Vpon sight of a Mouse," in *Spiritvall Intervals, Or The Soules Exercise. In Certaine Meditations on sundry objects and occasions* (London, 1641), 75-80.
⁷⁸ "The snare of the devil" in 2 Timothy 2:26 and 1 Timothy 3:7.
⁷⁹ See, among others, "For with the finest gold, is the bitterest Pill covered," in Morris Palmer Tilley, *A Dictionary of Proverbs in England in the Sixteenth and Seventeenth Centuries* (Ann Arbor: University of Michigan Press, 1950), P325, 539.

lothing of mana and earnest deasire of quales was instantly punished; for while the meate was yet in their mouthes, the wrath of God fell on them;[80] and thus Zimry and Cosby ware instantly slaine in their sinn, omnipotense som times not delayeng his judgmentes but instantly slayeng the offendares.[81] O Lord, I therfore humbly beseech thee, keepe backe thy sarvant from so much as lookeing at the intrapeing bates that Satan is continually layeng to gett [59v] such fast holde of me that I may neaver be able to eskape. And seeing ther is noe plase so seacure but that he will lay an ambuch in for me, lett me still be upon my garde, remembering that mistrust is the onely way to safety. And, therfore, lett me not so much as allow my eyes to wander towardes his disgised baites, but, Lord, doe thou keepe me by the powre of thee, my God, through faith unto salvation.[82]

Upon lookeing in a lookeing glase in the morneing to dresse my selfe[83]

[60r] How bise am I adresing my selfe and lookeing in this glase that I may apeare deasently before the compeny I am to converse with to day. But O, my soule, why am I not more carefull and conserned to dresse thee this morneing in the pure, unflatringe glasse of Godes worde, knowing that my inwarde setting out is observed by a more perseing eye then the world can possebly cast upon my outside and that the worde of God will show me all the spotes of my soule more trewly then my lookeing glase will show me the durty spotes of my skine. O Lord, I most humbly besiech thee, as much [61r] as my soule is more exselent then my body, so much more care lett me take to adorne the one then the other. O Lord, I humbly beseech thee, doe thou adorne me with all the graces of thy spirit[84] and make me be clothed

---

[80] Numbers 11:33.

[81] In Numbers 25:7-14 Zimri is the son of Salu killed by Phinehas along with the Midianite woman Cozbi, thereby turning God's wrath from the Israelites, who had been drawn to the worship of Baal. Another Zimri, in 1 Kings 16:8-20, killed Elah, seized power, and purged all males in the house of Baasha; besieged at Tirzah by Israelite forces, he committed suicide.

[82] 1 Peter 1:5.

[83] The looking glass is a common subject in meditations: Hall, "CXXXII Upon the Sight of a Looking Glass," in *Occasional Meditations*, 193-94; Spurstowe, "Meditation LV. Upon a Looking-Glass," in *The Spiritual Chymist*, 152-56; Boyle, "Reflection VI. Upon the sight of a Looking-glass, with a rich Frame," in *Occasional Reflections*, 5:88-90. On 6 December 1671 Rich lamented the vanity of adorning her body by looking in mirrors "to sett my selfe out with the neaglekte of my immortall Soul" (2/256v).

[84] "The spirit of grace and supplications" is both biblical (Zechariah 12:10, Hebrews 10:29) and common among seventeenth-century writers. Baxter, for example, echoes Hebrews in his depiction of Christ and Zechariah in his characterization of the grace and

with humility and have on the ornament of a meek and quiet spirit,[85] which is in thy sight of great valew.

[61v] *Upon goeing to walke in a very sereane and sunshine morneing but being instantly forsed to run home for feare of being wett by a great showre of raine*

[62r] How sereane and promising a morneing was this when by the sunes shineing I was invited to goe out and walke, but I had fetcht but a few turnes when I perseaved that it began to be over cast and that the blake cloudes gathering threatned a storme. But yet the hopes I had that it wolde blow over made me resolve to continue my walkeing, being drawne to doe so by the freachnes of the aire, and by the prity singeing of the birdes, and by the dealighting verdure of the wallkes, and by the prity primeroses wherwith the Willdernes was full both in the wodes [woody-part] and the bankes. But before I was aware, the storme of raine was so violent that it [63r] not onely made me forsake the plase I was so pleased to walke in but it made me doble my pase; and seeing that it selfe wolde not sarve my turne to keepe me from being wett, I was at last forsed to run for shelter in to the house. Wher I noe sonar was but that I instantly entertained my selfe with considering how fitly this unsartenty and soden change of the weather might be compared to the changes that are in all sublunary thinges, and how soon the most glitringe and most splended promiseing condition might be over cast with stormes of aflictiones, and how nesisary those tempestes ware to make us thinkeing of reaturneing [64r] home. For whilst we are seronded [surrounded] with numerous out warde mersyes, we are apte to forgett to turne homewardes, and to take upe with earth in stide of heaven, and to say, with the apostles (in another case), it is good to be heare.[86] But when God is so mersyfull as to send seasonable aflictiones, then, like the prodigall,[87] we begin to thinke of reaturning home to our father in heaven when we can noe longer feed our selves with the empty huskes of this worldes vanetyes. O Lord, I humbly beseech thee, lett me not stray from thee tell I am by a tempest driven home, but make me so ingenuous as to be drawne to thee by thy mersyes, and lett them be as so [64v] many

---

prayer God "poured forth" and "hath put into" the heart (*A Call to the Unconverted* [London, 1658], 227; *A Christian Directory,* Book Two, 21, 144).

[85] 1 Peter 5:5; 1 Peter 3:4.

[86] When Christ took Peter, James, and John to a mountain and was transfigured, Peter responded, "it is good for us to be here" and proposed the building of three tabernacles (Matthew 17:4, Mark 9:5, and Luke 9:33).

[87] Luke 15:11-32. Rich originally wrote "good Jacob."

cordes to tye me fast unto thee.[88] O lett thy mersyes make me give upe my selfe, my whole selfe, a liveing sacrefise unto thee.[89]

Upon seeing a birde fly very high in the aire; and though she desended doune againe to picke her meate, yet as sone as she had don, she flew upwardes againe singeing

[65r] How high was this poore birde just now in her aspireing flight towards heaven, soreing so high that I hardely thought she wolde ever have desended doune againe upon the earth. But at last she did, but stayde upon it noe longer then tell she had pickte her meate up and doune upon it; and then she, instantly singeing, mounted upe, as if she ware glade to reaturne againe towardes heaven and as if her leaveing it ware rather an efecte of neseasety then of choyce. O my soule, lett this observation make thee study how to reconsile Martha and Mary, the bisnes of the world and that of heaven.[90] And though whilst thou dwellest in this house of clay[91] thou must be upon earth, yet as sone as thou hast dispachte the neasisary workes of thy calling, still [66r] upon the winges of devotion monte alofte[92] and leave this earth behinde thee, and reaturne not to it tell thou arte

---

[88] Most commonly Christ draws with the cords of love, though the covenant and prayer were also seen in the seventeenth century as cords that draw toward God or bind him in love (Thomas Gouge, *God's Call to England, For Thankfulness after gracious Deliverances* [London, 1680], 135; Thomas Adams, *The Main Principles of Christian Religion* [London, 1675], 79; Jeremy Taylor, *The Rule and Exercises of Holy Living* [London, 1650], 290-91). Gouge cites Hosea 11:4 as a biblical source. Rich also describes former mercies as "Cordes to tye me faster unto thee" (17 August 1672, 3/49r).

[89] Romans 12:1; see above, n. 43.

[90] Martha, her sister Mary, and their brother Lazarus lived in Bethany (John 11:1-2). Rich has in mind Luke 10:38-42, where Jesus admonishes the woman who is "cumbered about much serving," "Martha, Martha, thou art careful and troubled about many things." Richard Baxter comments on this biblical passage, "Christ doth not blame *Martha* for her care and work, but for not preferring better: Nor speaks this so much to blame her, as to commend *Mary*, and to teach us all what to prefer" (*A Paraphrase on the New Testament* [London, 1685], C4v-D1r). In the many references in the diary, Rich expresses the traditional view of Mary as the contemplative and Martha as the active or busy (Mary Rose D'Angelo, "Mary 2," in *Women in Scripture*, ed. Carol Meyers [Boston: Houghton Mifflin Company, 2000], 119), comparing herself to Martha (e.g., 1/34r, 83r; 2/198v; 3/167r, 251v; 5/41r, 118v, 165r, 176v). Joseph Hall also admonishes in T*he Art of Divine Meditation*, "Trouble not thyself any longer, with Martha, about the many and needless thoughts of the world" (*The Art of Divine Meditation*, ed. Huntley, in *Bishop Joseph Hall and Protestant Meditation in Seventeenth-Century England*, 86).

[91] Job 4:19.

[92] Mounting with the wings of prayer, meditation, and devotion (cf. Psalm 55:6) is commonplace among seventeenth-century commentators on meditation; God is also seen as a refuge: "with the wings of ardent Devotion we should fly unto God for shelter, and for relief" (Isaac Barrow, "Sermon VI. Of the Duty of Prayer," in *The Works of the Learned*

nesesetaded to doe soe, and then lett that be an efecte of thy obedience. But doe not looke upon it as thy hapynes to be converseing in earth but rather wish that thou wert absent from the body that thou mightest be preasent with the Lord.[93]

Upon a poore womanes deasireing me to give her somthinge to cure a consumption which she was very dangereously ill of, though she looked very well

[66v] How earnestly dos this poore creature petition me to give her somthinge that may doe her good for her consumption;[94] and yet she lookes so well that if she did not pleade more moveingly to my eare then to my eye, I showld not be much moved to exsersise my charety towardes her. Yet to move me to compasenate her condition, she informes me that she has longe languished and decayde in her fleach before it was minded or taken notice of by her but that now she is grone so leane and weake that she beleeves she canot longe continue if she be not instantly releived by som good medsones [medicines]. Turn this, O my soule, into spirituall consideratones [67r] and thinke, if it be so disperate a condition to be sike of a bodily consumption, what is it then to be troubled with a spirituall one; and to have thy graces consume and decay before thou perseavest thay doe so; and though thou apearest to thy beholderes in the world in so seameing a good and thriveing condition, that thy inwarde lainguichinges are not conspikeous [conspicuous] to them. Yet if thou feelest thy spirites decay and that thy graces abate of their former strength and vigor, thou mayest upon this discovery conclude this is the dangerous disease thou arte pineing under. O thou great physician of soules[95] (as well as bodyes), who arte able to cure all maner of diseases wherwith thy poore creatures are opreste, I humbly [67v] petitione thee to prevent in me this dangerous consumption and lett my graces be so far from growing faint that thay may dayly increase in strinth [strength]. O Lord, when thou perseavest them to decay, then doe thou instantly strinthen [strengthen] in me that which is ready to dye and make me to thrive in spiritualles and to add one deagree of grace unto another.[96]

Isaac Barrow, D.D. Late Master of Trinity College in Cambridge, 2nd ed., 4 vols. [London, 1686-1687], 1:73).

[93] Rich deleted the rest of the sentence: "and that thou hadest winges like a birde that thou mightest flee away and be at rest" (66r), quoting from Psalm 55:6.

[94] Consumption: a disease that consumes or wastes away, specifically phthisis or pulmonary tuberculosis (*International Dictionary of Medicine and Biology*, ed. Sidney I. Landau, 3 vols. [New York: John Wiley and Sons, 1986], 1:629).

[95] See above, n. 2.

[96] Rich deleted the rest of the sentence: "tell I arive at the fullnes of the stature of Christ" (67v), quoting from Ephesians 4:13.

Upon lookeing in a prospective glasse

[68r] How pleaseing is the lookeing in this prospektive glase⁹⁷ to me because by the helpe of it I am inabled planely to deaserne thinges that are very distante from me and yet thay are in this glasse presented as very neare to me. But methinkes it should not onely be pleaseing to me but informeing too. O my soule, consider that though thou arte in this vale of teares⁹⁸ at a very remote distance from heaven and arte not able to see it, yet by the prospektive glasse of faith which God has given thee thou maist be helped to looke upe to it and, as Moses did, to see him who is invisible, and to be car'ed upe into Monte Nebow, and from thense have a prospecte in to the heavenly Cannane, and to discover on [68v] this side Jordane that it is a land that is so pleasant that it is worth parteing with all wordly acomodationes for it.⁹⁹ And make me parte with thinges temporale for the thinges that are eternall.¹⁰⁰ O make me seake after that site [city] that has a fondation whose maker and bildar is God.¹⁰¹

*Upon washing out with the helpe of a littell water a great deale of writing that was in a littell table booke and leaveing the leaves of it as white as if ther had neaver bene writeing in it*¹⁰²

[69r] How full was this table booke just now by my writeing doune my memorandums in it; but when I had done with them, how easely did I with the helpe

---

⁹⁷ Prospective glass: a telescope, e.g., Boyle's "Reflection X. Looking through a Perspective Glass upon a Vessel we suspected to give us Chase, and to be a Pyrat" (*Occasional Reflections*, 5:61-62).

⁹⁸ See above, n. 21.

⁹⁹ George Swinnock similarly writes, "I may with *Moses* go up to *Mount Pisgah*, and take a view with the *prospective glass* of faith, of *Palestine*, and that goodly land *flowing with milk and honey*. I may enter into the suburbs of the new *Jerusalem*, taste some clusters of the Grapes of *Canaan*" (*The Christian-Mans Calling: Or, A Treatise of Making Religion ones Business . . . The Third and last Part* [London, 1665], 442). In the mountainous region of Moab northeast of the Dead Sea, Mount Nebo is also linked in the Bible with "the top of Pisgah" (Deuteronomy 34:1). From this view are vistas of the Dead Sea, the valley of Jordan, and the desert of Judea. On this mountain, where he would die, Moses saw the promised land he would not enter (Deuteronomy 32:49-52, 34:1-8). In the diary's accounts of her meditations, Rich desires to be carried to the top of the mount and given a view of Canaan (18 December 1668, 1/146v-47r); God carried her there and gave a taste of heaven (11 March 1669, 1/303r-v; 19 November 1669, 2/3r-v; 8 January 1670, 2/33v-34r); heaven also appeared to her (28 January 1670, 2/46r).

¹⁰⁰ Cf. 2 Corinthians 4:18 and the collect for the Fourth Sunday after Trinity, "that we so pass through things temporal, that we finally lose not the things eternal" (*The Book of Common Prayer*, D2r).

¹⁰¹ Hebrews 11:10.

¹⁰² Among the occasional meditations Rich was reading on the morning of 20 September 1667 was one "upon washing out of a littell table booke a great deal of writeing

of a littell water wash them all out againe and lefte the table booke so cleane as if there had neaver bene any writeing in it. O my soule, translate this in to spiritualles and consider, though thy sines are noted in Godes booke, yet when thay are washt away with the blood of that emakelate [immaculate] lambe who can make skarlet and crimsone sinnes as white as snow,[103] there will not be any more apearance of them than if thay had never bene.[104] O Lord, I humbly beseech thee, therfore blot out that hande writeing of ordinances which is contrary [69v] to me,[105] and naile it to the crosse of Christ, and lett that blood which purefyes from all sines purefy my conchance [conscience] from all dead workes to serve thee, the liveing God.[106] And, I most humbly besiech thee, lett my sines be so washte out[107] that thay may neaver more rise upe against me to be my confusion heare or my condemnation heare after.[108]

Upon being awalkeing and feeleing a few dropes of raine fall upon my fase, and in a good time noe more, but at last a great showre falowde

[70r] These few drops I felte fall upon my fase made me aprehend being sone wett, and therfore resolve to keepe neare shelltar, and so continued my walke as long as I could. Which I did much longer without interuption then I expected, but at last a great and violent showre falowde those small dropes. Which made me compare my own condition, which I thought might not very unfittly be so to what had lately hapned. For when I have sett a day aparte from all other imploymentes to humble my soule before God and have indeavered to awaken it by the startling consideration of Godes judgmentes against impenitent sinnares and what he has prepared for the punishing of the presumptious despisers of his comandes, these thoughtes have made me drop now and then a single teare. But when God has bene so mersyfull as to give me a prospecte of a life full of unmerited mersyes uninterupted by all my disingenuous backslidinges from him, this has so throughly worked upon my harde and unsensible heart that, as if God had made a spirituall thawe upon my heart, I have shed showres of teares and have powred out my heart like water before the Lord.[109]

---

with the helpe of a littell water and leaveing the table booke as cleane as if there had neaver bene any writeing in it" (1/117r). The meditation is included among those for the year 1663.

[103] Revelation 7:10, 14; Isaiah 1:18 and cf. Psalm 51:7.
[104] 1 Peter 1:19, Revelation 7:14.
[105] See above, n. 31.
[106] Hebrews 9:14.
[107] Cf. Psalm 51:1-2, Acts 3:19.
[108] Rich deleted the rest of the sentence: "but lay them upon that skape goote Jeasus Christ that thay may be cared away that thay may neaver more be fonde" (69v).
[109] Recalling perhaps the tears in Jeremiah 9:1 and Psalm 22:14.

O Lord, I humbly beseech thee, lett thy mersyes allwayes melt my hard and rocky heart and lett thy goodnes leade me to repentance.

[70v] *Upon sealeing a lettar*

How carefull was I to have my seales in readynes that so when I had dropte the wax I might instantly whilst it was hot make in it the impression of the seale, knowing that it could not otherwise be done; for if I had stayde tell it had bene colde, it wolde have bene too late. O my soule, turne this into a spirituall consideration and be as watchfull when thy heart is hot, either by surpriseing providenses or by the warmeing consideration of the indearing love of God to thee, to have sensible impressiones made when it is so; and then to repent and put good resolutiones in practise of new obedience and wallkeing more closely with God; and not stay till thy heart is colde and unfitt to have any impression made.

O Lord, I humbly besiech thee, lett me strike whilst the irone is hott[110] and nott lett those impressiones which thou arte pleased to put upon my spiritt goe off, but lett me obay the santefieng motiones of thy blessed spiritt that so thay may have an abideing good upon my soule, I humbly besiech thee.

Upon lookeing in a very falte [faultie] *and flatringe glasse*[111]

[71r] How much more tolerably does my fase apeare to me as it is now represented me by this flatringe glasse then indeed it is and then it dos apeare to otherse who doe not see me in it. And though at first my vanity may tempte me to be lesse unsatesfide with this prospecte then with a trew representation of my selfe, yet when I come to consider that it is but a false beauty that I am pleased with, it presently stifulles [stifles] all the dealight of it. Thus it is with a flatteror whose false and smouth [smooth] tongue wolde represent to me my actiones as desaitefully as this glasse dos my fase. But when I com impartially to looke into my selfe and by that inwarde sight canot but be disabused from the beleefe of what that deceaver has tolde me, I am so far from being pleased with that unworthy persone who showde me a false picture of my selfe that I canot but dispise him and rather chuse to converse with those exselent persones whose goodnes makes them show me what I realy am by telling me truthes then with those that by telling me I am allredy posseste of those vertues I want wolde keepe me from the seakeing after them.

---

[110] Proverbial: "It is good to strike while the Iron is hot," in Tilley, *A Dictionary of Proverbs in England*, I94, 342.

[111] See above, n. 83.

[72r] Ocasionale Meditationes 1667 M Warwicke

[72v] *Upon layeng by som burnt endes of wode that thay might be usefull to rekindle a new fire*

[73r] How sone allready by these burnt stikes endes have I rekindled a fire. Which observation may be usefull to minde me how often by som meditationes that by Godes blessing have bene usefull to me I have againe by layeng them by in readines had my afectiones rekindled when otherwise I might unsouksessfully have spent a great deale of time before I could have fond any warmeth, as I might upon this fire have bestowde a great deale of blowing if I had not preaserved those usefull stikes.

O Lord, I humbly besiech thee, therfore by former warmeing meditationes of the greatnes and unmeritednes of thy love, reinflame againe my devotiones and heate the furnase of my affectiones seaven times hootar.[112] Lett formar meditationes warme my heart againe with a peaculiar and transendent deagree of love unto thy selfe.

[73v] *Upon ones payeng for a house but a littell fine but giveing yearly a great rente*

[74r] This may be usefull to minde me of the diferent wayes by which at furst convertion God is pleased to bringe home his last shipe [lost sheep].[113] Som have great terores, and have their fleach tremble for feare of him, and are afraide of his judgmentes, and goe morneing all the day under a spirit of bondage.[114] Other Christianes are drawne by the cordes of his love[115] and so with all the sweetnes imaginable com home from sinn to God. But yet though these more happy Christianes doe not pay to their great landlord so great a fine of grife and troble at their first turneing, yet thay pay him a more constant great rent of penitentiall sithes and teares for the unhappy miscarages of their unregenerate life, which is a constant springe that is neaver dry but allwayes runing out as long as their life lastes.[116]

O Lord, I doe most humbly besiech thee, lett me neaver keepe backe this rent but yearly pay thee all the grife I am able for my haveing ever bene so ungratefull and so disingenuous as to stoute it out against thee and to ofende thee

---

[112] Daniel 3:19.
[113] Matthew 18:12-14, Luke 15:4-6.
[114] Psalm 38:6; Romans 8:15.
[115] See above, n. 88.
[116] Fine: "A fee paid by a tenant to the landlord at the commencement of the tenancy to reduce the rent payments" (*Black's Law Dictionary*, ed. Bryan A. Garner, 7th ed. [St. Paul, MN: West Group, 1999], 646).

by my reiterated ofenses.[117] Lett me, as Mary went weepeing to the sepullcur,[118] so goe [74v] weepeing to my grave that ever I sined against thee.

Upon siting in my arbor in the Willdernes at Lees and heareing two of the laburing men discourse[119]

[75r] How much was I both surprised and trobled—when I had got into the pritty Willdernes a plase so soletary that I thought I had bene ther hid from all mortall eyes and freed too from all outwarde intangling destractiones and was indeavering to gett rid of all inwarde, too, that I might taste that deavine gustow that is to be fonde in converseing with God in solitude—to find this sweet quiet interupted by a loude voyce which gave me a very unpleaseing disturbance. Yet my curiosety sone drew my atention to harken who the persone was that had thus intruded into my privasy. Which I noe sonar had don, but I discovered it was two of the laburing men that looked to the garden and ware now imployde in rouleing a gravell walke in the Willdernes; which though at a very remote distance from the arbre where I was sett, yet their rude, loude mode of speakeing had made their voyce sone aproaech my eares. The one of them was ashewreing [assuring] his companion that thay rouled the worest way because it was somthing upe hill and the other was much the easiar. Upon which ashewrance the other without any debate was so fare convinsed that he presently went to begin at the tother ende of the walke. [75v] Which whilst he was doeing, I did, as Pharoues buttlar did, call my own falte to my rememberance;[120] for not unresemblingly [unresemblably] have I bene drawne by the great enemy of my salvation to quit my begun and intended journy to heaven because I som times fond it harde and was by him perswaded to beleeve that the way the world walkes in was best because most easy, not remembering that tis duty and not ease that a Christian is called to.[121] But, O Lord, I most humbly beseech thee, though I often trip in my journy to heaven,[122] yet lett me neaver forsake my purpose of goeing thiethar

---

[117] Stout: "to act in a defiant or stubborn manner" (*OED*).

[118] Mary Magdalene goes alone to the sepulcher in John's account of the resurrection; Christ appeared to her as she "stood without at the sepulchre weeping" (John 20:11).

[119] After Rich returned from London on 10 September 1667, where she had been for nine months, she wrote that she retired immediately the next day to the Wilderness (1/114v).

[120] Genesis 41:9.

[121] An echo of Ephesians 2:2 ("ye walked according to the course of this world") and Luke 17:10 (the "unprofitable servants: we have done that which was our duty to do"). The distinction between duty and ease is central to Richard Baxter's *The Saints Everlasting Rest*, 8th ed. (London, 1659). He dismisses the "worlds common, careless, easie way" and insists that while duty is insufficient "without Christ, so Christ will not do it without duty" (16, 17).

[122] WW notes that she uses this expression in the diary entry for 23 Sept. 1667 (75v).

nor be drawne from the performance of the striktest dutyes of relidgion because I find them harde; but lett me take the more paines to performe them, remembering that though the path that leades to life be straite and the gate narow, yet if I strive I shall enter into joy, but the brod way will bring me into everlasting tormentes.[123] O Lord, lett me neaver be so besoted as to preafer the pleasures of sinn, which are but for a moment, before those riveres of pleasures which are at thy right hand for ever more.[124]

[76r] *Upon stayeng betwene Chelsy and Lees to baite at Burnte Wode at dinar*[125]

With what chearefullnes and serenety of minde did I baire [bear] with all the inconvenanses and ill entertainement of this inne upon this consideration that what I met with there was not to last; but at night, when I came home to my own house, I should have abundante recompense made me by the good things I showld there injoy. O my soule, turne this into spirituall advantage and consider that all the ill entertainement I meete with in this vaine world is but the ill acomodationes of this great inne, the world. And when thou hast past through this howleing willdernes[126] and hast finished thy great journy, thou shalte come to heaven to thy home, wher when thou hast bene but one howre, it will make thee forgett all the trobles thou metest with in the way.

[76v] *Upon a begares beging of my Lady Robertes and she giveing him but a smale peece of mony, yet the man was at the receaveing it so much pleased that he cryde out with joy, what a gifte is heare*[127]

[77r] With what diferent eyes did the giver and receaver of this peece of charity looke upon what was given, the liberale bestowar thinkeing the gifte but smale

---

[123] Matthew 7:13-14. See also the straight path in Luke 3:4, Matthew 3:3, and Mark 1:3. Rich also strives in the diary "to enter in at the strait gate" (19 March 1672, 2/293r; 3 April 1677, 5/105r), perhaps having in mind as well Baxter's biblical summary, "*the gate is strait, and the way narrow, and we must strive if we will enter; for many shall seek to enter, and not be able*" (*The Saints Everlasting Rest*, 16).

[124] Psalms 16:11, 36:8.

[125] On 10 September 1667 the Riches probably stopped at Brentwood on their journey from Chelsea to Leighs (1/114r). The foremost inn at Brentwood (the burnt wood) was The White Hart, on the north side of High Street. The inn dates from the fifteenth century and is still open. Among other seventeenth-century Brentwood inns were The Crown, The George, and The Bell (*A History of the County of Essex*, in *The Victoria History of the Counties of England*, ed. W. R. Powell [Oxford: Oxford University Press, 1983], 8:93-94).

[126] Phrase from Deuteronomy 32:10.

[127] Other meditations on the beggar are Hall, "XXVII Upon the Sight of an Humble and Patient Beggar" and "CXXXVIII Upon an Importunate Beggar," in *Occasional*

and therfore intended the next time she met the begar to bestow upon him a more liberalle doule [dole], but the transported receaver in a great extasy of joy cryes out with admeration, what a gifte is heare. Thus it is often with the great God of heaven and poore indigent man when a poore creature out of ites sense of the great neseasety and want it has of grace beges with great importunety of God to give him grace needfull for him, and God in great mersy to that poore soule gives him som, yet dos not at the first grant him so great a proportion as he intendes him afterwardes, but intendes to try furst his thankefullnes for what he has allready receaved, and then intendes to give more grace that so he may grow in grace. But the happy receaver of it, knowing how unworthy he is of the least measure of grace and findeing that the littell he had already distrebuted to him has bene able to worke some sensible change in him and concur [conquer] some lustes which before concurde [conquerd] him, with transportes of joy falles of reaturneing glory to God by practesing the highest straines of gratetude, lookeing upon what he has receaved with eyes of admeration.

[77v] O Lord, I doe most humbly besiech thee, lett me lerne a leson of gratetude from this poore persone and be thankefull for the least deagree of grace thou hast bestowed upon me, cryeng out as he did, what a gifte is heare, that being thankefull for it thou maist bestow a greatar proportion that so I may grow in grace that my soule may prosper and I may be a thriveing, prosperus Christian.

Upon lookeing out of my window at Chelsy and seeing a littell cauke bote [cock-boat] *tide to a great bote*

[78r] How many waves have I with admiration observed to have tossed this littell cock-boat,[128] some of them so strongly beating against it that I thought it was impossible but it must sink, yet still I saw it safe. Which made me much

---

Meditations, 138, 196-97; Boyle, "Reflection V. Upon two very miserable Beggars, begging together by the High-way," in *Occasional Reflections*, 5:57-58; Bury, "Med. 60 Upon beggers at the door," in *The Husbandmans Companion*, 285-89. The Riches resided at Chelsea from December 1666 until March 1668, where Mary enjoyed the company of Letitia Isabella, the second wife of John Robartes (1606-1685), who served from 1661-1673 as lord privy seal and would become the first Earl of Radnor in 1679. Letitia Isabella was her husband Charles's cousin, the daughter of Sir John Smith and Isabella Rich, the sister of Robert Rich, second Earl of Warwick. The Robarteses resided in Chelsea at Danvers House, located at the end of the street by the same name and across from Crosby Hall, a residence Pepys found "the prettiest contrived house that ever I saw in my life" (Anne Duffin, "John Robartes, first earl of Radnor," in *ODNB*, 47:65-67; Randall Davies, *Chelsea Old Church* [London: Duckworth and Co., 1904], 145-48; Samuel Pepys, *The Diary of Samuel Pepys*, ed. Robert Latham and William Matthews, 11 vols. [Berkeley and Los Angeles: University of California Press, 1970-1983], 2:187-88).

[128] Cock boat: a small or light craft, a "small ship's boat" commonly pulled behind (*OED*).

wondar till at last I observed it was by a rope fastned to a great bote. This discovery made my admiration at the safety of the cock bote sease [cease] but raised it to consider the hapynes of a poore weake Christian. Who though often by the visesetudes [vicissitudes] and the troubles of this world tossed to and fro, and in such dangeres that the beholders canot but thinke it must peariech [perish] and can discover noe visible way for its safety, yet it being by faith united to Christ, it does like the arke still keepe above water and is safe from all the most violent tempestes it meetes with here below,[129] all the blustering windes it meetes with being but sarvisable [serviceable] to bring it safe to its harbore.

O Lord, I doe most humbly beseech thee, lett me be so tide to thee that I may still be safe even in the midest of all tossing providenses I meete with in this world that though thay may shake me, yet not overthrow me. O Lord, I know my safety is not in my holdeing thee but in thy holdeing me, for I showld sone lett goe my holde.[130] I [78v] know the divell wolde fain have me, but lett me be kepte by the powre of God through faith unto salvation. O, make me one of thy shipe [sheep] unto whom thou wilte give eternall life and none shall plouke [pluck] out of thy handes.[131]

Upon observeing the skies for som dayes togeather to promise raine, and yet it went off with onely raineing som few dropes

[79r] How many dayes has the most skillfull observer of the skies bene deceived in the weather, still beleeveing that there wolde be dayly raine in great plenty, and yet we could see nothing but now and then a few dropes. Thus it is often with a poore prodigall from God who has strong convictiones that if he dos not repente he shall perish, and dos thereupon promise both to God and man that he will instantly breake off his wiked life and be a trew converte, and dos so far convince his Christian friends of the trueth of his intended purpose as to shed a few penitentiall teares, which makes them confidently expecte he will be a trew converte; yet he being onely convinced and not converted, haveing onely a resolution to leave sinn but not being yet able to loeth it, he dos, as Pharow did, harden his heart yet againe[132] and so frustrates the confidence of his friendes by being, Agrippa like, but allmost a Christian.[133]

---

[129] The typology of Noah's ark and Christ's salvation is well-established; see, for example, John Milton's *Paradise Lost*, Book 11.

[130] Possibly Psalms 119:117, 18:35; see also the Coverdale version of Psalm 73:27 in *The Book of Common Prayer*, P1r, and George Herbert's "The Holdfast" (*The Works of George Herbert*, ed. F. E. Hutchinson [Oxford: Clarendon Press, 1967], 143 and n.).

[131] John 10:27-28.

[132] Pharaoh's heart hardens numerous times in Exodus, especially chapters 7-10.

[133] Festus brought Paul before Marcus Julius Agrippa (28-c. AD 100), the Herodian king who listened to Paul's defense of his Christian faith. "Then Agrippa said unto Paul,

[79v] *Upon seeing a blind minestur in Chelsy pullpett*[134]

[80r] How strangely was I both surprised and trobled to see a blind minestur in the pullpite, the sight of him makeing me thinke I had hitherto bene too unthankfull for the mersy of my sight, and could neaver for the time to com expresse my gratetude sofisantely for it, nor ever simpathise with him anufe to pity him sofisantly for his losse of it. But after the sarmone was ended, and that I had converste with him long anufe to find him a person of a very cleare understanding, and that I must by his holy discourse conclude him a very pious Christian as well as a very chearefull one, I began to thinke that he which before was so sad and mortefieng a spektacle to me was much lesse miserable then those unfortunate creatures who ware inwardely darke, haveing the eyes of their understandinges darkened[135] so as thay call good evell and evell good,[136] chuseing rather sinn that will damn them then Christ that wolde save them. O Lord, I most humbly besiech thee, make me rather chuse outwarde blindenes then inwarde; lett me not prefer eyes which doges and cates have before that which angelles are happy in, knowledge and grace.

Almost thou persuadest me to be a Christian" (Acts 26:28).

[134] On 6 July 1667 Rich heard a blind preacher's sermon and afterwards "had much good discourse and fond my heart much car'ed out to compasionate him and to praise God for giveing me my sight" (1/101v). WW suggests the blind minister was "very probably Mr Lucas" (79v). Richard Lucas (1648/9-1715), author and noted London preacher, did not become totally blind until several years after Rich's death. In any case, her diary account of the blind minister is dated 6 July 1667, when Richard Lucas would have still been a university student (Edward Vallance, "Richard Lucas," in *ODNB*, 34:688-89). Compare Hall, "LVII Upon the Sight of a Blind Man," in *Occasional Meditations*, 152; Reynolds, "XXVIII. Upon a blinde idle man," in *Spiritvall Intervals*, 105-8.

[135] Ephesians 4:18, 1:18.

[136] Isaiah 5:20.

[80v] *At Durdones.*[137] *Upon lookeing into a glasse bee hive, and expecting to see in it a great deale of hony, and finding nothing but blake, dry comes* [combs]

[81r] With what great expectation of store of hony did I looke into this fine glase bee hive;[138] but when it was opened, contrary to my hopes I fond onely a littell hony at the tape [top] and all the rest of the hive filded with nothing but dry, blake comes. Thus it fares often with us in our persutes after the pleasures of this world to which we come with raised expectationes of receaveing abundance of swetnes; but often we mite [meet] with very sensible defeates, finding most miserable disapoyntmentes, our blakest and bitarest crosses coming from those thinges wher in we expected our greatest solase. The pleasures of the world promiseing much at a distance but at the ende frustrate our expectationes.

O Lord, I most humbly beseech thee, therfore lett not my heart goe out too freely after any worldly pleasures, expecting much gustow from them, but lett me posses them as if I possesste them not.[139] O lett me looke after those pleasures that are satesfieng and lasting which are at thy right hand for ever more.[140] O Lord, I deasire noe other pleasure but the warmeth and fire of thy love; this, O Lord,

---

[137] On 7 August 1667 Rich went to Durdans or Durdens, the Surrey residence near Epsom of George Berkeley, first Earl of Berkeley (1626/7-1698), and his wife Elizabeth Massingberd (d. 1708), which John Evelyn describes as *"Durdens the Sweete Villa"* (*The Diary of John Evelyn*, ed. E. S. de Beer, 6 vols. [Oxford: Clarendon Press, 1955], 3:291). She returned to Chelsea on August 20 after tending to her husband, who was suffering from gout (1/108r, 110r). Her relationship with the Berkeleys was quite close: besides counseling their daughter Mary, Rich notes her "good" discourses with Lord Berkeley, for whom she wrote "Rules for holy living." Rich may also be Lady Harmonia, the "Excellent Saint" Berkeley praises for encouraging him to write *Historical Applications and Occasional Meditations upon Several Subjects* (London, 1670), A4v.

[138] Samuel Hartlib's *The Reformed Common-wealth of Bees* (London, 1655) describes a transparent hive given to John Wilkins, the Warden of Wadham College, and includes a drawing of a three-tiered hive with glass side doors (42, 50-52). Wilkins gave John Evelyn one of "the *Transparent Apiaries*, which he had built like *Castles & Palaces* & so ordered them one upon another, as to take the *Hony* without destroying the *Bees*; These were adorn'd with variety of *Dials, little Statues, Vanes* &c: very ornamental." Evelyn placed the hive in his garden at Sayes Court, and "many Yeares after," 30 April 1663, Charles II "came on purpose to see & contemplate with much satisfaction" (Evelyn, *Diary*, 3:110). On 5 May 1665 Pepys saw in this garden "a hive of Bees; so, as being hived in glass, you may see the Bees making their honey and Combs mighty pleasantly" (*Diary*, 6:97 and n. 2).

[139] Cf. 1 Corinthians 7:30.

[140] Psalm 16:11. Thomas Gouge, for example, encourages, "Oh think with thy self what a blessed thing it will be, to live in the vision and fruition of God himself: in whose presence there is fullness of joy, and at whose right hand there are pleasures for evermore" (*A Word to Sinners, And a Word to Saints* [London, 1668], 194).

in my deliberate [81v] thoughtes I prefer before the pleasures of sinn, which are but for a season[141] and which can hardely satesfy us for a littell time, much less for eternety.

Upon plokeing [plucking] *a rose and putting it in my bosom and then seeing it sone wither*

[82r] How much was I pleased with the vivid color of this rose, and the swetnes of it, too, did much dealight me; but when I had ploukte it and layde it in my bosome, I perseaved it sone apeared discolored and withered. Thus it is often with those admired and favorite relationes and friendes to which we lett out our afectiones too freely, thinkeing we can neaver lay them too neare our hartes. But when we inconsiderately sett them upon the throne of our heartes, God often is so mersyfull (to a soule he loves) as to throw doune our idole and his rivall and to make it ether seeme withered in our eyes by haveing a lesse blinded passion for that persone or else to ploke it away by the fattall stroke of death.

O Lord, I doe most humbly besiech thee, lett me neaver force thee to ploke away those friendes I love by laying them too neare my heart; but lett me still love creatures as I ought to love them, allowing them but sparkes but reaserveing my britest flames to blase towardes heaven. O Lord, I doe most humbly besiech thee, doe thou inflame my heart with a peculiar and a transendent deagree of love to thee, my God.

[82v] *Upon seeing a fagote that had a great many littell stikes in it; but as sone as that stike that goes ronde them was cutt, thay all fell asundare*

[83r] How fast ware all these stikes kepte togeather whilst that one we cale the band was rounde them; but as sone as that was cutt, thay all fell asundare. Thus it is often in great famelyes. Whilst the father of the famely lives, he keepes all his children and sarvantes togeather; but when once God cutes the thread of his life, thay doe many times fall to peeces amongest themsellves, and are often at a greator distance from each other then before thay ware neare, and all that before lived togeather are dispersed into seaverall famelyes.

O Lord, therfore I most humbly besiech thee, preaserve alive the rular of my famely that we may be preaserved togeather and may not all ether fale asundare or be dispersed one from another.

---

[141] Hebrews 11:25.

[83v] ~~Upon seeing it very faire aver head but very durty under feete~~[142]

[84r] Occasionall Meditationes M Warwicke 1668

[84v] *Upon seeing a very devoute persone very meanely clad*

[85r] How plain does this worthy persone appear to hur beholdures in her outwarde habite, which makes her often pass by disregarded, when on the other side our eyes are often helde with admiration to beholde the shineing aparrell of a glittering galant. But when we come to be aquainted with the persone so meanely drest and find that though she is but plane clouth [cloth] without, yet she is vellvet with in, and that the other persone that is like a painted sepullcur outwardely yet with in is nothing but dirte and rotones [rottenness],[143] sartenly [certainly] noe considering beholder but must in their deliberate thoughtes prefer the one in their esteem much before the other.

O Lord, I most humbly beseech thee, make me be like the kinges daughter all glorious with in;[144] make me put on the Lord Jesus; and make noe provision for the flesh to fullfill the lustes thereof.[145] Lord, lett me be adorned with the ornament of a meek and quiet spirit;[146] make me take care to dresse my soule, knowing that my inwarde setting out is observed by a more pure and perseing [peircing] eye then the world can possibly cast upon my outside. And, Lord, make [85v] me consider that if I had on the finest closes [cloaths] and the most exsaikte [exact] dresse that is possible, yet these fine close and this exsaike dresse must be pulde off at night. But if I be dekte with the graces of thy spirit, thay will make me fine to eternety.[147]

Upon ones takeing a great deale of paines in washing and scouring an olde pewtare diech [dish] *to make it looke very brite*

[86r] How much paines is taken with this olde dish to make it appear brite, yet all the washing and skoureing will not be able to make it looke neare so well as it did when it was new. Thus it is often with those persones who have bene cried up for great beauties and begin to find that age has made great decayes, yet the desire thay have to apeare still what thay ware rather then what thay are settes them upon useing all that arte can doe by washinges and putting on fresh colours, stodeing to appear beautifull. But their beholderes, perseaveing them to want that great varnish to beawty, youth, and that their spring is past and autome [autumn]

---

[142] This meditation appears on 108.
[143] Matthew 23:27.
[144] Psalm 45:13.
[145] Romans 13:14.
[146] 1 Peter 3:4.
[147] See above, n. 84.

come, despise that orange color on their cheekes which thay wold fane have to pass for freach [fresh] roses.

O Lord, I doe most humbly beseech thee, make me not to repine but be contented to find nature decay, and lett me neaver indeaver to repair it by arte as Jesobell did;[148] but though I should find my eyes grown dim, yett lett me be content as long as I am able to lifte them upe to heaven and to powre out with them penitentiall teares for my sines. And though my strength decayes, yet lett me [87r] not care as long as I am strong in the Lord and in the powre of his might.[149] And though the spring begin to disapeare in my cheekes and the winter begines to make ites aproaches, yet make me to consider that when that is come, that gray haires are a croune of glory if thay be fond in a way of riteousnes.[150] Therfore, O Lord, lett me not be so fooleichly besotted as to thinke it is possible so to repaire my house of clay[151] as to make it looke as well as it did at first, but make me consider it is mouldering into dust. Therfore make me looke after heaven where beauty paleth not, and where there will be noe decay, but where I shall be fresh and floriching for ever.

[87v] ~~Upon a littell strikeing clauke of my lordes~~[152]

Upon seeing a great blase but instantly goe out

[88r] How bright a blase was here just now, but how presently is it gone out. Which made me instantly in my thoughtes compare it to a wicked mans religion which is but as a pure blase and is soon exstinct. It makes in a devoute fitt a great show but is but like a morneing dew which sone passes away.[153]

O Lord! I doe most humbly beseech thee, lett me have a constant fire. Lett me walke in an even course of universall and uninterrupted sinseare [sincere] obedience, which though it dos not make so great a show, yet it will holde longer.

[88v] *Upon a Gloworme*[154]

[89r] How wholly undiscovered was this glowworme in a bright day; but when a darke night came, it shined so bright that all that were with in veiw of it could

---

[148] 2 Kings 9:30.
[149] Ephesians 6:10.
[150] Proverbs 16:31.
[151] Job 4:19.
[152] A meditation with this title or a similar subject is not in the manuscript.
[153] Hosea 6:4.
[154] Compare Hall, "XLIX Upon a Glowworm," in *Occasional Meditations*, 148-49. Kitty W. Scoular establishes some classical and contemporary significance of the glowworm in *Natural Magic: Studies in the Presentation of Nature in English Poetry from Spenser to Marvell* (Oxford: Clarendon Press, 1965), 103-8.

not but with delight take notice of it. Thus it is often with a pious Christian. In times of prosperity their patience and many other Christian vertues are by their beholders wholly undiscovered; but when a darke night of affliction comes and that they are put upon the exercise of those vertues that thay are by Godes grace possesores of, then thay are so conspicuous to all their beholders that thay canot but with admiration say that God is in them of a trueth and that the righteous is more excellent than his neighbour.[155]

O Lord, I doe most humbly beseech thee, doe thou make me like a glow-worme that shines brightest in the darkest night. When thou bringest the bitter-est cup for me to drinke, then lett me chearfully say, the cup which my heavenly father has given me shall I not drinke it?[156] O when thou bringest me upon the greatest exercise of my patience, then lett patience have her perfect worke and make me show that Christian fortitude that may convinse my beholders that by Gods supporting grace a Christian can doe more then others. O Lord, make me exceed all the unregenerate world in holyness to[89v]wardes God and in righ-teousness towardes my neighbour that so my light may so shine before men that others may see my good workes and glorify thee, my heavenly father.[157]

Upon observeing at table some with great dealight feed upon a dish that others naushate [nauseate]

[90r] How often have I at my table observed that one persone feeds with a kinde of epicurism upon some beloved dish that another nashates [nauseates] and is not able to indure. Thus it is often with a regenerate and an unregenerate per-son. He that is renewed in the spirit of his mind[158] by converting grace findes in the servise of his God sweetness and serves God in the beauty of holynes,[159] counting his ordinances priveledges, and the house of prayer a house of joy unto him,[160] and one day in his house to be better than a thousand ellse wher.[161] But the unregenerate person is so far from being of his minde that he cryes the bur-den of the Lord: when will the Sabbath be gone and when will all holy dutyes be done; O, what a wearisomness is it to serve God.

O Lord, I doe most humbly beseech thee, lett me not like children be frited from what I love because others make a mouth at it. Lett not the unregenerates dislike of thy holy wayes make me disrelish them, but make me finde a savour and gustow in them, and lett me some times have those regales which thou usest

---

[155] 1 Corinthians 14:25 ("God is in you of a truth"); Proverbs 12:26.
[156] John 18:11.
[157] Matthew 5:16.
[158] Ephesians 4:23.
[159] Psalm 29:2.
[160] Isaiah 56:7; see also above, n. 31.
[161] Psalm 84:10, 2 Peter 3:8.

to give thy children. O Lord, doe thou some times carry me into thy bainketing [banqueting] house[162] and refresh me there with those [90v] consolationes of God which are not small, with that joy which a stranger intermedles not with, that so haveing tasted that the Lord is gratious[163] I may be able to say [of wisdom, or religion,] all her wayes are pleasantness and all her pathes are pease.[164] And lett the besotted world dislike the way to heaven and chuse the pleasures of the world for their happyness; but, O Lord, doe thou lifte upe the light of thy countenance upon me[165] and lett me injoy comunion with thee, and I shall be satisfied.

Upon a kindeled stick of fire being car'ed from one house to another to kindle there new fires

[91r] How soon has this kindled stick by removeing it into another house made ther a new fire. Which makes me with admiration thinke of the providence of God in removeing pious Christianes from a religious famely into an ireligious one and making them there by their holy life and most pious advice instrumental to kindle new fires of devotion in the heartes of those persones who live in the same plase where God has been pleased to transplant them.

O Lord! I doe most humbly beseech thee, make me an instrument of good this way. Lett me by a devoute life and a warmeing conversation be an instrument in thy hand of kindling in the unregenerate new fires; make me by often speakeing all good of thee and of thy wayes bringe home rebelles to soubmit to thy septare [scepter] and to glorify thee with their bodyes and with their soules, which is but their resonable service of thee.[166]

[91v] *Upon ones being reatired for their devotiones, but upon hearing their husband come home, hudling them over to goe to him and then perseaveing* [perceiveing] *that he had a mind to be rid of her*

[92r] How bise [busie] is the great enemy of mankind in studying suteable temptationes either to diverte us from our duty or else to distracte us in it. Witness what he has now don with this pious lady, who being retired to converse with her God in solitude, he temptes her from duty to duty; for he perswades her that she hearing her lord come home, it was fitt for her to pay her duty to him by presently goeing to him. And he so far prevailed as she was contente to huddle over her devotiones

---

[162] Song of Solomon 2:4.
[163] 1 Peter 2:3; see also Psalm 34:8 and the version in *The Book of Common Prayer*, M2v.
[164] Proverbs 3:17. WW rather than Rich may have added "of wisdom, or religion."
[165] Psalm 44:3.
[166] Romans 12:1; see above, n. 43.

to come and converse with her lord.[167] Which she had done but a very little while but that she perceived in him a deasire to be rid of her company, which made her presently thinke that she was justly punished for her leaveing her God, who would not have been weary of her converse with him, considering those are well comest to God that come to him oftnest and staye with him longest.

O Lord! I do most humbly beseech thee, make this example be usefull to me; and make me punctually, as thou comandest me, pay my duty to my husband, neglecting noe thing that is fitt for me to doe both as a loveing and obedient wife;[168] but make me so discrete in chuseing the most convenientest times for my injoying communion with thee that I may attende upon thee without [92v] distraction and may not be tempted either to neglect quite my devotiones or slitely to performe them; and make me to consider that though I have often fonde even in my dearest friendes that though thay love me ever so well, yet my compeny may som times be unseasonable to them, and therfore for the present wold be glade to be rid of me. Yet in my longest and frequentest aproaches to thy divine majesty I never found that any howre rendered them unseasonable, and therfore lett this make me carefull to be less imployde in rendering my visittes to men and more inploy'd in converseing with thee, my God.

Upon laying the fire together and observeing it without the help of the bellas [bellows] *instantly to blaze*

[93r] How sone dos this fire blase even without the helpe of the bellos. Which mindes me of Godes mersyfull and soden somtimes aproaches to a devoute soule; who has noe sonar separated it selfe from compeny through a vement [vehement] deasire of injoyeng comunion with God, but that before it has by meditation sturde upe ites harte to lay holde upon God, it findes to ites unspeakeable joy its harte hot and ready to burne with flames of love to its deare Saviour.

O Lord, I doe most humbly blese thee for the many times that thou hast bene pleased thus on a sudden without any preparation of my parte to blow the languide sparke in my breste and to make me finde first those heavenly gloinges of heart that presently broke foreth into most glorious blases. O, that thou woldest be pleased thus often to prevent me with thy mersy and to doe that for me in a moment which without thy helpe I canot doe in the longest spase of time.

---

[167] Huddle: "indecent haste," "crowded together in hurried confusion," or "confused utterance" (*OED*).

[168] Ephesians 5:22, Colossians 3:18, Titus 2:5, and 1 Peter 3:1.

[93v] *Upon wallkeing in Chelsy garden and observeing that the frost had made whole bankes of emenes* [anemones] *hang doune their heades, but after the sunn shined thay ware againe revived*[169]

[94r] How much was I both troubled and surprised to see those curiously inameled emenes [anemones] by a colde frosty night so nipt that thay all lay along the bankes so discoloured and so shriveled that I thought thay wold neaver have revived againe. But being so much a florist as not to be troubled at this unpleasing prospect, I went into another parte of the garden; where, when I had continued my walke for about two houres in another walke, as I reaturned home by the same flowry bankes, I did much to my wonder as well as satisfaction perceive the same languishing flowres by the breakeing forth of that glorious and reaviveing creature the sun so reavived and florishing that thay did so delightfully attracte my eye that it was impossible for me to pershew [persue] my intended purpose of returning home till I had walked som turnes by those sweet bankes. Whilst I was doeing so, this occasional meditation presented it selfe to my thoughts: that the some houres before dying and now revived flowres might not very unfittly be compared to a poore disconsolate creature that when God has withdrawne his comfortes from it presently droopes and languishes; but when God is so mersyfull as againe to cause his face to shine upon it and to lett the sunn of righteousnes breake [95r] foreth with healeing in his wings,[170] then it recoveres vigor and life, flouriching like a garden which God has blessed, and appeares againe to the beholderes with a chearfull serenity and composedness of mind, its graces flourishing and prospering.[171]

O my most mersifull father, I doe most humbly beseech thee, lett me experience this trueth that thy face shineing upon me is able to revive and quicken me and to make my soule prosper and florish. O lett me see that one beame of light

---

[169] Rich mentions being in the Chelsea garden in 1675 and 1676 as well as in 1667. Charlotte Fell Smith states that while living in Chelsea Rich "went daily to Sir Hans Sloane's beautiful gardens (or, as she calls them, Chelsea Gardens)" (*Mary Rich, Countess of Warwick [1625-1678]: Her Family & Friends* [New York: Longmans, Green, and Co, 1901], 163). Conceivably the later but not the first place might have been the Apothecaries' Garden, which was founded by the Society of Apothecaries in 1673. Now known as the Chelsea Physic Garden, it is also associated with the name of Hans Sloane, who leased the land permanently to the holding in 1722 (Sue Minter, *The Apothecaries' Garden: A New History of the Chelsea Physic Garden* [Stroud, Gloucestershire: Sutton Publishing Limited, 2000]).

[170] Malachi 4:2.

[171] Jeremiah 31:12; Rich also cries out to God for a soul prospering "like a garden" (17 March 1677, 5/92r).

shineing from thy face is able to cheare and comforte me more then others are by the confluense of all worldly injoymentes.[172]

[95v] *Upon chuseing a patron* [pattern] *of a fine stofe* [stuff][173] *but thinkeing it much finar* [than] *when I veiw'd it in the shop*

[96r] How carefully have I viewed all the patterns that ware presented me to chuse one out of for my young ladyes gondes [gowns]. Which when I had done and afterwardes saw the stuff in the shop in the whole peice, I could not beleeve but that the mersare [mercer] had to my advantage changed what I fixt upon and given me a much bettar stuff, till he had undeaseaved me by ashewreing me the contrary. O my soule, thus will my mersyfull heavenly father deal with me when I come to heaven. Though he gives me here (as I may call them) patrones or taistes [patterns or samples] of glory which, as dasled as my eyes are, I canot but chuse before all [that] the world presentes me with, yet when I come to the heavenly Jerusalem, I shall to my unspeakable comfort find that place in holy writ verifyed (that eye has not seen, nor eare heard, nor has it entred in to the heart of man to conceive what God has layded upe for those that love him);[174] and that though I have on this side Jordan tasted some grapes of the land of promise,[175] yet I shall find that heaven shall as much transcend my expectation as my desert; and that though what I have injoyede of God sometimes in this life be ravishingly [97r] sweet and delightfull, yet it is nothing to what I shall injoy in the fruition of God in love when I shall, with those spirites of just men made perfect,[176] be ever with the Lord,[177] in whose presense there is fullness of joy and at whose right hand there are pleasures for ever more.[178]

---

[172] 2 Corinthians 4:6 and possibly Psalm 89:15, a consolation she finds a number of times in her writing.

[173] Stuff: a "textile fabric" or "woven material of any kind"; also a "woollen fabric" (*OED*).

[174] 1 Corinthians 2:9.

[175] Numbers 13:23. In *The Saints Everlasting Rest* Baxter encourages, with many scriptural tags, "take thy *heart* into the *Land of Promise*; shew it the pleasant hills, and fruitful valleys; Shew it the clusters of Grapes which thou hast gathered: and by those convince it that it is a blessed Land, flowing with better than milk and honey: enter the gates of the *holy City*, walk through the streets of the *new Jerusalem*, walk about *Sion*" (740-41).

[176] Hebrews 12:23.

[177] 1 Thessalonians 4:17. The burial service in *The booke of the common praier* (London, 1549) includes the epistle from 1 Thessalonians 4:13-18 when Communion was celebrated (Clxiiir-v).

[178] Psalm 16:11; see above, n. 140.

[97v] *Upon a spot in my gonde* [gown] *which I was impatient instantly to have waichte* [wash'd] *out*

[98r] How desires [desirous] was I of haveing this spot sone washt out. For though my woman ashewred [assur'd] me that I should the next day have it done, yet my impatiency was so great that I made her instantly doe it. O my soule, how much less care have I expreste for getting thee cleansed! For though I knew the blood of Christ could cleanse me from all the spots of sinn, yet I have lett those spots remaine without instantly goeing to that fountaine which is sett open for Judah and for Jerusalem.[179] But, O Lord, I doe most humbly beseech thee, lett me noe longer procrastinate the coming to that fountaine; but as sone as I fall into sinn by the prevalense of a temptation, lett me make as great haist [haste] to the blood of Christ to have that defileing spot washt out as I did to have this got away, knowing that the spots of my soule are more offensive to thy eyes then those of my closes [clothes] are to the most curious observer of them. O Lord, I doe beseech thee, doe thou wash me as cleane from the spots of my soule as the blood of a God can make me.

[98v] *Upon seeing my Lady Anne Baringtones picture that had a great resemblance to her though it was not very exsaiktely* [exactly] *drawne*[180]

[99r] Though I doe not with eyes of admiration looke upon this picture, yet I doe with pleased ones; for though I am not ignorante that it is but imperfectly drawne, yet the great likeness it has to my friend makes me highly to valew it. O my soule! lett this instrouckte thee to prize in saintes the likeness thay have to Christ; and where ever thou mitest [meetest] any that have those divine graces infused into them that makes them Christ-like, doe thou highly delight in them, though thay are not so perfect as their originall is; and the nearer thay come to that, the greator portion of thy delight lett them have. O, doe thou love Christs picture where ever thou seest it. And if thou seest them rich in faith and all other

---

[179] 1 John 1:7, Revelation 1:5; Zechariah 13:1, Joel 3:18-21. A similar desire to be washed in the fountain for Judah and Jerusalem occurs in the diary (22 July 1676, 4/40r).

[180] "I suppose this may be ye picture wch I have by me. W. W." (98v). Anne Barrington, the eldest daughter of Robert Rich, third Earl of Warwick, and a ward of Mary Rich, married Thomas Barrington, the son of Sir John and Dorothy Barrington, in Leighs Chapel on 8 November 1664 ("Some Specialties In the life of M Warwicke," British Library Additional Manuscript 27357, 32v). Their marriage led to legal challenges about the settlement and remained troubled, Anne preferring to reside in London and her husband the country. When Thomas Barrington died on 31 January 1682, they had five surviving children. Anne remarried soon after Sir Richard Franklin. (G. A. Lowndes, ed., "The History of the Barrington Family," *Transactions of the Essex Archaeological Society*, n.s. 2 [1884]: 47-50; J. T. Cliffe, *The Puritan Gentry Besieged, 1650-1700* [London: Routledge, 1993], 57-58.)

graces, though thay are contemptable in others eyes because thay are not sett off by a rich frame and [99v] haveing not the advantage of outwarde glory to make them conspicuous, yet doe thou love them in a poore, plane, ibeny [ebony] frame. Or ellse thou dost not love the picture but the frame.

Upon observeing a mower to goe some times to a whetstone to whet his scithe and then presently reaturne againe to his mowing[181]

[100r] I was by my wallkeing in the garden by a workeman, that I observed whilst he was mowing a walke to goe some times to whet his sythe with a whetstone and then presently againe reaturne unto his mowing, minded how neasesary it was to use som times lawfull recreationes which may be necessary when by too long studyes the minde is tired and therfore needs divertion from that constant fixtenes of mind or when by labour the body is by wearisomnes made unfit for further labour.

O Lord, I most humbly beseech thee, lett me neaver use even lawfull recreationes, but when I find an absolute necessity of them, to be as the mowers whetstone to make me more fitt to reaturne with more [100v] vigor and chearefullness of spiritt to the workes thou has sent me into the world to doe. O lett my recreationes be as my sauce, not as my full meales. O, inable me to be so good a houswife of my time as I may neaver spend one moment of it more than is neasisary [necessary] in any recreation, remembering that though time is not lasting, yet what dependes upon it is everlasting, and that time is the pralauge [prologue] to eternity. O Lord, give me, therefore, grace to spend it so that thou mayst neaver repent the bestowing nor I the receiveing of it from thee.

[101r] *Upon observeing in a fielde of corne two eares, the one standing upright but haveing nothing in it, the other eare hanging douneward full of granes of wheate*

[101v] How upright dos this empty, husky ear of corn stand without bending in the least dounewardes when as another ear that is filled with exselent graines of usefull wheate dos hang dounewarde. This observation may be usefull to minde me of being humble and to beleeve that those exselent Christianes that have most grace in them are the most lowly and lye most humbly prostrate at the feete of God under the sense of their coruptiones which still dwelles in them and which often hurries them inconsiderately into the actuall comition of the breach of Godes comandes. Wher [102r] as the unregenerate person who sees not his own sinfullnes, haveing a pharisaical spiritt,[182] thinkeing himselfe to be

---

[181] See also Hall, "CXXXI Upon the Whetting of a Scythe," in *Occasional Meditations*, 193; Reynolds, "XLII. Upon the sight of three men mowing downe grasse in my Meadow," in *Spiritvall Intervals*, 169-76.

[182] Luke 18:10-14.

better then his neighbour, walkes upright hautely, neaver humbling himselfe before God, begging that grace from him which he needs, because his pride makes him thinke him selfe allready possest of it.

O Lord! I most humbly beseech thee, make me walke humbly before thee, remembering that thou resistest the proud and givest grace to the humble[183] and that though every mountain shall be brought low, yet thou willt fill every vally.[184] O make me in lowliness of mind esteeme each other bettar then my selfe. [102v] O lett me be cloathed with humility[185] and allwayes walke before thee with a dew [due] sense of my own unworthyness, which may make me constantly confesse my selfe to be the chief of sinares and so trewly unworthy of the least of all thy mersyes.[186]

Upon an aple tree that grew in the high way

[103r] How many stikes has this aple tree throune at it to beate doune ites fruit, and how many rough shakeinges dos it undergoe that the trees that grow with in the inclosed orcharde escape. Thus it is often with a persone who makes choyce of a reatired life and one who is immersed in publike imploymentes. The reatired persone dos many times 'skape som of those shakeing tryalles that the other is often assaulted with, being freed from the hard and uneasy neaseasety of makeing his way to heaven not onely through his own coruptiones but through the coruptiones of otherse whome he converses with. Wher as the other [103v] in his journy to the heavenly Cannane mites [meets] from those he has to doe with all with many surpriseing temptationes which inconsiderately hurry him to the comition of those sinnes which he had neaver so much as thought on if he had bene freede from that insnareing company.

O Lord, I humbly besiech thee, lett this ocasinall meditation be so saintifide to me that I may more and more be confirmed in my opinion that it is a harde thing to goe to heaven from a croude[187] and that retirement is usually freede from many temptationes that are met with in the afaires and transactiones of this

---

[183] James 4:6, 1 Peter 5:5.
[184] Isaiah 40:4, Luke 3:5.
[185] 1 Peter 5:5.
[186] Jacob's admission in Genesis 32:10. In *A Christian Directory* Richard Baxter, for example, characterizes the humble man, "But of themselves they say, *I am a worm and no man: I am less than the least of thy mercies; less than the least of all Saints: the chiefest of sinners*: How unfit am I for so much love, and praise, and honour?" (Book One, 196). This was also George Herbert's motto, a poet Rich quotes in her diary (1/22r) and in the "Rules for holy living" addressed to George Berkeley, first Earl of Berkeley (Anthony Walker, *Eureka, Eureka. The Virtuous Woman found Her Loss Bewailed, and Character Exemplified in a Sermon Preached at Felsted in Essex, April, 30, 1678* [London, 1678], 133; Berkeley, *Historical Applications and Occasional Meditations*, 143-44).
[187] Richard Baxter, with whom Rich often conversed, had preached in a sermon, "To live as in *heaven*, in a crowd of business, and stream of temptations, from the confluence

world because ther I am [104r] to conflikte not onely with inward but outwarde enemies of my salvation. O make me every day more and more taist that deavine [divine] gustow that is to be found in converseing with thee in solitude that so I may finde noe want of the glitering gloryes of the world nor of the company by whose inticementes I may be shaken or drawne from my close wallkeing with thee, my God.

[104v] Upon being very much offended with one of my sarvantes for being dronke and then apeareing in publike to the disgrace of my famely

[105r] How aiengery was I with this untorde persone not onely because he had by his sinn dishonored God but because he had all so, being dronke, apeared in publike to the disgrace of my famely. But, O Lord, lett this meditation be instrouktive [instructive] and make me consider how much my sinnes dishonor God and how by the comition of them I give ocasion to the enemies of God to blasfeame [blaspheme] his name. And, O Lord, I humbly besiech thee, seeing I have to all the world avouched thee to be my God, lett me walke as becomes thy handmaide, doeing nothing that may be dishonorable to my heavenly mastur. O, make me obay thee, who hast comanded me to be holy and to walke worthy of the Lord unto all well pleaseing[188] that I may not by my loose and sensuall [105v] life bring reproach upon thy holy name.

Upon my Lady Anne Baringtones childes weaneing[189]

How aparantly is this littull prity creature changed, hur pale lookes and the abatement of her fleach [flesh] sofisiantly evinseing to us how much she is discontented at hur nurses haveing, by layeng som bitar thing upon hur breast, weaned hur from it; which makes hur so piveich[190] that she dos reafuse all the most inviteing meates is ofred hur, still cryeng aftur that milke which she used to lye and souke of.

Thus it is oftun with a discontented persone when God is weaneing them [106r] from som idolised dealight which he sees them over love, and in ordur to that mersyfull deasigne he dropes in wormewode and gall[191] to imbitare those comfortes or pleasures wher in thay expected the most solase and sweatnes.

---

of all worldly things, is so hard, that *few* such *come* to heaven"—*The Life of Faith, as It Is The Evidence of things unseen* (London, 1660), 59.

[188] Colossians 1:10.

[189] Rich notes in her diary the birth of a daughter, born on 27 August 1667 and christened 6 September (1/111v, 113v), who could have been weaned in 1669, the year before a second son was christened on 21 December 1670 (2/128r).

[190] Peevish.

[191] Lamentations 3:19.

Which showes them that though their pleasures promised them much at a distance, yet at the ende thay doe but frustrate their expectationes by sensible defeates. And then what was falsely layde to the charge of the miror of patiance (that he tore himselfe in his fury)[192] is trewly verefyde in them, for thay prove a torment to themselves by their willfull refuseing to take dealight in other mersyes because thay find it not in what thay saught it in and so by this fretfull humor disrealich all their other injoymentes.

[106v] O Lord, I doe most humbly besiech thee, lett me neaver be one of those who has such a discontented humor, but make me of the number of those happy ones whose will is wholy reasigned upe unto thy holy will in all thinges. O make me thankfully to injoy those mersyes thy wise providence sees best to intruste me with, and make me patiently to want those blesinges thou seest fitt to deany me. O lett me neaver so much deasire unposeste mersyes as ether to overlooke or disrealich my poseste ones. Amen.

[107r] Ocasionale Meditationes made by M Warwicke 1670 [and] 71.

[107v] *Upon walking and being much delighted with doeing so in a very glorious morning in which the birdes song very sweetly*

[108r] How much more ravishingly sweet and delightfull than ordinary is this morning (after my long reastraint from walkeing by the ill weathur), the sunn shining out so gloriously and the birds singing so chearfully and sweetly that I am almost transported with it. But O, my soul, lett these things (like Elias charett) carry thee up to heaven[193] and doe not heare terminate thy sight, but looke beyond things temporal to those thinges which are eternall[194] and consider: if the earth be so glorious when the sun shines upon it, O, what is heaven where there is noe need of the sun but the lambe is the light of it,[195] and where instead of these sweet birds singing thou shalt hear the songs of the heavenly Jerusalem sung by the sweat

---

[192] James 5:11. Seventeenth-century commentary supports the 1560 Geneva Bible gloss of Job 1:20: "in their pacience they fele affliction, and grief of minde: yet they kepe a meane herein" (223r). The "truly patient" bear God's strokes because they know they have sinned: "See an example of this in the mirrour of true patience, blessed *Iob*" (Arthur Hildersam, *CLII Lectvres Vpon Psalme LI* [London, 1635], 251). In his grief and humiliation Job nevertheless did "moderately bewail these afflictions" (Arthur Jackson, *Annotations Upon The five Books, immediately following the Historicall Part of the Old Testament* [London, 1658], 6; John Worthington, *The Great Duty of Self-Resignation to the Divine Will* [London, 1675], 166; George Abbot, *The Whole Booke of Iob Paraphrased, or, Made easie for any to understand* [London, 1640], 9).

[193] 2 Kings 2:11.

[194] Cf. 2 Corinthians 4:18 and above, n. 100.

[195] Revelation 21:23.

and melodious quire [choir] of angells and the soules of just men made perfecte,[196] [108v] who, beholding the beatifick vision, are in perpetuall extasies and are never weary of singing halaluias to him that sittes upon the throne and to the lamb who loved them and waichte [washt] them from their sinnes in his own blood.[197]

O Lord! I doe most humbly beseech thee, raise my thoughtes more from earth to heaven; and seeing that I hope to joyne with that heavenly host in celebrateing thy prayses for ever, lett me now begin my hosannos on earth that I may sing my halalulias for ever in heaven; where, I beseech thee, to carry upe first my heart, that though I am yet absent in body I may be present in spiritt; and haveing with thy blesed apostles my conversation in heaven whilst I am upon earth,[198] I may goe to heaven when I shall leave the earth and may then by thy [109r] mersy and through the merites of Christ have a wide entrance in to thy heavenly kingdome.

Upon a hen of my Lady Essex Richs[199]

I was surprised tother day to find a hen in the still house;[200] and inquireing of my servant that kept it why she would suffer her there, I was, by way of apology for her being so, informed by her that it was the hen that my Lady Essex had taken and bred upe from just being hatcht in the still house; and that when she was grown pretty big, because she use to wander aboute the house and durt it, I had ordurd she showld be removed from thense, which acordingly she was; and that she had not returned [109v] thithar in many monthes; but that now she would

---

[196] Hebrews 12:23.

[197] Revelation 1:5. Through meditation, Baxter proposes, "elevate thy heart" and "see for the present" the heavenly kingdom: "meditate of them, as if thou wert all the while beholding them, and as if thou wert even hearing the *Hallelujahs*, while thou art thinking of them" (*The Saints Everlasting Rest*, 752). Rich often strives for this elevated vision in the meditations of the diary.

[198] Philippians 3:20.

[199] Essex Rich (1651/2-1684) was the youngest daughter of Robert Rich, third Earl of Warwick; she and her sisters, Anne and Mary, were taken into the household of Mary Rich after their father's death in 1659. Essex married Daniel Finch (1647-1730), the son of Heneage (1621-1682) and Elizabeth Harvey (1627-1676), on 16 June 1674 at Leighs Chapel ("Some Specialties," 7/37r). She died in March, 1684 following the birth of their eighth child. Her husband then married Anne Hatton (1668-1743) (Henry Horwitz, *Revolution Politicks: The Career of Daniel Finch Second Earl of Nottingham, 1647-1730* [London: Cambridge University Press, 1968], 6-7, 37, 42, and "Daniel Finch, second earl of Nottingham," in *ODNB*, 19:554-57; Pearl Finch, *History of Burley-on-the-Hill, Rutland*, 2 vols. [London: John Bale, Sons & Danielsson, Ltd, 1901], 1:175-85).

[200] Still-house: a site for distilling. Anthony Walker's biography recalls that the "Closet and Still-house was their Shop for Chirurgery, and Physick, and her self, (for she would visit the meanest of them personally) and Ministers whom she would send to them, their spiritual Physicians" (*Eureka, Eureka*, 97).

in the morneings come and stand at the stillhouse doore till she came doun and opened it; and then would goe and in the same box where she her selfe was by her ladyes care of hur kepte and nourished when a chicken wold every day lay an egg and then be gone againe. Which relation, when I had heard and all so saw the trueth of it evinsed to me, I was so far from againe finding fault with hur being there that I commanded she showld have all the incoragement could be given her to come againe by laying in the box some hay for her to lay in. O my soule, turn this in to a good and profitable meditation; and learn a lesson of gratitude from this poore gratefull creture (whose action thou art so much pleased with); [110r] and consider if this poore harmeless hen expresses the highest straines of gratitude her nature is capable of by bringing the first and best she has as an expression of her thankfullness to the place and persones in it, who ware onely the preservers of her being but not the authours of it, how much showldest thou study and indeaver to returne thy first and best to him that was both the authour and is still the preserver of thy well-being and not dare to present him with any lesse expressione of thy gratitude than thy whole selfe, soule and body, which is but thy reasonable servise of him.[201] And, O Lord, inable me to offer this, my all, up as a burnte off'ring in flames of love.

[110v] *Upon putting some linnets in to the same cage with a canary bird and thay lerneing to sing like the canary bird*

How sone have this linnets learnt to sing the same notes with my canary bird and doe it so perfectly like that I canot by my eare without the helpe of my eye distinguish which it is that sings. This observation may be usefull to discover to me what inflewense [influence] company has. How many are there that by converseing with wicked and profane persones have from them sodenly learnt to swear the dreadfull oathes which thay have heard them doe and to deride also both the profession and practice of religion, and how many happy [111r] persones are there too who by Gods good providence to them being cast in to vertuous and pious persones aquaintance have by observeing their holy and good and profitable discourse learnt from them edifying and warmeing discourse such as will provoke their fellow Christianes to love and good workes.

O Lord, I doe most humbly beseech thee, lett this occasional meditation be so sanctified to me that I may now be more than ever carefull what company I keep; and though I may some times be cast in to ill company, yet lett me never chuse it nor find any satisfaction in any converse by which I may be taught ill but not good. And, O Lord, I beseech thee, lett me not onely carefully avoyde the openly profane but also, as much as in me lyes, those that are of a vaine conversation; and lett me be able to say with the man after [111v] thine own heart, I

---

[201] Romans 12:1; see also above, n. 43.

have not sat with vaine persones;[202] but make me chuse intimate familiarity onely with those who out of the good treasure of their heartes doe send forth good thinges,[203] that dealighting to keape compeny with thy saintes on earth[204] I may be able to say (with a holy man when dying), I am goeing to change my place, but not my company; I have kept compeny with saintes on earth, and I am now agoeing to keepe compeny with them in heaven.[205]

Upon seeing some grond that was dry have great cracks in it

[112r] How strangely does this ground gape, and yet some neare it, though as dry, does not so. Which mindes me of the great difference there is betwene necesitous persones. Som who have had an ingenuous and plentyfull education and afterwardes are by Godes providence reduced to want are many times content rather to conflicte with great neaseasetyes then by opening their mouthes to beg declare their sad condition. Where as otheres who want the modesty which the others brideing [breeding] has given them noe sooner have any manur of want of former plenty but presently seeke relief by proclameing with open mouth their necessities to be great and insupportable, though indeed much less then the otheres who conceale them. O Lord, I beseech thee, grant that this consideration may be so usefull to me that I may not in the [112v] dispenseing of my charity thinke I am bond to give most to them that aske most but may rather chuse by my inquiries to find out the most neaseasitos [necessitous] persones, though more silently so then otheres, and so powre in to that grond that is dry though not so gapeing.

Upon observeing a sheepe to bite very close to the earth[206]

[113r] I have observed this poore sheepe to bite so close to the grond that I could not but wonder to see how it was possible for it to feed it selfe, and yet it does by

---

[202] Psalm 26:4.
[203] Possibly like the householder in Matthew 13:52.
[204] Psalm 16:3.
[205] Variations of the statement are attributed to the divine John Preston (1587-1628). Edmund Calamy, for example, quotes the dying man, "I shall change my place, but not my company" (Calamy et al., *An Exact Collection of Farewel Sermons*, 409). Samuel Clarke records that Preston on his deathbed assured others, "I have accompanied Saints on earth, and I now shall accompany Angels in Heaven (*The Lives of Thirty-Two English Divines*, 3rd ed. [London, 1677], 113). The change of place but not of company, kindred, or principle was also in the seventeenth century a general maxim (Andrew Gray, *The Mystery of Faith Opened up* [Edinburgh, 1669], 76; Thomas Watson, *A Body of Practical Divinity* [London, 1692], 256; Philip Traherne, *The Soul's Communion With her Savior* [London, 1685], 169).
[206] WW: "I suppose this Observation was made at or on the Tree, in Little-Leighes Park, wch she call'd her stand, near ye Wilderness" (112v).

that short provision keape it selfe, I perseave [perceive], fatt and in good likeing. O my soule, turne this observation in to a usefull occasionall meditation and consider from hence how Godes providence in this world provides for his sheep who, though thay be his jewelles and are the excellent of the earth, much more exselent than their unregenerate neighboures, yet God is pleased for good and wise ends to himselfe knowne to make even these, his own pretious people, many times to feed close and to fare hardly when their ill neighboures injoy all manner of plenty and abundance of these creature comfortes. O Lord, I humbly beseech thee, lett this consideration make me consider that there is neither love or [113v] hatered declared by all that is before us; and therefore lett me not esteem them to be hapy in thy favour who, Dives like, live in plenty and prosperity though unsanctified;[207] but lett me esteem them so who, though poore in the world, are yet rich in faith[208] and who shall in heaven have an abundant amendes made them for their necesitous and straite condition here in this their pilgrimage on earth.

Upon seeing the sunn shine when it rained

[114r] With how plentyfull showres is the earth watered even whilst the sun shines out most gloriously. Which mindes me of Gods dealinges some times with his poore creatures. When he has, as it were, opened a spring of godly sorrow in their heartes at the rememberance of their disingenuous sinning against him even whilst thay are watering their couches with penitentiall teares,[209] he is so mersyfull as of a sodain to reafresh them by letting the sun of righteousnes shine bright and gloriously to them so as thay are able to say that even in the time of mourneing thay have had comfort.[210]

O Lord, I bless thee that I am able experimentally to say[211] that I have had some times the greatest comfortes when I have been able all so to say rivers of

---

[207] Dives, derived from the Vulgate Latin for wealthy or rich, is the name traditionally given to the unnamed "certain rich man" in Luke 16:19-31. In the seventeenth century "the *Dives-es* of this world," "*Dives*-like," and "like a *Dives*" were synonymous with sumptuousness, luxury, gluttony, disdain, and oppression: George Abbot, *Brief Notes Upon the whole Book of Psalms* (London, 1651), 186; William Gouge, *A Learned and Very Useful Commentary on the Whole Epistle to the Hebrewes* (London, 1655), 307; Richard Baxter, *A Christian Directory,* Book One, 317.

[208] James 2:5.

[209] Psalm 6:6.

[210] Malachi 4:2; Matthew 5:4.

[211] A common seventeenth-century phrase for the personal experience of religion: having read the life of Christ in Scripture, John Everard, for instance, notes in *The Gospel-Treasury Opened* (London, 1657), "you shall be able *experimentally* to say, and cry out, Alas! *this day is the Scripture fulfilled in me*" (79). Rich uses it as well in the diary, e.g., 9 March 1673 (3/140r).

waters have run down myne eyes for my sinnes.[212] Which made me thinke how sweet musick is upon the water. [114v] O, blessed God, lett me often thus morne that I may be comforted by haveing beames of light shineing from thy face which may make more and more cleare to me the pleasantness of religion that can make even penitentiall teares more deasirable then all the pleasures the unregenerate world have in their mirth and jollity.

Upon coy duckes bringing in many with them

[115r] How diligent are these coy duckes to bring in otheres, and how souksesfull [successfull] are thay often in their attemptes goeing out and allureing in great numbers with them.[213] Which mindes me how usefull a chearfull Christian may be to bring in otheres to imbrace and practise religion, thay being often allured at first to it by perceiveing the pleasant conversation of devoute persones.

Oh Lord! I humbly beseech thee, make me serve thee with chearfulnes of heart in the plenty and abundance of all thinges; and haveing tasted that thou arte gratious,[214] and that all thy wayes are wayes of pleasantness, and all thy pathes are peace,[215] lett me by my chearfull caredge [carriage] adorne the Gospell and indeaver to greaten thee in the world and to be instrumental to bring in many [115v] to thy service by showing to them a constant serenity of mind and a great chearfullness in thy sarves [service], and by this way may declare to them how good a master I serve and so may allure them to taste and see how gratious thou art[216] by disabuseing them first from the false suggestiones that the divell and wiked men would impose upon them the beleefe of that religion is a melancholy and sowre thing. O! as I am really convinced of the contrary, so lett me every day evince it more and more unto others by goeing on in a constant course of chearefull and universall obedience that so it may be my great care to save my own with others soules.

[116r] *Upon letting the fire in my chamber goe allmost quite out for want of care to renew it by putting on now and then a stick of wood*

How warmeing and cheareing a fire was here just now; but for my want of care to preserve it by renewing it now and then by putting on another stick, it is allmost

---

[212] Psalm 119:136.

[213] Decoy ducks were trained to fly near dusk among passing ducks, drawing them down to bodies of water and into nets, often baited with grain. Arthur Aikin describes how men and dogs trapped the wild ducks after the decoy escaped by diving through the bottom of the enclosure: *The Natural History of the Year* (London, 1798), 175-76. WW dates this meditation about four years after one was built at Pond Park (114v).

[214] 1 Peter 2:3; see also Psalm 34:8 and above, n. 163.

[215] Proverbs 3:17.

[216] 1 Peter 2:3; see also Psalm 34:8 and above, n. 163.

quite gone out, and there remaines nothing of the late blaseing fire but som few languid coles [coals]; which makes me find great dificulty to rekindle a new fire. Turn this, O my soul, in to spiritual advantage and sadly reflecte how often thou hast by Godes mercy to thee found the warmeness and fire of his love in thy heart; but by thy carelesnes, [116v] or by being too much emerest [immerg'd] in worldly transactiones, or ellse too much diverted by the inticeing, deluding pleasures of the world from attending upon God, thou hast for want of frequent returnes to him by short ejaculationes lett this heavenly fire goe allmost out; where as by frequent and expedite motiones to heaven thou mightest much longer have preserved its heate, where as now thou arte fain to take much paines in indeavering to blow up those allmost exstinguished sparkes.

O Lord, I doe most humbly beseech thee, saintefy [sanctify] this occasionall meditation so to me that I may for the time to come be more carefull to preserve those heavenly glowinges and heart warmeinges thou voutesafest me some times, [117r] and may even in the midest of the performeing the dutyes of my calling send upe my heart often to thee, and so by makeing frequent, though short, visitts to heaven keep up heavenly affectiones. O doe thou be pleased to heate the furnace of my affectiones seven times hootar [hotter];[217] and seeing thay are, as it ware, the feet of my soule, lett me by them run nimbly in my Christian course and lett my love blaze with more than seraphick heat.[218]

Upon seeing young aples before thay ware ripe lye dead under the tree

[117v] How many aples that are so young that thay have not yet attained to their maturity lye dead allready upon the grond. Which mindes me of Godes somtimes makeing young children dye as sone allmost as they are borne, or ellse before thay have come to their full yeares of discretion dos he make them fall by the irresistable stroke of death and turne them to rotones [rottenness].

O Lord, I desire to adore thee for thy great mersy to poore babes whom thou takest, as I charitably hope, to glory before thay have been polluted by any actuall transgressiones or ever knowne any of the trobulles and miseryes of this life.

---

[217] Daniel 3:19.

[218] The coal one of the seraphim placed on Isaiah's tongue suggests the prophetic (Isaiah 6:6-7); seraphic heat also described in the seventeenth century the charity the Holy Ghost brings (Jane Lead, *The Revelation of Revelations* [London, 1683], 90) and the love for God (Thomas Ken, *The Works of the Right Reverend, Learned, and Pious Thomas Ken, D. D.*, 4 vols. [London, 1721], 1:484). "Seraph" comes from the Hebrew for "burning" or "fiery."

[118r] *Upon observeing a snail crepe constantly forward in the walke without turneing backe*

I have observed with great admiration that this poore snail, though it creepes so slowly that I could hardly perseave [perceive] it did so at all, yet in the time I have bene walkeing, by keeping on forward still and never turning back, I plainely perceive, it has crepte a good way in the walke before me and made a longer progress in its journy in this small time then if I had not taken notice of it I could have beleeved it possible for it to have don in a much longer space of time.

[118v] O my soul, turn this in to a usefull and incorageing occasionall meditation and consider that though thou dost not tread nimbly in the path that leades unto eternall life, yet if thou doest pershew [persue] thy intended journy, and stedfastly settest thy face to goe towardes the heavenly Jerusalem, and every day makest some farther progress in it without turneing back to Sodom, thou mayst at last attaine to heaven, though thou dost not run thy Christian course with so much swifteness as some more happy Christianes doe.

O Lord, I doe most humbly beseech thee, though I doe but slowly creep to thee, yet lett me never forsake my intended purpose of makeing towardes thee; and though I doe too often break my good resolutiones, yet lett me never quite renounse them by turneing backe againe unto my sinnes, but lett me still goe forward till at last I finish my course[219] and attaine through thy mersy the [119r] end of my faith, the endless salvation of my pretious and immortal soule.

Upon observeing a snaile that where so ever it crept it left some slime[220]

How plainely doe I perceive where this snaile has been, for both upon the wainescote and the boardes in every room I deaserne [discern] by its slime where it has been.

This ocasionall meditation may be usefull to teach me a lesson of humility by makeing me sadly to reflecte upon that indwelling corruption that still remaines in me and is so defileing that in every place I live in I evince to others (as well as experience in my selfe) that filth of originall sinn [119v] which staines and blemishes all I doe and makes others take notice of my depraved nature and of my wretched heart that is still casting out slime and filth, this poyson being allwayes breaking out at some creane or other.[221] O Lord, I humbly beseech thee, every

---

[219] Cf. 2 Timothy 4:7.

[220] Other views of the snail, beside those found in emblems, are Hall, "XXIX Upon the Sight of Two Snails," in *Occasional Meditations*, 139; Bury, "Med. 71 Upon a snail," in *The Husbandmans Companion*, 333-37.

[221] Rich similarly writes in her diary about the poison sin in her body "still breakeing out at some Creane or other" (3/87v). "Crevice" is written above the world "Creane," which is not defined in the standard dictionaries.

day more and more humble me for my carrying a nature about with me which is so displeaseing unto thee, my God, and which does so plainely discover upon every occasion to my fellow Christianes my wretched and defiled heart, and doe thou wash me as cleane from the guilt of the sinn I brought in to the world with me and my actuall sines, too, as the blood of a God can make me.[222]

[120r] *Upon observeing a candle a little before it went out to give a more then ordinary light*

This candle giving so much more light then ordinary before it went out made me take notice of it and minded me of some pious Christians that, though their graces were very conspicuous before and that thay were so happy as to obey that precept of letting their light so shine before men that others might see their good workes,[223] yet before God called them from grace to glory thay have so apparently to the eyes of all about them shined so much more bright than before that thay ware taken notice of to grow more heavenly and spirituall than thay had been, their [120v] warmeing and heavenly converse showing to what place they ware goeing, their soules thriveing and prospering like a garden that the Lord had watered and blest.[224]

O Lord! I doe most humbly beseech thee, lett me every day grow in grace and make me meet to be a partaker of the inheritance of the saintes in light.[225] And, Lord, as I grow nearer my death, make me fittar for it; lett me grow in grace and make my graces more conspikeous [conspicuous] to my self and others; give me more of the grace of heavenly mindedness. Doe not take me away till I am ripe, but fitt me for thy self. Fill me with thy self and at last take me to thy self that I may be ever with the Lord,[226] in whose presence is fullnes of joy and at whose right hand are pleasures for ever.[227]

[121r] *Upon the sudden putting out of a candle*

This candle being so sodenly put out mindes me of Godes many times sending out a swift arrow and strikeing some of his creatures with a soden death,[228] their

---

[222] 1 John 1:7, Revelation 1:5.
[223] Matthew 5:16.
[224] Jeremiah 31:12; see also above, n. 171.
[225] Colossians 1:12.
[226] Cf. 1 Thessalonians 4:17 and see above, n. 177.
[227] Psalm 16:11; see above, n. 140.
[228] The version of Psalm 64:7 in *The Book of Common Prayer* has "shoot at them with a swift arrow" (O2r); also *The Psalter of David: With Titles and Collects according to the matter of each Psalme*, 3rd ed. (London, 1647), 116. Zechariah 9:14 is another possible biblical source, which supports the view of the Almighty's "swift arrow."

breath instantly goeing out; and thay returne to their earth, and in that day their thoughtes doe peariech [perish].[229]

O Lord! seeing there is but a breath in my nostrills betwene me and eternity[230] and that I am ignorant how soon thou wilt stop that and send me into it, O lett me allwayes waite till my great change by death shall come that whether thou art pleased to snatch me away by [121v] a sudden stroke or to lett me lye languishing by a consumeing sikness, I may be allwayes prepared that when thou callest me I may have nothing to doe but to dye. And when I am goeing to doe a worke I neaver did, Lord give me a strength I neaver had; and lett me not feare that king of terores,[231] but looke upon it as a friend, remembering that death will doe that for me which all my graces canot, for it will free me from all my sinnes (for thou hast told me that he that is dead is freed from sinn).[232] O lett me live with dying thoughts that I may dye with liveing hopes;[233] and lett me entertaine my death not onely patiently but with raptures of joy, knowing that as sinn brought death in to the world, so nothing but death will carry it out of the world.[234]

[122r] *Upon being told that where the rich mines are the grounds about them are barren*

This information that is given me of the barrennes of the ground that is about the rich mines makes me consider how often I have (as well as others) observed that thay that abound most in wealth are often very barren in good workes, the places where thay live being not much inricht by their wealth.[235] Which makes them about them not thinke them hardly worth a prayer for their life nor a tear at their death, but thay dye undesired because thay lived unusefully to their poore fellow [122v] Christianes.

---

[229] Psalm 146:4.

[230] Cf. Isaiah 2:22.

[231] "*But when thou hast said all,*" Baxter concludes in *A Christian Directory*, "*Death will be Death, the King of Terrors*" (Book Two, 147). Numerous authors recognize that "*Job* calls it, the *King of Terrors, Job* 18.14. The black prince or the prince of clouds and darkness, as some translate those words" (John Flavel, *Two Treatises: The first of Fear* [London, 1682], 45). Thomas Watson also includes Aristotle together with Job (*A Body of Practical Divinity*, 865); death is also "accounted the King of Terrors" in *Epicvrvs's Morals, Collected Partly out of his owne Greek Text* (London, 1656), 123. On 15 August 1677 Rich, for example, meditated on "fearefull thoughts about that King of terrores" (5/170r).

[232] Romans 6:7.

[233] WW: "This was my good Fathers expression in his Family prayer" (121v).

[234] Romans 5:12, 21.

[235] A 19 December 1675 entry in the diary paraphrases a later sermon by George Gifford: "where the golde and silver mines ware there all the grounde about them, from whence they ware digged out ware usually very barren" (4/93r); see below, n. 607.

O Lord! I beseech thee, lett this ocasinall meditation be so sanctified to me that I may not be a burthen to the earth by being useless to my fellow Christianes but may poure out to them of what thou pourest in to me, remembering that they that water shall be water'd of the Lord;[236] and make me rich in good workes, that improveing the talent thou art pleasd to intrust me with[237] and makeing my selfe friends of the unrighteous Mammon when thay faile, I may be received into everlasting habitations.[238]

[123r] *Upon observeing in the court yard many severall paths towardes the house*

How many several pathes are there made in this court to the house, and yet by every one of them thay are brought in to it. Thus it is often in religion there are severall opiniones about the way to heaven, and many (even holy Christians) differ about it and canot agree about seremones [ceremonies] and some lessar things; yet as long as they agree in the fundamentales, and continue stedfast in the apostlles doctrine[239] and in the trueth as it is in Jesus, and tread in the holy path that is sett out for them to walke in,[240] and by persevering obedience doe [123v] continue in it unto their deathes, thay will (I doubt not) at last meete hapyly together in glory and there agree for ever in celebrateing the high prayses of their great redeemer.

O Lord, I doe most humbly intreat thee, doe thou by this occasionall meditation make me more and more stedfast in my resolution of loveing all my fellow Christianes that doe differ from me in the lessar thinges of religion as long as thay agree in the fundamentalles, remembering that those shall agree well in heaven that canot doe so upon earth. O make me to love those that are holy, spirituall Christianes though thay be not in all things of my judgment. O make me so charitable to them as not by my severe censures [124r] to unsainte them and shut them out of thy eternall rest, who through thy mersy and the merites of Christ shall have a wide entrance administred unto them into thy heavenly kingdome.

Upon finding in my selfe a great backwardness to cast up my accountes when I feared I showld by doeing so find I had run in depte [debt]

How often have I defer'd the looking over my accounptes, being loth to cast them upe for feare when I had done so I showld discover that I had [124v] by my ill

---

[236] Proverbs 11:25; Walker stresses Rich's generosity, noting that she gave away "for charitable uses" a third of her "separate maintenance or allowance, settled by Marriage Articles" (*Eureka, Eureka*, 99, 98).
[237] Matthew 25:14-30.
[238] Luke 16:11, 16:9.
[239] Acts 2:42.
[240] See also *The Book of Common Prayer*: "and do all such good works as thou hast prepared for us to walk in" (F1v).

husifry [houswifery] run in to debt. Thus it is too often with me in my great accounptes I ought to cast upe for heaven, by which I may find out some of those vast debts I owe to the great God of heaven by my iterated sinnes, yet I find often a great reloukstancy [reluctancy] to this most usefull worke.

O Lord, I doe beseech thee, pardon me this great fault and lett me not for the time to come be so backward in lookeing in to my selfe to find out how it stands betwene thee and mee, but lett me be diligent and faithfull in this business of so high concernment. And lett me not in this case doe, as the unjust steward did in another, sett doune fifty for a hundred;[241] but lett me indeaver to find out every sinn, though the smallest [125r] of my faultes, remembering that in an acounpte the farthinges helpe to make it upe as well as the shillinges and the poundes. And, Lord, make me, when I have searcht my heart as narrowly as I can, yet doe as thay that draw a map of the world: when thay have done so, thay allwayes leave a spase for the unknowne part of the world. So, Lord, lett me leave place in my prayures for acknowledging my unknown sins, for, Lord, who knowes how often he ofendes. O, doe thou cleanse me from my secret sinnes[242] and make me now every day at night cast upe my debts to thee that so when I come to dye I may have but 24 howres of my life to cast upe. O lord, I know my debts to thee are vast and great and thou mightest for them justly cast me into the prison of hell, but, Lord, I tender upe my shurety for my full discharge.[243] [125v] He has satisfied thy justice to the full; O doe not exsaikte [exact] that of me for which he has suffered, but crosse out all my deptes and wash them all away in the blood of Christ that they may be like the sinnes of Juda that shall be sought for but shall not be fond.[244] O blot out that hand-writing of ordinances that is against me[245] and naile it to the crosse of Christ that my sinnes may never more rise upe against me either to confond me here or to condemn me here after.

[126r] *Upon observeing after a great storme a great many fine peaches and much other fruit blown doun*

How many lovely peaches and other beautifull fruites has this very boyseterous and rough storm blown doune which ellse wold longer have bene preaserved still flouriching upon the trees.

---

[241] Luke 16:6.
[242] Psalm 19:12, which has "faults," not "sins."
[243] Surety: a formal pledge, bond, or assurance; also "A person who is primarily liable for the payment of another's debt or the performance of another's obligation." Discharge: release or free from obligation; "payment of a debt or satisfaction of some other obligation" (*Black's Law Dictionary*, 1455, 475).
[244] Jeremiah 50:20.
[245] Colossians 2:14; see also above, n. 31.

Thus it is often with appeareingly flourishing Christianes. Till a storm of persecution arises thay stand fast, but then thay presently fall [126v] from their apeareing stedfastness, not being able to indure any persecution or aflictiones for their conchanses [consciences].

O Lord, I doe most humbly beseech thee, lett not the most boyseterous stormes I can mite [meet] with drive me from thee, but lett me own thee and thy truthes. Though it showld cost me the losse of all my worldly injoymentes and my life, lett me be ready (with thy blesed apostle) not onely to be bound but to dye for the name of the Lord Jesus.[246] And if thou callest me to sofer [suffer] persecution, lett me imbrace it, rejoyseing that I am found worthy to suffer for thee, and not think it much or strange to follow a crucified saviour with a crosse upon my back.

[127r] *Upon eating my meate without salt*

How unsavoury and ill dos this meat taste for want of salt. Which mindes me how little relish there is in all our possest mersyes without the injoyment of that great earthly blessing, health, which gives the gustow and realiech [relish] to all our other mersyes.

O Lord, I do desire to bless thee, and O that all that is with in me might truly blesse thy holy name[247] for so many yeares injoyment of my health. O Lord, when I consider how [127v] many diseases this poore fraile body of mine is subject unto, and yet that this house of clay[248] has been for the most part of my life kept from them, and that thou hast onely now and then given me some taste of sickness to make me the more prize my health,[249] and by those craikes [cracks] in my claye-house hast onely minded me that at last it must turn to dust and rotones [rottenness], I canot but admire at thy unmerited mercy to me that when others of my fellow creatures are roreing upon a bed of sickness and at morneing wishing it ware evening and at evening wishing it ware morneing, that I showld be at ease and by being so am able to taste and relish thy mersyes. Lord, lett me not forfett my health by my unthankefullness for it and by my not improveing it to thy glory.

---

[246] Paul, who responded to the prophecy that he will be bound and delivered to the gentiles, "I am ready not to be bound only, but also to die at Jerusalem for the name of the Lord Jesus" (Acts 21:13).

[247] Psalm 103:1.

[248] Job 4:19.

[249] The diary records earlier headaches, colds, fits of spleen, and vapors.

[128r] *Upon observeing a mother before she layd her child to sleep kiss it*

My observeing this kind mothers caredge to her child, who before she layd it to slepe she kiste it, minded me of Godes mersyfull dealeing many times with his deare children. Before he makes them to sleep in Jesus,[250] he does to disarme that terrible of all terribles, death, give them a lively sense of his love; which makes them willing to sleep in the dust and makes them look death in the face with an undaunted courage, knowing that thay have a life hidden with God in Christ and that when Christ, who is their life, shall appear, thay shall appear with him in glory.[251]

[128v] O Lord, I doe most humbly beseech thee, before I sleep the sleep of death[252] lett me have such a full assurance of thy speciall love to me that I may desire to be dissolved and to be with Christ,[253] which is far better for me. Lett me not then languish under an over clouded and eclipsed assurance, but lett me be thought worthy to know my name is written in the Book of Life.[254] Lett me not onely looke upon my dissolution but allso upon my conjunction with Christ; make me, haveing thy face shineing upon me, goe triumphing to heaven, knowing that there I shall be ever with the Lord,[255] in whose presence is fullnes of joy and at whose right hand there are pleasures for ever more.[256]

[129r] *Upon observeing that when a glass was very full it was apt to spill*

How much care does the person that cares [carries] this full glasse take to preserve what is in it from spilling. Which makes me consider the danger that is in a full and great condition in this world. For if the possesors of great fullness be not very carefull, they are apt to be in danger of miscareing [miscarrying] by being

---

[250] 1 Thessalonians 4:14.

[251] Colossians 3:3-4.

[252] Psalm 13:3.

[253] Rich often longs in the diary to be dissolved and to be with Christ, recalling Philippians 1:23 and "a desire to depart, and to be with Christ; which is far better." The biblical passage in the Vulgate has "dissolvi et cum Christo esse," which in the Douay-Rheims version is "having a desire to be dissolved and to be with Christ." In his often-published *The Practice of Piety: Directing a Christian how to work that he may please God* (London, 1669), Lewis Bayly cites Philippians 1:23: "When *Paul* once had seen this blessed sight, he (ever after) counted all the riches, and glory of the world (in respect of it) to be but *dung*; and all his life after was but sighing out, *cupio dissolvi, I desire to be dissolved and to be with Christ*" (129). Nathanael Ranew hopes that in meditating on his death "I may be greatly desirous to be *dissolved*, and be thereby with Christ, which is best of all" (*Solitude Improved by Divine Meditation* [London, 1670], 170).

[254] Revelation 13:8; 17:8; 20:12, 15.

[255] Cf. 1 Thessalonians 4:17 and see above, n. 177.

[256] Psalm 16:11; see above, n. 140.

drawne by things temporall to the undervalewing and disregardeing of God and thinges eternall.[257] Which occasioned that caution to the children of Israell given in those God-breathed oracles[258] that thay showld take heed that when thay had possest the land of Cannane and were fed there to the full, thay did not then [129v] forgett God.[259] And we see that Nebuchadnezzar, when he was possest of great Babylon, ascribeing all to himselfe without at all owning the great God that gave it him, cryes out, is not this great Babylon that I have built for the house of the kingdom by the might of my power and for the honour of my majesty.[260] And we read how sone from this splendid and full condition the voyce fell from heaven that told him the sad newes that the kingdom is departed from him.[261]

O Lord! I doe most humbly beseech thee, lett this occasionall meditation be so sanctified to me that I may be carefull in a prosperous condition (in which I am at present by thy unmerited mersy to me sett), that I be not drawn by temporalls from thee and so miscare [miscarry] and grow worse for thy goodness to me. But lett me when I am fed to the full [130r] then blesse the Lord my God, and make me to serve thee with chearefullness of heart in the plenty and abundance of all thinges.

Upon hony combes and observeing that those combes that run freely unprest ware the purest and best hony

[130v] How plentifully do these hony combes run, and how pure is the hony that unforest [unforced] comes from them, where as those other combes that are fain to be preste yield nothing so pure nor good hony. Which observation makes me consider of the difference there is between legall and evangelical sorrow.[262] Those

---

[257] Cf. 2 Corinthians 4:18; see above, n. 100.

[258] Contemporaries characterized the Scriptures as God-breathed oracles. "God-breathed" is from Greek exegesis, *theopneustos*. 2 Timothy 3:16 ("All Scripture is given by inspiration of God") and Romans 3:2 (unto the Jews "were committed the oracles of God") are also relevant. The term *theopneustos*, translated as both breathed by and inspired by God, has been linked with Greek sources and figures prominently in modern commentary on the passage from Timothy (e.g., Luke Timothy Johnson, *The First and Second Letters to Timothy*, in *The Anchor Bible*, 35A [New York: Doubleday, 2001], 420; P. W. Van Der Horst, *The Sentences of Pseudo-Phocylides With Introduction and Commentary* [Leiden: E. J. Brill, 1978], 201-2).

[259] Deuteronomy 6:11-14.

[260] Daniel 4:30. Nebuchadnezzar ruled Babylonia from 605 to 562 BC; besides the Summer Palace, walls, and ziggurat in Babylon, he built the Hanging Gardens (*Anchor Bible Dictionary*, 4:1058-59).

[261] Daniel 4:31.

[262] Legal repentance: "when a person is brought to the sight of his sin, without beholding any pardon in Christ." "Evangelical, or Gospel-repentance . . . is a transformation or change of minde and heart, wrought by the holy Ghost, through the power of the

hapy children of God that are throughly wrought upon and have felt their hearts softned by the melting considerations of Gods great free and disinterested love (as if God had made a spirituall thaw upon their before hardned heartes) feel them dissolve so as thay are able to say rivers of water have run down my eyes[263] and, as the prophet Jeremiah phraiseth, powre out their heart like water before the Lord in penitentiall teares for their base, ungratefull, and disingenuous sinning [131r] against so good a God.[264] Where as those who are onely legall penitentes and have onely bene frighted for feare of hell into atrision [attrition] but never attained contrition, and so neaver mourned for sinn as it was dishonorable to God and as it grieved his holy spirit, have onely forest [forced] now and then a teare but neaver found the kindly meltinges of love.

O Lord, I doe most humbly beseech thee, give me to mourne for sinn as sinn not onely because it will damn me but because it has bene committed against so much mersy. And, Lord, doe thou make my heart, as it ware, a spirituall limbeck [alembic] out of which thou mayst extracte the teares of godly and childlike sorow, that unforest by any other consideration but that of thy great and ineffable love I may bemone my sinnes with a flood of penitentiall teares that I may with the penitent Mary make a bath of teares to wash the fete of my Saviour.[265]

[131v] *Upon my haveing many yeares agoe a very dangereous fitt of siknes and yet by reason of a distemper in my head beleeved my selfe to be well*

[132r] How dangereously ill was I in this great and languishing distemper, my docteres lookeing upon my condition as very doubtfull; and yet when I was inquired of by them how I felte my selfe, I answered, well; and so, indeed, I did beleeve my selfe to be. Which made my kind and most concerned friendes troubled to see my great insensibleness under so palpable and aparant hasarde of my life. But when by the blessing of my mersyfull God upon the meanes used by my physitian I began to mend, and being asked by him how I then felte my selfe, I

Word" (Christopher Blackwood, *A Treatise Concerning Repentance* [London, 1653], 4). "It is the grace of the Spirit of God; not a *Legall* grace: for the Law knoweth neither repentance for sinne, nor remission of sinne" (Thomas Taylor, *The Practice of Repentance, Laid downe in sundry directions, together with the Helpes, Lets, Signes, and Motives*, 4th ed. [London, 1635], 19). See also Rich's summary of Henry Wilkinson's sermon, 164–65 and below, n. 581.

[263] Psalm 119:136.

[264] Jeremiah 9:1.

[265] The woman who washed Christ's feet is unnamed (Luke 7:38). Mary, sister of Martha, is sometimes linked with this anonymous figure (D'Angelo, *Women in Scripture*, 119-20). Above Mary in the diary is written Magdalene (11 February 1667, 1/62r). Baxter, on the other hand, does not identify Magdalene with this woman in his *Paraphrase on the New Testament* (M1v); however Blackwood, as well as others, does (*A Treatise Concerning Repentance*, 13).

answered, ill, and began to make moveing complaintes of my distempered and pained body. Which made him then conclude I began to mend and give my inquisitive and allmost disparreing friends hopes of my yet continueing amongst them in the land of the liveing.[266]

[132v] Turne this, O my soule, in to a usefull meditation and consider how much danger there is in insensibilety under soule distemperes; for whilst thou beleevest thy selfe well and therupon cryest, peace, peace, under a mistaken opinion that thou hast made thy peace with God,[267] some discerning spirituall physitian may say unto thee, what hast thou to doe with pease whilst so many unmortified coruptiones evinse to others (though not to the selfe) that thou arte yet in danger of eternall death.

O Lord, I doe most humbly beseech thee so to sanctify to me this ocasionale meditation that I may not beleeve my selfe well when under dangereous symptomes of spirituall distemperes, but, Lord, be pleased to show me my danger that I may then flee to thee, my spirituall physician, who arte able to cure all my soule diseases. O lett me never sinn without sense,[268] but lett the pressing sense I have of my danger make [133r] me run to thee for the trew universale remedy for sike [sick] soules (the preatious blood of my deare Saviour). O wash me as clean from the guilt of all my sinnes as the blood of a God can make me,[269] that those observing beholders of my life that before lookt upon my condition as very dangereous by beholding my cure may take notes [notice] that I have bene with Jesus; and the more thay have with justise discomended my formar life, the more thay may commend my physician.

[134r] Ocasionall Meditationes made by M Warwicke 1671

[134v] *Upon the filere hedge that grew before the* [great] *parlor dore*[270]

[135r] How much was I surprised and trobled to find after som nippeing fro<st> nightes this fine filere hedge was dead, and how uneasy was it to me to part with

---

[266] Psalm 142:5.

[267] Jeremiah 6:14, 8:11.

[268] In an often published work dedicated to Mary Rich, John Gauden offers the assurance that God gives grace to the humble, "for humbled we may be, when prest down under the weight of punishment, but humble we cannot be less laid low in the sense of Sin, without this sense of Sin, we shall be as far from being humble, as from having Grace" (*The Whole Duty of a Communicant: Being Rules and Directions for a worthy receiving the most Holy Sacrament of the Lord's Supper*, 2nd ed. [London, 1685], 72-73).

[269] 1 John 1:7, Revelation 1:5.

[270] Phillyrea: "also called *jasmine-box* or *mock privet*" (*OED*), this species of evergreen shrub is, according to John Evelyn, "equal our *Holly*, in suffering the extreamest rigours of our cruellest *Frosts*, and Winds"; used as hedges, it thrives especially against walls (*Sylva, Or a Discourse of Forest-trees*, 3rd ed. [London, 1679], 128).

it when I saw it cut quite down to the very rootes that there by the gardnar might indeaver to make it afterwardes florish and prosper againe. But after it was so, it did to my amasement as well as satisfaction come upe againe with so much a purer verdure and lovelynes as did much delight me to behold it.

Turne this, O my soule, into a usefull ocasionall meditation and consider that thou oughtest not to mourne for the deaths of thy regenerate friends or indeared relationes as those that have noe hope of their riseing againe,[271] but as a Christian be comforted and consider that nothing dyes finally and totally in a child of God but sinn.[272] And remember that their dead bodys shall rise againe and be more glorious; [135v] for though thay be sowne naturall bodyes, <ye?>t thay shall rise spirituall bodyes.[273] And lett this consideration, too, make thee be willing to dye and not feare to sleepe in Jeasus,[274] knowing that though thou must for a time lye in a cold grave, yet from thense thy vilde [vile] body shall com forth and then shine as the sunn in the kingdome of thy father.[275]

O Lord, I doe most humbly beseech thee, lett these thoughts be so sett home to me that I may onely have life in patience, but death in deasire, and lett me often meditate upon that sweet and comfortable plase in thy inspired volume: (As for me, I shall behold thy face in righteousnes, and I shall be satisfy'd when I awake with thy likenes).[276] And lett the considration of my future glory make me deasire to be dissolved and to be with Christ;[277] lett me have my part in the first resurrection that so the second death may have noe power over me.[278]

[136r] *Upon a great and fruitfull aple tree that grew before the parlor doore, but being blown down by a great storm was taken up and a young, unfruitfull one planted in the place*

How loth have I been for a long time since the blowing downe of the fine tree to walk in that walk; and thou<gh> ther be another young one now planted in the room of it, yet it dos appear to me so far from filling up that place that I care not to cast my eye that way. Yet when at last regardlesly I did so, it minded me of the death of some good father who had most excellently fill'd up that relation in his own family and was, too, very usefull in the place God had sett him as a good neighbour abounding in good works and being fruitfull [136v] in every good

---

[271] 1 Thessalonians 4:13-14.
[272] Possibly Luke 20:36.
[273] 1 Corinthians 15:44.
[274] 1 Thessalonians 4:14.
[275] Matthew 13:43; see also above, n. 6.
[276] Psalm 17:15.
[277] A common desire in the diary; see also above, n. 253.
[278] Revelation 2:11, 20:6.

worke:²⁷⁹ relieving the distressed and, given to hospitality, letting noe poore lazarus's goe unrealived from his gate.²⁸⁰ But when by death he made rome for a young son to come and aire [heir] his estate, he was so far from filling upe his room that the neighbourhood could not but strangely miss him; the young aire [heir], being indeed in his fathers place but not doeing that good he had done, was as unpleasingly regarded by his beholders as my young tree was by me when I saw noe fruit upon it and consider'd there was plenty upon that it came in the place of.

O my soule, turn this consideration into a charitable meditation and lett it provoke thee to love and to good workes; lett thy own, not indureing that with any delight in thy garden that was unfruitfull, make thee indeaver to be usefull in that station God has putt thee least he showld say to thee as he did to the fruitless fig tree that produced nothing [137r] but leaves, cut it down; why 'cumbers i<t> the grond?²⁸¹

Upon my forgettfullnes to wind upe my watch

My forgettfullnes to wind upe my watch made me by my so doeing miss being informed how the howres paste and made me see a neaseasity [necessity] of being more mindful of it for the time to come. But as it convinced me of the fault of my memory, so it made me call to mind the usefullnes of winding upe my affectiones by heavenly meditationes; for as my watch will, unwond up, stand still, so will my affectiones, without being exsited up by warmeing and moveing consideratories, grow dead and unusefull to me.

O Lord, I doe humbly beseech thee, make me more then ever indeaver to wind up my affectiones to the highest pitch I can by the [137v] constraineing and most powerfull engine, thy free and unmerited love to me meditated upon. O make me by the consideration of thy goodness keep up lively and most vigorous afectiones that my meditationes may be as usefull to my afectiones as the bellowes are to blow upe the fire to make it blase and burn. So, O Lord, lett my inlivenieng thoughtes make my love blaze that my languid sparke may breake forth into a most glorious flame that so I may upon the wings of my affections mount upe to thee.

Upon viewing a map

[138r] This map evinces to me that the contery [country] it describes is good and shows me in it great stroukutres [structures], noble and well situated seates. Yet

---

[279] Colossians 1:10.

[280] Lazarus: a beggar at Dives's gate (derived from Luke 16:19-31; see above, n. 207).

[281] Luke 13:7. For her remissness in duty, Rich writes in her diary that she deserves to be cut down like the barren fig tree (30 December 1676, 5/62r).

one that has travelled into it and deliberately veiw'd it, as he makes himselfe more particular observationes of the excelencyes of it than those which the map represented to him, so he can describe it to others at a better and more takeing rate.

Thus it is with those who have had onely religion recomended to them by others who have told them that it was most exselent, usefull, and advantageous; and have onely, as Job phrases it, heard of God by the hearing of the eare;[282] and therupon concluded it was admirable. But when thay have by a selfe devotedness given up them selves to God, and have traveld in that straite and holy path that leades to the heavenly Jerusalem,[283] and have by the eye of faith [138v] lookte into the glorious rest that remaines for Godes jewelles,[284] and have, too, experimented the sweatness that is to be fond in the soules approaches to God in actes of solemn adresses to him by which thay have tasted that the Lord is gratious,[285] haveing had som of the warme and lively comfortes of the Holy Ghost, then thay descry themselves before unseene atraktifes [attractives] and make to others too the most clearly convinseing notiones of its exselencyes.[286]

O Lord, I doe most humbly blesse thee for the experimentale divinity[287] I have lernte from som of thy old desipulles [disciples], those experienced Christianes haveing often taught me more of thee by telling me of thy goodnes to them in all their straites and of thy manifestationes to them in their searchings after thee in thy prescribed dutyes then the most eloquent orator that had onely read of thee in bookes and knew thee noe otherwise could doe.

[139r] O Lord, I doe most humbly beseech thee, lett this ocasionall meditation be so sett home and sanctified unto me that I may more than ever chuse and

---

[282] Job 42:5.

[283] Hebrews 12:22.

[284] Malachi 3:17. The phrase "eye of faith" does not appear in its biblical counterpart Matthew 9:29, though it is very traditional in the seventeenth century. Baxter, quite typically, exhorts the readers of *A Christian Directory*, "Open the eye of Faith and Reason, and behold thy God." Those who do may see the love and redemption "in Christ clearly represented" as well as "foresee your end" and even behold "thy salvation" (Book One, 121, 58, 218; Book Two, 160). Thus Rich sees the joys and glory of the Church Triumphant (10 March 1673, 3/141r; 6 April 1677, 5/106v; 15 August 1677, 5/170v).

[285] 1 Peter 2:3; see also Psalm 34:8 and above, n. 163.

[286] John Edwards draws a similar analogy in describing "a sensible Experience of those Divine Truths which are recorded in Holy Scripture, there is an experimental feeling of the Truth and Reality of them, which is far different from a meer speculative notion of them. This latter is like seeing a Country in a Map only; the former is like Travelling through it, and being intimately acquainted with the several parts of it" (*The Doctrin* [sic] *of Faith and Justification Set in a True Light* [London, 1708], 86).

[287] Though theologically "the method of dealing with the conscience and religious feelings" (*OED*), the term might also suggest the confirmation of doctrines by experience.

dealight in those spirituall and exselent persones conversationes, who can by their experiances bring me more to adore thee and dealight in thy wayes and people.[288]

Upon the opinion of some that water that has bene onse heate afterwardes is colder

This water that has been heat and afterwardes (as som observe) is colder[289] mindes me of those persones that by having had a religious education have appeared forward in the wayes of God; and have had warme affectiones; yet haveing not had a real and a [139v] sanctifying work of God upon their heartes, have afterwards, when they have faln in to insnareing and unsaintefide company, been by them drawne to be the greatest opposers and despisers of religion and have plainely appeared to be worse then those that never made a show to be religious.

Upon a childes falling in to the dirt and goeing to his parent to have it washt off

[140r] This childe, when it had faln in to the dirt and come and complained of its so doeing to the indulgent parent and cryd to have it washt off, has not onely got the spot it had cleansed but has all its face and hands, too, washt clean.

Thus it often hapens to a child of God, who by a sudden, and sutable, and a surpriseing temptation is drawne to fall in to a sinn against God; and not being able to indure that filthy spot upon his soul, he instantly flyes to his heavenly father and cryes to him to wash him from it. And God, like a most indeareing and indulgent parent, not onely waiches [washes] away that in the pretious blood of his son, but also out of his over flowing goodness washes him all over in that fountaine which is sett open for the house of Juda, and so makes him clean from the gilte [guilt] of all his sinnes.[290]

[140v] O Lord, I doe most humbly beseech thee, saintefy this meditation so to me that I may upon any sinn I wretchedly comit against thee presently fly unto thee to take it away; and, O Lord, be pleased then to wash me all over in that

---

[288] Rich deleted the rest of the sentence as well as the next: "and to take upe alone with thee alone for my fealisety. O Lord be thou unto me all in all infenettly above all and bettar then all" (139r).

[289] Pliny's account of the emperor Nero offers a source for the statement that "water once heated, and cooled again, is by so much the colder" (Edmund Bolton, *Nero Cæsar, or Monarchie Depraued* [London, 1624], 284); see also Pliny the Elder, *The Historie of the World: Commonly called, The Natvrall Historie of C. Plinivs Secvndvs. Translated into English by Philemon Holland Doctor of Physicke*, 2 vols. in 1 (London, 1634), 2:407. Rich's brother Robert also concerned himself with the belief that "Water once heated and againe expoz'd to the Cold, contracts a more Intense Degree of that quality then it had before" (*The Aretology*, in *The Early Essays and Ethics of Robert Boyle*, ed. John T. Harwood [Carbondale and Edwardsville: Southern Illinois Press, 1991], 118 and n. 53).

[290] Joel 3:18-21; also above, n. 179.

Occasional Meditations

pretious blood, one drop of which is eficatious anufe [enough] to wash away the sinnes of the whole world.[291]

~~Upon a shell snale~~[292]

Upon two persones deportments under the carrying of two equall burthens

[141r] How readily and easily does this persone take up this burden and with what chearefullnes does he carry it; where as the other is so far from doeing so that he complains, and murmurs, and is not able to stand under it.

O Lord, I doe most humbly beseech thee, sett home this ocasionall meditation so to me that it may make me consider that some Christians doe with Christian courage and patience bear the trying burthen of afflictions which others stand complaining under and repining at. And O, make me to take up with readynes my crosse;[293] and the cup which my heavenly father has given me, lett me drinke it, though it be ever so bitter.[294] Lett me not murmur at any burthen thou art pleased to lay upon me, but lett me have that subjection of soule that I am convinced a creature ought to have to his creator. And that I may not faint when I am corrected of thee, lay under thine everlasting [141v] armes and doe, like Simon of Sirenea, helpe to beare the crosse.[295]

~~Upon taisting citron water~~[296]

[142r] *Upon letting blood*

I have observed that some persones have bene so much opprest that thay have not bene able without great difficulty to breathe, and yet by opening a vein they have fond present relief and ease. Thus it often happens to an opprest mind which is so much so that it can find noe relief from it by any thing till it retires to God and by secret prayer opens its heart to the great searcher of it. And then when it has poured out its soul (as pious Hanna did), it findes present ease, and (as she did) went away from prayer, and their countenance was noe more sad.[297]

---

[291] 1 John 1:7. Less immediate are Matthew 26:28, Romans 5:9, Ephesians 1:7, Colossians 1:14, and Revelation 1:5.
[292] The snail appears in no later meditations; previous meditations are on 91.
[293] Matthew 16:24, Mark 8:34, Luke 9:23.
[294] John 18:11.
[295] Deuteronomy 33:27. Simon of Cyrene, the Cyrenian compelled to help bear Christ's cross (Matthew 27:32, Mark 15:21, Luke 23:26).
[296] This meditation appears on 107.
[297] 1 Samuel 1:15, 18. The childless Hannah "prayed unto the Lord, and wept sore," asking God for a son; later she rejoiced (1 Samuel 1:10-11, 2:1-10). Rich also meditates

O Lord, I blesse thee that I have experienced this trueth my selfe and can from my own experience asserte it that when I have been opprest with the great and oppresing burthen of sinn and of afliction, too, I have in my aproaches to thy divine majesty by secret prayer found such heartes ease as [142v] instantly cheared me and made me able to say with Luther (that I still fond prayur the leech that soukte [suck'd] out all my cares).[298] O lett the former supports I have found by my approved remedy, prayer, for the future make me know whither to goe for relief; and that my prayers may come up before thee as incense,[299] lett me pray yet more earnestly, remembering that it is the fervent prayer that availes much.[300] O, therefore, lett me pray as if my soule ware sitting upon my trembling lips ready to take her everlasting flight and I were goeing to say, Lord Jesus, receive my spiritt.[301]

[143r] *Upon ones stealing by a private way in to the house*

This person entering by a private door in to the house, by so doeing has his coming in unsuspected and unregarded, too. Thus it is often with some formal, sivell [civil] person that by his beholders is — not observed to have a private sinn — loved and allow'd; yet by his indulging him-selfe in one, he does, as it ware, steale in to hell without any bodies takeing notice of his so doeing.

Upon observeing a childes being frited from what it likte because others made a mouth and laught at it

This poore childes quitting what it was imployd in with much dealight because a gaser on it made a mouth and laught much at it mindes me of a much more [143v]

---

on the example of Hannah's prayer and solace (29 April 1668, 1/182v) and compares her own absence of sorrow after meditation to that of Hannah's (28 August 1666, 1/21v).

[298] Melchior Adam, *The Life and Death of Dr Martin Lvther* (London, 1644), says Luther assured Philipp Melanchthon, "He who is become our father, will be the father of our children. I pray for you earnestly, and I grieve that you make my prayers, the most violent sucking-leech of cares, to be fruitlesse" (80). In a 20 February 1676 letter to Essex Finch, whose first child died on January 28, Rich quotes Luther's assurance about prayer, the "leech that sucked out all his cares" (HMC, *Report on the Manuscripts of the Late Allan George Finch, Esq., of Burley-on-the-Hill, Rutland*, 3 vols. [London: His Majesty's Stationery Office, 1913-1957], 2:27). In the midst of her own troubles about her husband's suffering, Rich recalled on 8 December 1669, "Luther sayd he still fond prayer the leech that suckt out all his cares" (2/12r).

[299] Psalm 141:2.

[300] James 5:16.

[301] Stephen's dying words in Acts 7:59. Rich deleted the next sentence, which alludes to Genesis 32:26 (see below, n. 337): "O lett mee Jacobe like rasle with thee and not lett thee goe tell thou haste blessed me."

ridiculous action that people of more age (that therfore should be wisar) doe, who suffer themselves to be laught out of the practise of realidgion which before thay likte because som of their vaine relationes or their carnall friendes make a disdainefull moueth at it and dearide it. But, O Lord, I doe most humbly intreat thee, lett me neaver be of that besotted number that, because som senseles fooles loudly evince their being so by breakeing a wiked, profane jest, indeaver to make relidgion appear ridiculous (but doe indeed by so doeing discover them selves to be so), be laught out of my indeavering the practesing of strikte holynes. But, Lord, make me skarne [scorn] the scorner[302] and goe on in serveing and owning thee most avoudely [avowedly] in that company (if I should by thy providence be cast in to it) where I am sure I shall be most derided for it. O lett me never be ashamed of thee here that thou maist not be ashamed of me here after.[303]

[144r] *Upon blowing of a fire to warme another and finding my selfe heated whilst I was doing it*[304]

Whilst I am blowing this dull fire that I might by makeing it burne heat another, I find my selfe by my takeing paines to blow warmed. Thus I have often experienced that whilst I have been indeavering by holy and warmeing discourse to exsite in others (that are under my charge)[305] lively afections to the supreame good, I have fond my own cold and allmost before frosen heart toucht with celestiall love and by that have fond it warmed and revived.

O Lord, lett the experience I have fond that by indeavering to doe good to others I have fond good my selfe make me more then ever consider my fellow Christians to provoke them to love and to good workes. O make me be often in this charitable duty, in the exsersise of which thou art pleased to give me a present reward by finding the languid sparke in my own breast many times ready to breake forth [144v] in to a most glorious blase and by letting me, too, be instrumentall som times to kindell som fire in others brestes towardes thee, my God.

[145r] *Upon tasting some drops of citron water*

These very few drops when tasted discover to me the excellency and fragrancy there is in citron water, which makes me keep the pleasant tast of it in my mouth som time afterwardes.[306] Which may be usefull to mind me of the relish and

---

[302] Proverbs 3:34.
[303] Mark 8:38, Luke 9:26.
[304] Compare Hall, "XXII Upon the Blowing of the Fire," in *Occasional Meditations*, 135.
[305] Among them perhaps her nieces Mary and Essex.
[306] Citron or lemon water, a distillation of citrus peels or fruit steeped in alcohol; it "comforts the brain as well as stomach" (George Smith, *A Compleat Body of Distilling*

divine gustow I have some times had by a previous gust of heaven and by relishing, as it were, a grape of the blessed land of promise.[307]

O Lord! I doe most humbly beseech thee, lett me have a tast of the lambes maredg [marriage] supper;[308] and though in this valley of teares I am not permitted to drinke so abundantly of the rivers of thy pleasures[309] as those hapy soules that have finished their course here[310] and are now triumphing with thee in glory, yet, Lord, lett me have some larger earnest of heaven than ever yet I have had. O lett [145v] me have much of heaven lett doune in to my heart that I may, as it were, taste some cromes [crums] and pareinges of glory,[311] which may keepe som realich of heaven in my mouth, which I may find so ravichingly sweat that I may disdaine and dispise all the ragoues the world would allure me to taste.

[146r] *Upon seeing it very fair over head but finding it very dirty under feete*

How cleare a day is here above, the skye being so free from black cloudes that it does not so much as threaten a storme, and yet under feet there is nothing but dirt and mire. Thus it is often with a Christian. Whilst he is in his pilgrimage towards heaven, he some times has the transporting satisfaction of seeing from above clear, unclouded dayes where in he deasernes [discernes] the sun of righteousness appearing gloriously to him;[312] yet when he lookes down and mindes what is underneath, he findes he must meet with some trobelsome dirty steps whilst he is treading in the strait path that leades to life eternall,[313] there being many dificultyes to incounter with in the finishing our journy towards heaven. O Lord, I doe most humbly beseech thee, lett me see all clear above; lett me [146v] by the spectacles of faith see a beame of light shining from thy face.[314] O lett there be curtains drawn by and unvailed discoveryes made to me out of a God

---

[London, 1725], 111-12; William Salmon, *The Family-Dictionary; Or, Houshold Companion* [London, 1696], 57; George Hartman, *The Family Physitian* [London, 1696], 299). Though "true citron water" required the peels of the West Indies citron, lemons were the more common ingredient. Among recipes, those in *The Queens Closet Opened*, 10th ed. (London, 1696), 251, and *A Queens Delight* (London, 1671), 91-92, steep slices of lemon with various spices and herbs in two pints of white wine; when distilled, sugar and ambergris are added.

[307] Numbers 13:23; see also above, n. 99 as well as 79 and n. 175.
[308] Revelation 19:7, 9.
[309] Psalm 36:8; see also valley of tears, above, n. 21.
[310] 2 Timothy 4:7.
[311] Cf. Matthew 15:27, Mark 7:28, Luke 16:21.
[312] Malachi 4:2.
[313] Matthew 7:14; see also above, n. 123.
[314] 2 Corinthians 4:6 and possibly Psalm 89:15; eye of faith: see above, n. 284. "Prospective" (a telescope) is written above "spectacles."

reconciled to me in Christ that so I may tread nimbly through all the durty way I meet with in my journy to the heavenly Jerusalem.[315]

Upon observeing that a stomakefull child has by refuseing to beg his parents pardon after it onse was whipt drew upon it selfe by its after sobbing and crying a more severe whipping than for its first fault[316]

[147r] I have observed that this untoward child, when it was corrected by the parent, in stead of begging pardon and confessing its fault by its great stomake exprest, by afterwardes sobbing and crying has irritated its provoked father more by that then by the comition of the first fault, and so has justly drawne a more severe whiping upon it selfe then it before had. Thus it often hapens to poore dealuded and rebellious creatures. When their great father in heaven is chastiseing them for their sinnes to prevent their relapseing in to the same inormates [enormities] or comitting greater, thay doe, in stide of falling before the offended diety humbly prostrate at his feete to implore his pardon, by their impatiante beareing what he inflictes and by haveing workeinges and riseinges of heart against what he has layd upon them neasesetate him to bring upon them a more trying and smarteing afliction then [147v] the first.

O Lord, I doe most humbly implore that thou woldest by this observation make me so wise as, when thou art next as a most mersyfull and indulgent parent chastiseing me for my good, make me heare the rod and consider who has appoynted it;[317] and so by takeing notes [notice] of the first corection, and by humbling my selfe, and laying my mouth in the dust,[318] and with justise acknowledging that thou art righteous in what afliction so ever thou art pleased to lay upon me, I may not draw from thy divine majesty a more severe and smarting one then the first. But, good Lord, be pleased to make me say, it is the Lord, lett him doe what he pleases with me; I will beare the indignation of the Lord because I have sinned against him and because in this and all my other crosses he has layd upon me he has punished me farr less then myne iniquites deaserve.

---

[315] 2 Corinthians 5:18; see also Colossians 1:20 and Romans 5:10. Christ is the means of overcoming God's anger at the transgression of Adam and Eve. Among others, Baxter states, "God the Father offereth himself to be my God reconciled in Christ, and so my chief good; and by voluntary receiving Baptism, I do signally profess my Acceptance of him so offered" (*Certain Disputations Of Right to Sacraments*, 2nd ed. [London, 1658], 69).

[316] Other children's reactions are the subject of Hall, "XCVIII Upon a Child Crying," in *Occasional Meditations*, 176-77; Thomas Fuller, "Personall Meditations, XII," in *Good Thoughts in Bad Times* (Exeter, 1645), 29-31.

[317] Micah 6:9.

[318] Lamentations 3:29.

[148r] *Upon the quenes ballett*[319]

This fine ballett, that has to see the great splendor of it drawne together so vast a concours of great personages that have made their way to it through vast croudes, was yet by the wise designers of it chose to have its apearance be by night, well considering that the jewelles and all the numereous wax lights that were sett upe to discover the glittring gloryes of it would not so delight and dasle the beholders if before they drew their curtain God had not first drawne over the canopy of night by which he does from us mortalles conceal till morneing his astonishing workes of wonder. For how pitifull a light wold that of many candells appear if that [148v] glorious creature the sun were not shut out, and how dispiseingly meane and pitifull would all the painted seanes [scenes] (in some of which in their representationes thay draw a sky) bee if the bespangled firmament that showes Godes handy-worke[320] were not hid from them that are at preasent so taken with the painted one onely because that either by shutters or night the other is kepte from their viewing it.

O Lord, I humbly beg of thee so to sett home to me this occasionall meditation that the searious consideration that the heavenes that declare the glory of thee, my God,[321] is allwayes carefully shut out before any of our admired and costly representationes are showd may make me still goe on to disesteme those tinsell pageantry gloryes which some others looke on with eyes of admiration; and make me [149r] be often lookeing up to those never anufe [enough] admired lights of heaven, with which I may delight my selfe allmost dayly without crouding to doe so and which when view'd will make me as much despise the other as the light a glowworme gives is when the sun shines.[322] O lett me find, too, that one beam of light shining from thy face is anufe [enough] to eclipse all the glory of this world in its highest lustor.

Upon a birds being kept fast by being onely tyde by one leg

[149v] I have observed that this poor bird being tyed onely by one leg yet by that is kept as fast a prisnor as can be. Which mindes me of the great enemy of man-kindes some times by one beloved, indulged sinn keaping the poore sinner as sure his own as if he ware guilty of more, because one sinn resolvedly lived in

---

[319] Queen Catherine danced in a "grand ballett" elaborately staged and performed at Whitehall three times in February 1671. Rich would not have witnessed the splendor since she was at Leighs in 1671. Evelyn saw the queen dance here and at another "magnificent Ball or Masque in the *Theater* at Court" in February 1667 (*The Diary*, 3:569, 476). See also the contemporary account in Eleanor Boswell, *The Restoration Court Stage (1660-1702)* (Cambridge, MA: Harvard University Press, 1932), 138-39.

[320] Psalm 19:1.

[321] Psalm 19:1.

[322] See also "Upon a Gloworme," 74–75.

and allow'd is not (by divines) held to be consistent with a state of grace.³²³ O Lord, I doe humbly beg that thou woldest never lett me live in any sinn alowedly, remembering that one pistol is as able to kill one as many are, and that one hole in a boat will as well sink it as many, and that Gideones one bastard son was the destruction of all the rest,³²⁴ and that one bastardly coruption chearished will be my eternall ruin if I perseveringly live in it. O lett not, therfore, any one sinn have dominon over me for Christ Jeasuses sake.³²⁵

[150r] *Upon a birds when it flew doune being caughte in a snare*

<Wh>ilst this pretty birde was flying upwardes and warbeling out hur takeing notes, she was pleasant and safe; but when by an inticeing bait she was brought doune upon the earth, she was presently taken in the snare. Thus it is too often with us poor deluded mortalles. Whilst we are obeying that inspired precept of setting our affectiones on thinges above³²⁶ and by an eye of faith are lookeing towards our eternall rest, we are happy and secure;³²⁷ but when we deasend [descend] from the contemplateing of thinges eternall to the intiseing snares that are by the divell covertly layd for us,³²⁸ we are then instantly tangled and so fast keacht [catch'd] that unless he that is stronger in us then he that is in the world come to our rescue, we canot [150v] escape.

O Lord, lett this consideration make me keep my thoughtes and my afectiones much above, remembering that all is safe, sereane, and quiet there; and lett me never more by the false delusiones of Satan be intangled; but, Lord, grant I may so resiste the divell as I may neaver more by him be caught.

---

³²³ John Tillotson, among others, warns that "living in any one known Sin, is enough to expose us to the dreadful wrath of God" ("Sermon LVII," in *The Works of the Most Reverend Dr. John Tillotson*, 2 vols. [London, 1717], 1:401).

³²⁴ Robert Boyle writes in *The Aretology*, "One neglected Leake is enuf to sinke the greatest Ship," an observation that has a parallel in Thomas Fuller's *The Holy State* (Cambridge, 1642), 20 (*The Early Essays and Ethics of Robert Boyle*, ed. Harwood, 107 and n. 22). Abimelech, the son of Gideon and his concubine from Shechem, killed all but one of his father's seventy sons, Jotham having escaped. After ruling Israel for three years, Abimelech was mortally wounded in battle against the forces of Shechem (Judges 8:31; 9:5, 53-54).

³²⁵ Romans 6:14. Rich deleted the rest of the sentence: "but thou whose prerogative it is to soubdew eniquitise sobdew all mine" (149v).

³²⁶ Colossians 3:2.

³²⁷ See above, n. 284.

³²⁸ 2 Timothy 2:26, 1 Timothy 3:7.

[151r] Upon observeing that every place was the better where the sheep were folded

How usefull creatures are these pretty sheep. Every place is enricht where thay are folded, and they stay noe where but thay doe good. This may put me in mind of the advantage the flauke [flock] of Christ are to kingdomes, tounes, and famelyes, thay makeing every place the bettar where the providence of God is pleased to cast them. Thus Potifers house was blest for godly Josephs sake, and Labans for Jacobs.[329]

O Lord, I doe most humbly beseech thee, doe thou so sett home this meditation to me that I may more then ever be ambitious of haveing many of thy sheep in my family, and make me still more to reverence and esteem them where ever I find them dispersed in the world, knowing that those most [151v] exselent persones ought to be highly valewd by thy creatures when thou hast bene pleased thy selfe to give such high and honorable titells to them as to call them thy jewelles.[330] O make me to see that the righteous is more exselent then his neighbour,[331] and to love them here, and fitt me to live with them for ever here after.

[152r] Upon bending a young twig

This twig I find noe difficult thing to bend which way I please now 'tis young; but if I stay till by age it has got a stifned hardness, I may bestow much unsouksesfull [unsuccessfull] strength upon it and must be forced at last to leave it without effecting my designe. This may put me in mind of the wisdom there is to be used in the educateing young ones, who whilst thay are so may by carefull and discreet governement be made pliable to good and may then be taught those excellent preceptes that may be of highesst advantage to them afterwardes.[332] But if for want of prudent care they be onse suffer'd to grow hard'ned in ill customes and so grow too big before they have their willes broke, one may take much labor to make them yield and yet [152v] neaver make them to doe so.

Upon a spoon full of strong orange water[333]

How much more strength is there in one spoonfull of this strong orange water then there is in many of cold ordinary water. This makes me to reflecte and consider how much a fervent prayur, though shortar, is to be valewd before a cold,

---

[329] Genesis 39:5; Genesis 30:27.

[330] Malachi 3:17.

[331] Proverbs 12:26.

[332] See the advice in Proverbs 22:6.

[333] A cordial made from peels of oranges steeped in wine, sack, or brandy and then distilled, orange water was "very good in pestilential Fevers: It strengthens the Heart and the Brain"; it was also carried on a sponge to ward off the plague: Salmon, *The Family-Dictionary*, 243; Kenelm Digby, *Choice and Experimented Receipts in Physick and Chiru-*

heartless one that is longer. O Lord, be pleased to so sett home this meditation unto me that I may in my humble addresses to thee be fervent in spiritt whilst I am serving the Lord and may indeavour to worshipe thee, who art a spiritt in spiritt a<s?> in trueth.[334] O lett my heart goe along with my petitiones, and lett me indeaver to storme heaven by my importunate prayures.[335] O make me as my blesed Saviour did, who in the days of his fleach offard upe strong cryes with teares,[336] and make me to pray yet more earnestly. Make me Jacob like.[337]

[153r] Occasional Meditationes made by M Warwicke 1672

[154r] *Upon my being exsidingly affected with the consideration of the very sad condition of those persones who ware in the plague time forced to be shut upe with their dead relationes*[338]

How many affecting thoughts have I had for the trying, deplorable condition of those unhappy wives (or mothers) who in the sad visitation of the plague were necessitated for some time to be in the room with their dead husbandes or children, their neighboures being afrade to receave them out of their infected houses for feare of their bringing with them the contagion in to theirs.

Oh, my soule, lett this ocasional meditation awaken thee to consider, [154v] if it be so sensible and allmost overcoming a grief to be kepte with an indeared relation that dyde onely a naturall death, which is comon to all mortall creatures and possibly by doeing so is made eternally happy being one of those that onely

---

rgery, 2nd ed. (London, 1675), 130-31; Hannah Woolley, *The Accomplisht Ladys Delight* (London, 1675), 32-33.

[334] John 4:24.

[335] The biblical justification for taking heaven by storm is Matthew 11:12, and the means is often prayer: "Heaven sometime may be forced by storm; (or by the assaults of extremely-fervent prayer)." Isaac Barrow, "Sermon VI. Of the Duty of Prayer," in *The Works*, 1:76. See also in the diary 27 June 1675, 4/30r, and below, n. 407.

[336] John 11:35.

[337] Who wrestled with an angel (Genesis 32:24). In a passage she deleted on 142v, Rich importunes God, "O lett mee Jacobe like rasle with thee and not lett thee goe tell thou haste blessed me." Prayer was the common means of wrestling with God, e.g., "I should be like unto *Iacob*. . . . I should wrestle, and tugge, and strive, and hold fast by faith in my *prayers*, and my *teares* too, as Iacob did" (John Featley, *A Fountaine of Teares Emptying it selfe into three Rivelets, viz of Compunction. Compassion. Devotion* [Amsterdam, 1646], 134).

[338] Compare Hall, "LXXII Upon the Red Cross on a Door," in *Occasional Meditations*, 161; Elizabeth Delaval, "Meditations writ upon the continuance of the plague," in *The Meditations of Lady Elizabeth Delaval Written Between 1662 and 1671*, ed. Douglas G. Greene, Publications of the Surtees Society 190 (Gateshead: Northumberland Press Limited, 1978), 91-92.

sleepe in Jesus,[339] how much more shouldest thou compasionate those miserable persones whose husbandes or children are dead in trespasses and sinnes. Who are necessitated to be with those who are spiritually dead, and some for many yeares together see with sad heartes dead husbandes and children and weepe for their being so.

    O Lord, I doe most humbly beseech thee, make me by this consideration be put upon pittying those of my relations that are yet dead in a spirituall sense, and lett it put me uppon coming to thee for to raise them from this spirituall death. And, O thou to whome nothing is impossible,[340] raise my dead [155r] relations. I know noe less powere is required to doe it then that which raised Christ from the dead; but, O Lord, I beseech thee, put forth thy allmighty power and lett them have their part in the first resurrection that so the second death may have noe power over them,[341] and give me cause, Lord, rejoyceingly to say these, my relations, were dead but thay are now alive.[342] That as I have formerly poured out my heart like water for their deathes and with a flood of teares mourned for it,[343] so now I may weep as much for joy at their resurrection. And seeing thou hast in thy sacred oracles told us that there is joy in heaven over a sinar that repentes,[344] O make me to experience some of that heavenly joy here upon earth, and lett me here joyne with that heavenly host in singing glory to God on [155v] high.[345] Lord, I know, though thou hast the halleluliahs of the Church Triumphant, yet thou dost not disdaine the hosannas of thy saints upon earth. Lord, give me cause upon this acounpte to sing hosannas here and fitt me to sing halleluliahs for ever in heaven.

Upon a doctors cutting and scarifying his sike [sick] *patient*[346]

[156r] With how many sad sighes does this poore sick persone mourne and complaine to his friends of the great smarting paines his physitian putts him to. Yet though their indearing kindness makes them (with very sensible concern for him) compationate his sad case, yet because what he indures is in order to his cure, they are more pleased with this way he takes than they would have been

---

[339] 1 Thessalonians 4:14.
[340] Luke 1:37.
[341] Revelation 20:6.
[342] Luke 15:24, which has "son" rather than "relations."
[343] Having in mind perhaps the tears in Jeremiah 9:1 and Psalms 22:14, 119:136.
[344] Luke 15:7.
[345] Luke 2:13-14, Revelation 19:1.
[346] Scarifying entails either cuts, punctures, or scratches on parts of the body correlated to the malady; heated glass cups, when used, helped draw the blood. Nicholas Culpeper lists the illnesses scarifying relieves in *Two Treatises: The First of Blood-letting, and the Diseases to be cured thereby. The Second of Cupping and Scarifying* (London, 1663).

with his letting him alone, giveing him over as desperate. And all the while the patient cryes out the skillfull doctor still goes on without being moved by his so doeing to quit his designed cure, knowing tis much more mersyfull to him to doe so then to suffer him to perish.

O Lord, I beseech thee, sanctify this occasional meditation to me that I may not chuse either for my selfe [156v] or most indeared relations rather to be given over as desperate then to have a cure perfected upon us by smarting paines. And oh, thou great physian of soules as well as bodyes,[347] use what meanes thou pleasest to save our soules from eternall death. If thou seest it fitt by bodily torments to mind us of fleeing from eternall ones, send what ones thou seest fitt. And, Lord, lett this meditation, too, mind me that I doe not yield to any temptation that the divell would tempt me with to thinke thou dealest cruelly with some of my relations because thou torturest their fraile bodyes, but make me rather conclude from that thy kindness to them, who art so mersyfull as rather to use meanes for their recovery than to give them over as desperate. O Lord, I am convinsed it is one of the saddest judgments on this side hell to be left un[157r]punished for sinn, and therfore in thy God-breathed oracles thou threatenest (thy people) that if their daughters commit whoredoms thou wilt not punish them.[348] O therfore lett me not so strongly cry to thee to spare their bodys as to save their soules, and lett me trust thee, the great and mersyfull physisian, how long thou seests fitt to keepe on thy smarting coresifes [corrosives]. Onely, Lord, I humbly beseech thee to perfect the cure and lett this be the fruit of their punishment to take away their sinn that they may at last have cause to say it was of faithfullnes thou didest afflict them. For before they were so, thay went astray; but now they have learnt thy word, and have heard the rod and [him] who has appoynted it,[349] and have lost nothing in the furnace of affliction but their drosse.[350]

[157v] *Upon the pitty I have had for som poore dwarfes I have seen*[351]

How compationately have I lookte upon some little dwarfes I have seen; and yet, wretch that I am, how littell sensible have I been of my own being so in Christianity and have not bemoned my want of growth, being too much contented with out doeing so where as I should have indeavoured to have grown in grace and to have added one cubitt to my spirituall stature.[352] Lord, make me now to have my soule prosper and thrive like a garden which the Lord has blest.

---

[347] See above, n. 2.

[348] Hosea 4:14; for the characterization of Scripture see above, n. 258.

[349] Micah 6:9.

[350] Isaiah 48:10.

[351] Also Hall, "CXXXVII Upon the Sight of a Dwarf," in *Occasional Meditations*, 196.

[352] Matthew 6:27.

[158r] *Upon lookeing over a hedge in to a garden which I could not gett in to*

How plesant is this prospect to me though I can but looke over the hedge in to this fine place, being hindred by this fense from entering in to this garden, which it is not fitt for me to breake over in to though it is to looke into it.³⁵³ Oh, my soule, lett this occasional meditation make thee to consider that though thou must not breake in to heaven but must wait till God gives thee enterance, yet thou mayest be often lookeing, as it ware, over the hedge in to it, though thou must not breake over it, and that thou mayest be often opening thy windowes to looke towards the heavenly Jearusalem to view and consider well her palaces³⁵⁴ and take in the delight and comfort of that, being thy designed inheritance. [158v] Oh lett the joy of spring goe before the joy of harvest and make me to find that title is somthing with out present possesion.

[159r] *Upon the opinion that moules* [moles] *neaver have their eyes op'ned till just before their deathes*

This opinion that the naturalists have that those poore little moles that digg up the earth are all their life time blind and never see till just they are dying³⁵⁵ mindes me of those sadly to be deplored creatures whom the divell has so far blinded by the insnareing, bewitching things of this world that thay discern not their spirituall condition till thay are by their physitians told thay must soon dye; and then many times the eyes of their understandinges are inlightned,³⁵⁶ and thay begin to discern some thing that before thay never saw. O Lord, I doe beseech thee, lett me not be blind all my [159v] life time till my death, but open my eyes that I may now see the thinges which belong to my peace before thay are hid from my eyes.³⁵⁷

---

³⁵³ The enclosed garden may also suggest in this context Song of Solomon, 4:12, which the 1612 edition of Wilson's *Christian Dictionarie* links with "The Kingdome of Heauen" as well as "The true church" (185-86).

³⁵⁴ Psalm 48:13.

³⁵⁵ Sir Thomas Browne offers a number of traditional sources for his contention that the common belief "Moles are blind and have no eyes . . . is received with much variety," concluding that they have "both eyes and sight" (*Pseudodoxia Epidemica*, in *The Works of Sir Thomas Browne*, ed. Geoffrey Keynes, 4 vols. [Chicago: University of Chicago Press, 1964], 2: 219). The belief that they regain their sight is not apparent among naturalists nor has been located in folk tradition.

³⁵⁶ Ephesians 1:18.

³⁵⁷ Cf. Psalms 119:18, 13:3.

Upon a day when the sunn appeared not

[160r] This day for want of the sunns apearing in it seems to me to be very sad and disconsolate, yet I comfort my selfe with this consideration: that there is still a sunn in the firmament as well in this darke, cloudie day as in those where in that glorious and reviving creature shines britest forth.

 O Lord, I most humbly beseech thee, lett this occasional meditation be usefull to comfort me by considering that though there are some dayes in which the sunn of righteousness[358] dos not cause his face to shine upon me[359] and make such cleare discoveries of himselfe to me as at som other approaches to my soule he does, yet that thou arte still in heaven and my God as sartenly [certainly] as when I have been able to say, I have seen the Lord (by the eye of faith); he has indeed appeared unto Mary.[360]

[160v] *Upon two fishes, a live one swiming against the streame and a dead one that was car'ed doune with it*

[161r] This dead fish that is so swiftly car'ed downe with the streame does mind me of dead sinnars who as the God-breathed oracles speake of those widowes that live in pleasure are dead whilst thay live,[361] so these persones have a name to live but are dead in a spirituall sence and sadly evince their being so by being so fashionable in their practise that they will be car'ed with the streame of the times (and goe with a multitude to doe evill, though that in sacred writ is forbidden them).[362] But yet they are resolved to doe as the most doe; and if religion it selfe be by them derided and the practicers of it laught to scorn, thay will goe along with them even in these horridly wicked practices rather then not be thought modish persons. [161v] But the live fish that swims against the streame makes me compare it in my thoughtes to a good, warme, and lively Christian who is resolved to be so unmodish as against the fashion of these loose times to walke in that straite and holy path that leades to life eternall;[363] and will not be car'ed with the most to follow their profane examples; but will rather chuse to goe alone, though with much difficulty striving against his coruptiones and the grand enemy of mankindes temptationes, who wold perswade him to goe with the stream, rather than to offend his good and gratious God; being resolved what ever affronts and jeares he meets with to own God and his people and not to be

---

[358] Malachi 4:2.
[359] Numbers 6:25.
[360] Mark 16:9; John 20:11-18. See also above, n. 284.
[361] 1 Timothy 5:6; see also the characterization of Scripture above, n. 258.
[362] Exodus 23:2.
[363] Matthew 7:14.

ashamed of the chief good here that he may not disown him at the last and great day before the glorious angells.³⁶⁴

O Lord, I doe most humbly implore thou wouldst be pleased to make this ocasionale [162r] meditation usefull to me to caution me against being drawn to doe as the most doe. O lett me rather chuse to be one of those that indeavour to bring religion in to fashion than of those that stay till it be soe. And lett me constantly and undantedly own thee thy truthes and thy servants where I am sure I shall be most laught at for doeing so. Lett me consider that those deriding libelles that are by the profane made on me upon that acounpte here will be panejerikes [panegyricks] in heaven. And, Lord, grant that when the profane are most bold in deriding religion I may be as bold in owneing it, that I may there by evince to them that thou hast some as resolute friends as enemyes.

[162v] *Upon a cabinet of my Lady Broghilles*

[163r] This cabinet of my Lady Broghilles,³⁶⁵ though she has bene mistress of it many yeares, yet she has all that while bene ignorant of the gold that was in a secret drawer of it consealed from her discerneing it, though she did very frequently look in to it and never her selfe found the hid treasure, but it was fond out by another for her.

Oh my soule! turne this in to a usefull meditation and consider that though thou hast often lookt in to the close cabinet of thy heart and because of the secret and cunning concealed corners of it canest find skairse [scarce] any thing that is pretious in it, yet thou mayst have some concealed grace in it. Benjamin had treasure in his sacke, and yet he knew it not.³⁶⁶ And therfore, O my soul, doe not be too much dejected and pass too sad a dome [doom] [163v] upon thy selfe because thou hast not found that which all the gold of Ofor is not worth (the graces of Gods spiritt),³⁶⁷ but goe to the great searchar of the heart who made it and beg his discovery of it to thee. And, oh Lord! I humbly beseech thee, examine and prove me; try out my reines and my heart and discover my selfe unto my selfe.³⁶⁸

---

³⁶⁴ Mark 8:38, Luke 9:26.

³⁶⁵ Margaret Howard (1623-1689), daughter of Theophilus Howard, second Earl of Suffolk, and his first wife Elizabeth Home, married Rich's brother Roger Boyle, Lord Broghill (1621-1679), on 27 January 1641. Her husband, who became in 1660 the first Earl of Orrery, played a role in both the political and literary worlds. (Toby Barnard, "Roger Boyle, first earl of Orrery," in *ODNB*, 7:109-14.) Rich was the godmother of their son Lord Broghill's child, christened on 21 March 1676 (4/132v).

³⁶⁶ Genesis 44:12.

³⁶⁷ The Old Testament often associates an especially fine grade of gold with Ophir, a seafaring nation that has been variously located in Africa and India.

³⁶⁸ Reins: kidneys or more generally the loins, a seat of feeling, affections (*OED*). Rich echoes Psalm 26:2, "Examine me, O Lord, and prove me; try my reins and my heart." See also Jeremiah 11:20, 17:10; Revelation 2:23.

And if I have any true saveing grace, manyfest it clearly unto me that so I may rejoyce with thy people and be glad with thine inheritance.[369]

Upon a tree in atome [autumn]

[164r] I did observe in my walkeing tother morneing that a tree that grew pretty neare the bainketing [banqueting] house had on it such yellow, ugly, discolourd leaves as made it by me taken notice of because that in the spring this same tree that now was so disagreeable to me to behold in September[370] in Aprill and May, when it first put forth its leaves, had so pure and dealightfull lovely a verdure that it often with pleasure drew my eyes that way. But some dayes after I saw those leaves which before ware so changed faln on the ground, and many remaineing ones fell in my sight. Which ware the occasion of this meditation that the difference of this tree might not very unfittly be compared to that which is observed in persones in the May of their lives and in the winter of it. Those very lovely persones whose [164v] beauty attracts the eyes of all that are in view of them to behold the freshnes of the spring in their looks and the whiteness of the milke represented in their skins, yet when age makes its very unwellcome approaches to them, their admired beauty changes into so unpleaseing, discoloring a change as makes the very idolisares of beauty see cause with the great experimenter of the world to conclude bewty is vanity.[371] And it may, too, make these cry'd up beauties consider that this so apparent allteration in their claye-houses[372] is but the foreruner of their aproaching goeing to the earth and there turneing to dust and rottennesse. O Lord, I doe most humbly beseech thee, lett this meditation make me consider what thy inspired volume tells me: that wee all doe fade as a leaf;[373] and lett me not be of the number of those that have gray haires here and there and yet perceive them not;[374] [165r] but lett those and the change that is so discernable in my vile body be my monitors to provide for my great change and to mind me of turneing to dust. And, O Lord! grant that when my body dos lye down in the bed of darkeness my soule may pass into the region of light where I shall for ever shine as the sun in the kingdome of my father.[375]

---

[369] Psalm 106:5.

[370] During September 1672 she wrote occasional meditations on the sixteenth, twenty-first, and twenty-third (3/63v, 66r, 67r).

[371] "*Solomon* was a great Experimenter of all Sorts of things in the World" (John Edwards, *A Brief View of the Mistakes about Happiness, Or, the Chief Good of Man* [London, 1724], 99, 2). Without mentioning beauty, Ecclesiastes insists that all is vanity; Proverbs 31:30, however, specifically states, "Favor is deceitful, and beauty is vain." About this time in the diary Rich especially stressed vanity.

[372] Job 4:19.

[373] Isaiah 64:6.

[374] Hosea 7:9.

[375] Matthew 13:43.

[165v] Upon walkeing in atome [autumn] *amongst dead leaves*

[166r] These dead leaves among which I walkd this fall mindes me of the great unpleasantness that is in being amongest dead persones, though we took great delight in them whilst alive, and we are, too, the less able to indure them for that reason. For whilst these now dead, rattling leaves ware alive, haveing a vegetive life, made it very sweet and deasirable to walke where they were because their shadow was sweet and refreshing from the hott beames of the sun. But now thay lye dead, I am impatient to have them removed out of my sight, as the father of the faithfull was desireous to have even his beloved wife buried out of his, not being able to be with one dead that was so comfortable to him when living.[376]

O Lord, lett these thoughtes make me consider how much reason I have [166v] to valew and love best the soules of those indeared relations, that their bodyes are but the cabinetts of and that have noe life nor motion but what they have from them. And when once thay have out of them taken their flight, their bodyes are not indured to be viewd or stayd with. O make me, therefore, prize above all their immortall part that is by being so freed from death and from being either frightfull or displeaseing to me. With which, if thay are renewde in the spiritts of their minds[377] and I by thy grace sanctified, I may with them live for ever hapy in the injoyment of thy selfe in a plase where even death it selfe shall neaver part us.

Upon an old broken cabinett of my Lady Lakes that was with great store of gold by her left to her son Sir Lancelott Lake

[167r] This old, hordeing, cunning woman for feare of haveing her treasure by rude breakers in to hur house found and stolen, to prevent that had deasigneingly [designedly] put in a very fine cabenett onely som few hundred pondes but had in an extrordnary ugly, broken one that was in a cornar of hur closett, where it was seamely [seemingly] flung by as useless, put all hur gold.[378] And that great wealth she left hur sonn, who after hur death coming in to hur closett to see

---

[376] When Sarah died in the land of Canaan at the age of 127, Abraham sought to "bury my dead out of my sight" (Genesis 23:4); he buried his wife in a cave in Hebron (23:19).

[377] Ephesians 4:23.

[378] Mary, the wife of Thomas Lake (1561-1630), was the daughter of William Rider and the mother of Lancelot (1609-1680). Lancelot's older brother Arthur (d. 1633) had married Lettice Rich, the daughter of the first Earl of Warwick and aunt of Mary Rich's husband; and the account of the gold discovery may well have been part of the family history, since Lady Lake died in 1642. Lancelot, who married Frances Cheke, was knighted 6 June 1660; he resided at Canons Park, Stanmore, Middlesex, and was elected a member of parliament the same year. (*Le Neve's Pedigrees of the Knights*, ed. George W. Marshall, Publications of the Harleian Society 8 [London: Harleian Society, 1873], 63-64, 243-44; Robert Lockyer, "Sir Thomas Lake," in *ODNB*, 32:247-49; *The History of Parliament: The*

what so many yeares scraping had for him produced, was sadly frighted to find onely the small sum in the fine cabenett. But after a long, diligent, fruiteless searching which made him allmost conclude that his mothers treasure was before his coming stole, he, wondering to see in that odd place of the room the old, before mentiond [167v] cabinett, out of a designe to remove so ill a furniture out of that rome went to take it out; but when he attempted doeing so, much to his comfort found it so very heavy that by the waite [weight] of it he was pretty well informed of the worth of it; and when he open'd it, found that great sum of gold that she had hid in it for him, though she never before her death durst trust even himselfe so as to informe him where it was. This may be usefull to mind me not to despise persones who have possibly unhandsome outsides but may for all that be very much richer in the graces of the spiritt of God then many of those fine, glittering persones that like the fine cabenett have but little of worth in them. O Lord, I humbly beseech thee, make me so wise as not to despise or valew persones by their outward beauty or by their want of it. [168r] Lett me never be so foolish as to chuse onely by my eyes, but make me make use of my understanding in my choyse. And if I find in unhandsome outsides inward riches, lett me not disdainefully entertaine mean, unworthy thoughtes of them, but make me imitate thee, my God, who hast in thy divine oracles told me that thou lookest not at the outward appearance but at the heart.[379] And though thou hast also there informed me that though thou onely knowest the hearts of the children of men,[380] yet thou hast also instructed me that a good tree brings forth good fruit and that by their fruit we shall know them.[381] And therefore, O Lord, if I see them by their holy life evince to me their inward piety, make me by that conclude thay are worthy to be highly prised that I may this way show my love to him that begetteth by loveing those that are begotten.

[168v] *Upon the sunns setting in a cloud*

[169r] I have observed that though the sun has for the most part of the day shined forth cleare and bright, yet that it sett in a cloud. Which observation minded me of the deathes of many pious Christians who have for the most part of their lives by all their beholdars been taken notice of for their exemplary piety and have obeyed that inspired precept of letting their light so shine before men that others seeing their good workes may glorify their father which is in heaven.[382] Yet before their deathes, at which time many of their frendes have come to them, being

---

House of Commons 1660-90, ed. Basil Duke Henning, 3 vols. [London: Martin Secker & Warburg Limited, 1983], 2:704-6.)
[379] 1 Samuel 16:7.
[380] 2 Chronicles 6:30.
[381] Matthew 7:17-20.
[382] Matthew 5:16.

full of most raised expectationes to heare som thing extraordinary from them, thay have bene far from saying any thing that was so, but have appeared clouded, and have not gone so triumphingly to heaven as was expected by their beholdars; which cloud might be occasioned either by Gods withholding from them at that time his usuall comfortes or from the force of the disease that seising [169v] their spirittes has much dispirited them and so for the preasent dampt them. Which makes me to conclude that it is best not to judge of persones so much by their deathes as by their forepast lives.

Upon a piece of sullied gold

[170r] This gold, though I see it by dirt much sullied, yet I doe not refuse it for that reason, because the piece when it was tryde was found to be trew [true], though sullied, gold. This may be usefull to mind me of the great goodness of my gratious God to his poore saints who have bene by his holy spiritt renew'd in the spiritt of their mindes and so have true grace in them,[383] though by reason of the indwelling coruption that still in this life remaines in the best (in som degree) are by that originall corruption much sullied. Yet God is so mersyfull, as finding in his children truth of grace when he has tryd them, he dos not for that inward coruption which defiles them reject them but mersyfully in Christ accepts them.

O Lord, I bless thee for thy great mersy to lost men in generall and, in particular, for acsepting [accepting] me, thy unworthy servant, and lookeing upon me in and through my sweet and lovely Saviour, in whom thou art well pleased.[384] And O, that all that [170v] is with in me might bless and prayse thy holy name[385] for thy acseptation of so deafiled a wretched person who am, I acknowledg, sadly sullied with sinn. But, O Lord, if the roote of the matter be in me,[386] doe not reafuse me, but lett me be accepted in the beloved; and being washt in that fountaine that is sett open for Juda and Jerusalem to wash in,[387] lett me be owned and taken by thee in the day when thou makest up thy jewelles[388] and hear thee pronounse that sentance on me, come ye blessed of my father; inheritt the kingdome prepared for you from the fondation of the world.[389]

---

[383] Ephesians 4:23; 1 Peter 5:12.
[384] Matthew 3:17, 17:5; Mark 1:11; Luke 3:22; 2 Peter 1:17.
[385] Psalm 103:1.
[386] Job 19:28.
[387] Joel 3:18-21; also above, n. 179.
[388] Malachi 3:17.
[389] Matthew 25:34.

Upon my haveing but very little windowes for some time in my closett and afterwardes haveing bigger ones

[171r] This clossett when I was first mistress of it had so little windowes that not without some difficullty could I see out of them, but now I have got so large ones that I can sitt in the room and with much cleareness and ease see more out of them. This may be usefull to mind me of some good Christians that when they were first saveingly wrought upon had but littell light and could hardly deaserne [discern] spirituall thinges, but afterwards God was pleased so to open the eyes of their understandings that thay did not onely see those things which before thay did but difficultly doe but thay also clearly saw much more then formerly. O Lord, I doe most humbly beseech thee, lett this meditation be usefull to cautione me against either despiseing or quarelling with my fellow Christians if they doe not with as much cleareness as my selfe see som truthes. Oh! lett me neaver thinke it fitt to quarell with them because thay have not so big windowes as my selfe, but make me to remember that I had not some yeares since my selfe so large ones as [171v] now I have and possibly some yeares hence thay may have much wider ones then I now have. But if thay have not, and I perceive the light thay see is but like one that sees but at the small holes of a lattisse window, yet lett me not be angry with them, but thanke thee, my God, for giveing me more then them, and make me willing to impart to them what I see more then thay yet doe.

Upon a candles being sett against a wall which, though it could not burne it, smutcht it

[172r] This candle that has been putt against the wall, though it could not burne it, yet it has smutcht it and plainely discovered to me by its doeing so that it was sett there.

Turne this, O my soule, into a usefull ocasionall meditation to caution thee against ill company who, though thay canot by their inticements draw thee to those sinnes which wold quite destroy thee, as the candle could not burne doune the wall, yet thay may by vaine and frothy discourse sett thy coruptiones at worke by which thay may smutch and sully thy soule. O Lord, I humbly beseech thee, make me a companion of all them that fear thee and who will by their warmeing, heavenly discourse doe me good, and lett me not chuse those which will necessitate me with difficulty to make my way to heaven, not onely through my own coruptiones but through the coruptiones of those I converse with. And oh, make my sadly bought experience of the sully I have con[172v]tracted from them make me for the time to come carefully avoyd them.

Upon smelling spice after it had been bruised

[173r] This spice till it was bruised in the morter never sent forth so sweet and fragrant a smell. Though it was in it selfe sweet before, yet it was not deaserned

[discern'd] to be so by others. Which observation mindes me of those holy and spirituall Christians who never so clearely evince to others their graces (though thay ware before posest of them) as when thay are by aflictiones prest and bruised, and then their patient bearing them discovers to their beholdars what thay before ware ignorant of.

[173v] *Upon a birdes hopping from one bough to another and fixing noe where*

[174r] I have observed this pretty but inconstant bird how it hovers about without fixing any where but still hops from one bough to another. Which mindes me of the inconstansey and unfixedness of my some times roveing thoughtes, which, O, canot posibly keep any where but will be gadding from one place to another. O Lord, therfore I doe most humbly beseech thee, doe my impossibles and inable me with the man after thy own heart to say, my heart is fixed.[390] O Lord, seeing that thoughtes are the consepsion of the mind (as spich [speech] is the bearth [birth] of it), O make me carefull what is there conseaved [conceived] and lett me have holy and pious thoughts. And if vaine and ill thoughtes be by my grand enemy now and then darted into me, Lord, keep me from entertaining them; lett me give them a quick dispatch that they may not lodge and abide with me. Make me to consider that thoughtes are pretious, being the immediate fruites and budds of an immortall nature. And therefore make me able to say with an inspired writer, [174v] how pretious are thy thoughtes unto me, O God; how great is the sum of them! If I showld count them, thay are more in number than the sands,[391] that so my heart being taken up with thoughtes of thee, my God, I may not have so much room for parleys, and interviews, and chattings [which] my mind too often has [had] with things lett in to it that are but frothy and vaine.[392]

Upon lookeing in to the glass bee hive that is in the garden

[175r] The lookeing in to my glass bee hive[393] and there seeing how busy those littell but usefull creatures are in working to finish their combs may be nesisary to mind me of the great worke I came in to the world to doe, which I have hitherto been too unmindfull of and too seldome busily imployd in.

O Lord, I doe most humbly beseech thee, lett this occasional meditation be an awakening one to me that I may now be as busy as a bee, and may not stand all

---

[390] Psalm 57:7; 108:1.

[391] Psalm 139:17-18.

[392] In his only comment on the emendations, WW notes, "Somewhat concise and obscure, and therefore I have inserted two words, wch I think make ye true meaning" (174v). The words are in brackets.

[393] See above, n. 138.

the day idle,[394] but may now look to my finishing work, and may not any longer be a drone, but may now worke whilst it is day because the night will come when no man can worke.[395] O, make me now be so diligent in my masters business that at last thou mayest say, well done good and faithfull servant.[396] And the more I have loyter'd hitherto the more lett me thinke my selfe obliged to worke harder now. O lett me not be idlely busie, but make me to be [175v] imployd in doeing that which will make me happy here and, through thy mersy and the merits of Christ, eternally so here after.

Upon goeing to visitt a friend, resolved not to make there any long stay

[176r] I did when I went to visett my friend goe resolved against makeing at present a long stay, but finding whilst I was with hur so much comfort and satisfaction in hur wellcoming me express by much indeareing kindness that it was impossible for me to quit her pleaseing and delightful conversation till I had injoyd it for some long space of time. Which yet seemed not so to me, nor could I thinke the houres ware past which others as well as the clauke [clock] informed me ware so after my reaturne home. O my soule, lett this be usefull to mind thee of the many times thou hast in thy visitts to heaven thought not to stay long with thy highest and best friend but to make a quick returne to other, though not so necessary, business and so thought onely to have had a runing bainket [banquet] of heavenly meditation. But whilst thou hast been conversing with thy God in solitude and by heavenly meditationes been car'ed up where thy chief good is, he has bene pleased to give [176v] thee such a wellcome as has made thee say, it is good for me to draw neare unto God,[397] and has evinced to me that he that makes all others good company is best himselfe.[398]

O Lord! I doe most humbly beseech thee that thou wouldst be pleased to make me thankefull for the unvalewable kindness I have had from thy great and divine majesty, who has been pleased to stoope so beneath thy greatness as to converse with such a crawling worme as I am, and to give me such a wellcome as has made me forgett all my imployments that when I went in to thy preasense wold have ingaged me to a quike reaturne, and has made me say, one day in thy

---

[394] Matthew 20:6.
[395] John 9:4.
[396] Matthew 25:21.
[397] James 4:8.
[398] Rich advises Lord Berkeley to set time aside for meditations, for "the way not to be alone, is to be alone"; "God that makes all others good company, must needs be best himself" ("A most pious Letter," in Berkeley, *Historical Applications and Occasional Meditations*, 150, 151; in Walker, *Eureka, Eureka*, 135, 136).

courtes is better then a thousand ellse where,[399] and has made me thinke the howres I have spent with thee but as moments.

[177r] *Upon lookeing in to a barne*

Onely lookeing into this barne wold at first sight have made me beleeve there had skairse [scarce] bene any thing ellse in it but chaff and straw; but afterwards I perseaved it contained much valewable and usefull wheat which was, before it was thrasht out and winowd, hid by the straw. Which minded me of the great number of the wiked world who are in Godes inspired volume called the chaffe, which are there condemnd to be burnt up with unquenchable fire, and of his preatious jewells, which are called his wheat and are ordered to be gathered in to his barne.[400] And this sight has made me too consider how in citys, countreys, and families the number of the wiked are usually so great that hardly the holy, pious persones are amongst them considerable anufe [enough] for their number to be taken notice of; and therefore [177v] many times those that doe onely come in to those places without making there any stay are apt to feare there is nothing but chaffe—as the prophet [Elijah] mentioned in the Old Testament did beleeve himself to be the onely persone alone that was left, though he was informed of thousands that had not neither bowed to Baal.[401] But after thay that at first sight beleeved so come to stay som time in those before mentioned places, thay find many pious sanctified persones who are highly to be prized.

O Lord, I humbly beseech thee, lett this meditation caution me against censureing all to be chaffe when I see great numbers that are so, but make me amongst them find out those that are thy corne and ordred to be layd upe in thy barne, and not despise them because they are yet mingled with much chaffe. O make me consider that one bushell of wheat is worth many of chaffe and that one of thy own saintes are exsidingly more usefull and [178r] considerable then vast croudes of the unregenerate persones.

Upon a damm that was made to stop water

This dam I toke notice of the other day, which was made with designe to stop the water and did so for som time, I now perceive has but a littell while kept it from passing, for it has made its way at last over it. Which made in my thoughtes compare it to carnall relations who stand betwene us and God like this dam to stop our pasage to him. And though some times by their inticements or restraintes thay may a while retard our running to him, yet that soule that is in earnest in its pershutes

---

[399] Psalm 84:10. The same belief is also in the diary—11 October 1668, 1/249r; 7 February 1669, 1/291r.
[400] Matthew 3:12.
[401] 1 Kings 19:18, Romans 11:2-4.

after God will at last breake over all difficultys and come to him as pious Chrisistan resolved to doe, who sayd that though his father, and his mother, and his sister should all hang about him to hinder his goeing to Christ, yet he wold trample upon them and fling them off [178v] to come to his deare Saviour.⁴⁰²

Upon this pasage in the life of Alexander the Great that hee was troubled because in his great garden at Babylon ivie would not grow

[179r] My reading this pasage in the life of great Alexsander, that had councurd [conquer'd] so much of the world, that he showld be troubled because in his spatious and fine garden in Babylone in which he had all that was valewable in gardens he found not ivie growing, made me (not without som astonishment) consider that so great a monark as he was, who made the great Persian empire furst tremble and then fall, could take notice of so inconsiderable a thing.⁴⁰³ But much more did I wonder that he could express discontent at the want of it. But whilst I am with some disdainefull thoughtes censureing him for this strangely trobling himselfe for want of it, I am with King David censureing my own action in anothers persone.⁴⁰⁴ For how many times (wretched creature that I am) doe I find my selfe uneasy and vexed that I have not all my foolish fansy causes [179v] me to deasire, though ever so undesirable in the opinion of others more wise then my selfe. And how much can I torment my selfe for the want of it when yet God has been pleased to give me with a bountifull and liberall hand variety of greater and more excellent mersyes to take comfort in.

---

⁴⁰² WW glosses Chrisistan as Chrysostom (178r), but the source is Jerome, who has in mind Luke 14:26 (see also Matthew 10:37). Jerome's letter to Heliodorus exhorts, "Though your little nephew hang on your neck, though your mother with dishevelled hair and torn raiment show you the breasts that gave you suck, though your father fling himself upon the threshold, trample your father underfoot and go your way, fly with tearless eyes to the standard of the Cross": *Select Letters of St. Jerome*, trans. F. A. Wright (London: William Heinemann Ltd, 1933), 31-33. Among seventeenth-century variations are Isaac Ambrose, *Media: the Middle Things*, 3rd ed., in *Prima, Media, & Ultima: The First, Middle, and Last Things*; in *Three Treatises* (London, 1657), 107; Thomas Watson, *The Duty of Self-denial Briefly Opened and Urged* (London, 1675), 40-41.

⁴⁰³ According to Plutarch, Alexander the Great gave his lieutenant and governor of Babylon the task of planting "all maner of plantes of Graece" in the palace gardens and along the walks. Harpalus failed, however, to introduce ivy; "it ever dyed, bicause the heate and temper of the earth killed it" (*Plutarch's Lives of the Noble Grecians and Romanes Translated by Sir Thomas North*, 8 vols. [Stratford-upon-Avon: Shakespeare Head Press, 1928], 5:215; in the 1579 edition, 742). Rich's observation about Alexander's "strangely trobling himselfe" appears neither in Plutarch nor in Samuel Clarke, *The Life & Death of Alexander the Great* (London, 1665); Quintus Curtius Rufus, *The Life and Death of Alexander the Great* (London, 1661).

⁴⁰⁴ See above, 47 and Psalm 73:22.

O Lord, I doe most humbly beseech thee, doe thou so saintifye this meditation to me by which thou hast bene pleased often to make me call my own faults to my rememberance that I may neaver more be so foolishly besotted as to trouble my selfe for little things, but make me be chearefully thankful for what I have and not disrelish my possest greater mersyes. For every trifeling thing that crosses me, O give me allwayes a meek, quiett, contented spiritt which will make me happy to my selfe and which is, too, in thy sight of great valew.

[180r] *Upon observeing that my coach-horses when I was neare home went much faster then thay did in all their journy*

These horses when thay ware once with in view of their home did plainely evinse to me their desire to be at it by the swiftness of their pace, which thay seemed to me to double. Which mindes me of some happy, pious Christians to whom God has by an eye of faith given a prospect of their everlasting rest, carrying them, as he did his servant Moses, in to the mount,[405] and by discovering to them the plase he had prepared for them and giving them some secret hopes of their being soon there, has made them goe faster in their journy towards heaven, running in the wayes of his comandements,[406] knowing thay had now [180v] but a little time to finish their great journy in.

O Lord, I doe most humbly beseech thee, make me so wise as to go nimblar and swiftar than ever in my journey towards heaven, being somond [summon'd] by my yeares to believe that I am neare home and that I may take the kingdome of heaven by violence and press hard forward.[407] Lett me see by the prospective glass of faith those glorious mansions that are prepared for thine.[408] O lett me have a sight of my eternall rest, and lett that make me goe and not be weary, and run and not faint.[409]

Upon my friends begining a journy when the sunn was neare setting

[181r] This late setting out of my friend did make me wonder at his indiscretion in so long deferring to begin his intended journy, the sunn being neare setting before he began to sett out though he had a good way to goe. This may be usefull

---

[405] See above, nn. 284 and 99.
[406] Psalm 119:32.
[407] Matthew 11:12: "now the kingdom of heaven suffereth violence, and the violent take it by force." In the diary Rich would also take heaven by violence (3 April 1677, 5/105r). Baxter quotes the passage from Matthew in counseling "daily travellers for Heaven" that "There must be violence used to get the first fruits, as well as to get the full possession" (*The Saints Everlasting Rest*, 673, 16). See also above, n. 335.
[408] John 14:2.
[409] Isaiah 40:31.

to mind me of what the inspired volume tells me of beholding the mote in my brothers eye and not perceiving the beame that is in my own, being uncharitably apt to condemne others and pharesaiecaly [pharisaically] to justifye my selfe though guilty of greater enormityes.[410] For whilst I am with some amasement thinkeing of his procrastinating his going to his deasigned plase, I am guilty of a much more dangerous one in not setting out betimes in my grand journy towards the Jearusalem that is above,[411] not remembering that the night of death is drawing on and that if before that comes I have not finished my journey for heaven I am undone, where as my delaying friend may have another day if he have [181v] unadvisedly lost one to goe where he intended.[412]

O Lord, I doe most humbly beseech thee, so sett home this ocasional meditation to me that I may neither be a lazy nor a delaying Christian; but seeing I have a great way to goe before I have finished my course,[413] make me every day to goe some of my straite way that leades me to my journyes end.[414] And the longer I was by the insnareing temptations of my grand enemy[415] and by my own coruptions been detained from setting out, the faster lett me now run that my sun may not be sett before I have finished my Christian course. Which I beseech thee to grant that I may doe with joy that at the end of my dayes I may attaine the end of my faith, the salvation of my soule.[416]

[182r] *Upon observeing that some leaves continued a great deale longer upon the trees then others but at last thay all fell downe*

Though these leaves have, as I have observed, continued much longer upon the trees then the rest that grew with them, yet I see they are now at last faln too. Which mindes me of some long lived persones to whome God has given a longar time of continuance in this world than he did to those that once lived with them,

---

[410] Matthew 7:3; Luke 18:10-14.
[411] Galatians 4:26.
[412] Thomas Watson similarly writes, "So we have a long journy, and the night of death is drawing on, how should we use spurs to our sluggish hearts, that we may go on more swiftly" (*Heaven Taken by Storm: Or, The Holy Violence a Christian is to put forth in the pursuit after Glory* [London, 1670], 157).
[413] 2 Timothy 4:7.
[414] Recalling Matthew 7:14: "strait is the gate, and narrow is the way, which leadeth unto life."
[415] See 2 Timothy 2:26 and 1 Timothy 3:7.
[416] "Hope" is written above the word "faith."

yet at last thay drop to the dust.[417] For it is apoynted unto all men once to dye, and what man is he that lives and shall not see death?[418]

O Lord, I doe most humbly beseech thee so to sett home this observation to me that I may often thinke upon and seariously prepare for my dissolution, knowing that it is sarten [certain] it will come but unsarten when it will [182v] doe so. For though thou hast bene pleased allready to lengthen out my life longer then thou waste pleased to doe to my onely sonn,[419] yet lett me reflect and consider that if it be so done to the greene tree, what shall be done to the dry;[420] and that though thou hast not yet given death the comission to cutt me down (which, Lord, thou mightest, I confess, justly have done for my unfruitfullness), yet that it will not be long before I shall goe hence and be seene noe more.[421] And therefore, O Lord, I implore that when I am goeing to doe a worke I neaver did, I may have a strength I neaver had and may not be surprised by that king of terrours;[422] but being every day expecting it, I may deasire to be dissolved and to be with Christ, which is far better.[423]

[183r] *Upon a sparke of fire*

This littell sparke has by its burneing a hole evinced to me that it is trew fire and may, too, be usefull to comfort me for my haveing yet attained so little grace, considering that if it be true though small, it may by Godes mersy be accepted, the promises in the God-breathed oracles being made to sinceare grace.[424] O therefore, my soul, be carefull to search for truth in the inward partes;[425] and though thou must be farr from being satisfied with what thou hast allready attained to, but

---

[417] Job 34:15, Ecclesiastes 12:7, Psalm 104:29. Rich may have had in mind acquaintances or perhaps even the list of Adam's long-lived descendents in Genesis 5:1-32: Seth lived 912 years; Enos, 905; Cainan, 910; and Methuselah, 969. Adam lived to be 930.

[418] Hebrews 9:27, Psalm 89:48.

[419] Her son Charles died on 16 May 1664 at the age of twenty.

[420] Luke 23:31.

[421] Psalm 39:13.

[422] See above, n. 231.

[423] See above, n. 253.

[424] 1 Peter 5:12 stresses "true grace"; other New Testament statements on grace include Ephesians 2:8, 4:7; Titus 2:11, 3:7; Hebrews 4:16. The phrase is common among seventeenth-century writers who sometimes link love and grace. "Sincere Grace," Baxter insists, is the love of God and not the world; "it is not the measure of Grace, but the Truth; not the Quantity, but the Quality that we must judge our selves by" (*The Saints Everlasting Rest*, 481). "Sincere Grace," for John Flavel, "is Gold tryed by fire" (*The Touchstone of Sincerity: Or the Signs and Symptoms of Hypocrisie; Opened in A Practical Treatise Upon Revelations III 17, 18* [London, 1698], 51). See also above, n. 258 and the characterization of Scripture.

[425] Psalm 51:6.

must grow in grace and add one degree of it to another, yet doe not conclude sadly against thy self that thou arte not a Christian because thou hast not attained yet so great a proportion as som more holy and thriveing [183v] Christians have done. But remember a child, though little, may as well be loved and owned by the indulgent father as a big and grown man who is come to full maturity.

[184r] *Upon an hour glass*

As sone as I had turned this glass, the sand by which we measure the time began to run, and I observed that those graines of it that first did so made way for the rest and did as well contribute to the hours passing as the last that fell did to the finishing of it.

Turn this, O my soul, in to a usefull occasionall meditation and consider that it is not onely the last and finishing actes of ill that thou must avoyde but those first motions and actions that doe goe before, and make way, and so do contribute towards it.

O Lord! I doe most humbly beseech thee, lett me take care of the first inticements which I am tempted unto, remembering that they will, if harkened to, make way for more and so contribute [184v] to my finishing actes as well as my last actions will.

[185r] *Upon the skye when it was full of bright stars*

This bespangled firmament that showes us so many glittering stars whose glorious brightness dos attracte us with admiration to view them and excites us to admire the maker of them mindes me of the great and glorious promises that God has in the inspired volume scatt'red through the whole booke,[426] which are as usefull and comfortable to a poore disconsolate soul that is, as to his spirituall condition, in darkness and sees noe light as these twinkling stars are to light the benighted traveler that has long wandred in the dark.

[185v] O Lord, as I doe with the man after thine own heart admire the firmament which showes thy handy worke,[427] so, O Lord, I doe, too, with adoration of thy goodness and mersy to thy poore creatures admire thy care of poor lost persones to whome thou hast given so many free and gratious promises of all kindes that the heirs of promise[428] might have sure hope. For thou hast not onely made conditional but absolute promises, haveing not onely made promises to grace but of grace; and thou hast furnished thy sacred writ with comfortable promises for all conditions and exigences to which we poor mortalles in the time of our sojourning here may be exposed; and thou hast comanded us noe duty,

---

[426] 2 Samuel 22:29; Psalm 112:4; John 8:12, 12:46.
[427] Psalm 19:1.
[428] Hebrews 6:17.

but thou hast also anexed a promise of inabling us to doe [186r] it. O Lord, I doe from my soule bless thee for thy sweet promises, and I doe desire never to stagger at thy promises through unbelefe but really and firmly to rely upon them for my eternall salvation, knowing that thay are in thee, yea and amen.

Upon observeing that as sone as one of the birds that was in my cage began to sing the others that were in it began to doe so too

I have often taken notice that as sone as one of these pretty birds begins to sing the rest that are in the same cage neare it doe instantly acompeny it in doeing so and so together sweetly [186v] gine [join] in warbling out their pretty, takeing notes, by which thay doe in their kind and as far as they are able sing forth their makers prayse. This minded me how usefull a thankefull Christian may be to others. For whilst they are imployd in that pleasant as well as heavenly imployment of prayseing God, they by their good example may excite others to helpe them to returne glory to God as King David did when he sayd to his fellow Jews, (come and lett us magnify the Lord, and lett us exalt his name together);[429] and as if these ware not by him judged sufficient to prayse their great and glorious creator, he calls allso upon the inanemett [inanimate] creatures to doe it.[430]

O Lord, I doe most humbly beseech thee, make me much in this evangelical worke. O lett me begin my hosannas on earth that I may by them be fitted to gine [join] with that heavenly host in singing halaluihas for ever. O Lord, grant [187r] that I may be usefull, too, in setting on others to reaturn glory to thee, my God.

Upon a bird that I have kept alive ten yeares in a cage[431]

How many birdes have bene of late brought in which ware caught many seaverall wayes, som by a sparow hauke, som ware shott, and som with snares, but all have bene destroyde; whilst I have yet alive in my cage one that has there allready now bene preaserved more then ten yeares. Which observation may be usefull to make me consider how much more safety there is in a retired then in a publike life. For though these birds that by their not being confined had therfore liberty to fly when and where thay wold, yet by haveing that priveledge thay ware often exposed to many dainegurs [dangers]. [187v] Which though by flying from the hauke thay escaped then, and by the swiftnes of their flites at other seasons did, too, gett away when thay ware shott at, yet not allwayes so cleare but that thay in their goeing lost som times a wing and some of their feathers and at last thay ware taken; whilst the inclosed bird has not onely escaped those dainegurs but is

---

[429] Psalm 34:3.
[430] Psalm 148 exhorts all life forms and created things to "Praise the Lord."
[431] Another meditation with a similar title is Bury, "Med. 68 Upon a Bird in a cage," in *The Husbandmans Companion*, 319-23.

still singing quiet and safe. Which makes me conclude that though company is by most (though not by my selfe) thought most pleasant, yet reatirement is useally most safe.

O Lord, I doe most humbly beseech thee so to sett home this ocasional meditation to me that I may be more and more confirmed in my long time received opinion that in retireing from the noyse and crowd of the world there is more safety than there is in incountering with these temptations which are useally mett with abroad in the world. O Lord, as I am really convinced that in reatirement there is not onely security but unspeakeable pleasures to be mett with in [188r] reatireing to thy divine majesty fr<om> other compenyes, so, O Lord, make me be drawne by it to more frequent aproaches to thee, who art sofisiant [self sufficient] and all sufficient to make me happy, without needing to run and flutter about from one place to another to pershew [persue] my happyness in variety of objectes and places.

Upon my Lord Grayes house at Eping that fell sudenly doune flatt to the grond

This great and fine house which appeared so strong and likely to continue to all its beholders was yet to the great amasement of all with in view of it faln in a very small space of time flatt to the ground, as was afterwards fond, by a fault in the fondation which was not well layd.[432]

Turne this, O my soule, in to a usefull meditation to caution thee against building thy spirituall building upon any fondation but the Rock of Ages, where alone there is safety, [188v] and where no thing can overthrow <it>, nor rough stormes either of afflictions or persecutions can th<row> it downe, amen.[433]

---

[432] The Greys' manor at Epping was in Waltham Hundred, Essex. William Grey, first Baron Grey of Warke (1593/4-1674), was alleged to be part of a planned 1653 uprising against Cromwell, along with the second Earl of Warwick and John Robartes (Cliffe, *The Puritan Gentry Besieged*, 16); his wife Cecilia, the daughter of John Wentworth of nearby Gosfield, was also mentioned as a frequent visitor in the diary (Fell Smith, *Mary Rich, Countess of Warwick*, 335). Rich was the godmother of "Grayes daughter," possibly their grandson Ford's daughter Mary (18 May 1675, 4/19r). William Grey died on 29 July 1674; within a year his son and heir Ralph also died, and the barony went to Grey's grandson Ford Grey (*A History of the County of Essex*, in *The Victoria History of the Counties of England*, ed. W. R. Powell [London: Oxford University Press, 1966], 5:118-19; Philip Morant, *The History and Antiquities Of the County of Essex*, 2 vols. [London, 1768], 1: part three, 47; Sean Kelsey, "William Grey, first Baron Grey of Warke," in *ODNB*, 23:896-97).

[433] Rock of Ages, perhaps most widely associated with Augustus Montague Toplady's eighteenth-century hymn, has no precise biblical counterpart. Seventeenth-century writers commonly used the phrase, however, in reference to God (Isaiah 17:10), Christ (1 Corinthians 10:4), and Peter (Matthew 16:18), rocks of support and fortresses of defense. See, among others, Everard, *The Gospel-Treasury Opened*, part two, 38-39; Thomas Hill,

[189r] Ocasionale Meditations made by M Warwicke 1673

[190r] *Upon the cutting down of the Willderness*

This sweet place that I have seene the first sprouting, growth, and florishing of for above 20 yeares togeather and allmost dayly taken delight in, I have also now to my trouble seene by my lords command the cutting downe of in order to its after growing againe thicker and bettar, though I often interceeded with him to have it longer spared. This brought to my sad rememberance afresh the death of my onely son, whom I had also seene the first growth of in his childehood, and the florishing of to my unspeakeable satis[190v]faction for allmost twenty one yeares, and in a short space of time to my unexpressable grief by my great Lordes comand cutt doune by death that he might rise againe in a bettar and more florishing condition, though I often implored that if it ware agreeable with the divine will he might be longer continued to me.[434]

O Lord, I doe most humbly beseech thee that thou wouldst be pleased by this ocasionall meditation to mortifye me not onely to the sweet places where I have taken greatest and lawfullest delightes but to the persons in whom I have done so, too, by remembering me that I can sett my heart upon noe worldly object but that sodenly that which I dote on most may be taken from me or I from that by death. And, O Lord, I beseech thee, grant, too, that the consideration that my [191r] son shall rise againe may be a reaviveing [reviving] cordiall to me for my being for some time separated from him. O make me to remember that I shall shortly goe to him, though he shall not return to me, and that I shall then see him cloathed with immortality,[435] and florishing, and glorious to eternity.

[192r] *Upon the Indians being fond of colord beades and exchangeing for them pearls*

Whilst I am from those that have travelled in to the Indies heareing the relation how highly the inhabitants of it doe desire our gaudie colloured glass-beades, which thay valew at a rate that makes them exchange for them perles that are much more valewable and lasting,[436] their very readikeleous [ridiculous] and

---

The Spring of Strengthning Grace In the Rock of Ages, Christ Jesvs (London, 1648); Richard Baxter, *The Crucifying of the world, by the Cross of Christ* (London, 1658), d1r. Other possible biblical sources include Psalms 18:2, 28:1, 31:2-3, 62:2, 71:3, 92:15 as well as Matthew 7:24-27 and Luke 6:46-49. On 15 June 1667 Rich wrote she had God, "the rauke of ages to fly to" (1/96r).

[434] Rich commemorated yearly the 16 May 1664 date of her son Charles's death.
[435] 1 Corinthians 15:53-54.
[436] Among the references to "Ignorant," "silly," and "foolish *Indians*, who sell their Gold, and their Pearls and other precious things for Brass, and Iron, and Glass Beads": John Cockburn, *Fifteen Sermons Preach'd upon Several Occasions, and on Various Subjects*

strange choyce makes me thinke of a much more irationale one of poore deluded Christians who, too, often prefer the gay and tinsell glittering thinges of this world before the pearl of greatest price[437] and those eternall gloryes which Christ has purchased for those who in their deliberate choyse prefer and deasire him above all thinges.

[192v] O Lord, I doe most humbly beseech thee, lett me never prefer tinsell above gold or the uncertain thinges of time before the sarten [certain] and lasting thinges of eternity. O make me so wise as to count all thinges but as dung and dross to gaine the unvalewable pearl which is infinitely above all and better then all.[438]

Upon observeing that a fire made with billets would not burne till some chips and shaveings ware put to it, and then it instantly did [439]

[193r] I have observed that these billets wold not burne till some chips and shaveings of wood and little sticks were fetcht; which when thay ware so and put to them, they then instantly sett the great blocks and billets afire. Which minded me how usefull many times heavenly, warm, and lively Christians though of lower and meaner parts may be to those who are of more raised and refined ones, for by their most heavenly warmeth thay may exsite and stir up in more knowing persones life and heate.

O Lord, I doe most humbly beseech thee, lett this ocasionall meditation make me never dare [193v] to disesteme any of those excellent ones that have truth of grace because thay have not so great partes as som others have, but make me to love and desire their companies, knowing how usefull their holy conversation may be to draw out in som measure the strength of my affections. O make me more to prise in others and to deasire for my selfe grace then partes, remembering that partes are given me for others, but grace for my selfe. And, O Lord, I humbly beg that when by thy good providence to me I am cast in to such good company, make me so to improve those opportunitys that I may find them good fires to warme my selfe at that so by [194r] their warmeing discourse I may be inabled to find somthing of the warmeness and fire of thy love in my heart.

(London, 1697), 224; Edward Reynolds, *True Gain, Opened in a Sermon Preached At Pauls, Nov. 9. 1656* (London, 1659), 30; Cotton Mather, *Small Offers Towards the Service of the Tabernacle in the Wilderness* (Boston, 1689), 81.
  [437] Matthew 13:45-46.
  [438] Matthew 13:45-46.
  [439] Compare Boyle, "Reflection II. Upon his making of a Fire," in *Occasional Reflections*, 5:85.

Upon a dispute with a friend

How deepe and sensible a trouble doe I find of this ill reaturne my friend has made me for my real, obligeing expressions of my kindness to him by which I did designe to overcome him, and I did beleeve that my declaration I made him of it would sartenly [certainly] have done it. But [194v] now that to my great grief I find that it has not; but, on the contrary, whilst I was heapeing oblidgeing and indeareing kind expressions upon him, his reaturnes to my doeing so ware cruell and despitefull wordes, he speakeing like the pierceing of a sorde [sword] and saying all he could that he fansed would displease and disoblidge me, I find my selfe so much irritated by this usage that it does much more grieve me than all I ever mett from him before.[440] And were it not that I have the inward comfort and support that attends obaying that great soveraine who has comanded me to overcome evill with good,[441] I showld have been ready to sinke under this otherwise insupportable burthen.

[195r] Turne this, O my soule, in to an heart-humbling meditation and consider how justly the offended deity may say to thee, as Joseph did to one of his brethren, wherefore have you requited me evill for good.[442] And if what thy fellow creature has done to thee in this kind is so grieveing and so highly disingenuous, what is it then for thee to commit it against thy great creator?

O Lord, I humbly beseech thy majesty so to sett home this consideration that it may turne all my sorrow in to the right chanell that my teares may noe more be powred out for my friends ill usage of me, but grant that I may powre out my heart like water[443] before thee for my crimsone sinnes[444] against thy constant and unmerited goodness [195v] to me. O Lord, I doe acknowledge that these are the transgressions that cry loudest to thee for to punish them; but, O Lord, I humbly implore that when my sinnes, like the sinnes of Sodom, come upe before thee for vengeance,[445] then lett the cry of my deare Savioures blood be

---

[440] An entry for 9 October 1670 describes her husband's unprovoked but "violent pasion" that caused him to "speake like the persing of a sword" (2/95v); on 27 July 1673 he "broke out of a soden to speake like the pierceing of a sword" when she tried to reprimand him for dishonoring God (3/198r). The phrase recalls Luke 2:35, Simeon's prophecy to Mary.

[441] Romans 12:21.

[442] Genesis 44:4.

[443] Rephrasing Psalm 22:14: "I am poured out like water."

[444] Isaiah 1:18. On 11 April 1673 Rich also "grieved for . . . my Crimson crying Sinnes against mersyes, and my not profiting under holy ordinances" (3/157r).

[445] On 5 December 1669 she lamented her shortcomings and "did trewly confess it would be more tolerable for Sodom and Gomora then for me" (Matthew 10:15, 11:24; Mark 6:11; Luke 10:12) (2/10v). Genesis 13:13, 18:20, and 19:1-29 mention the sins and destruction of Sodom and Gomorrah; the sinful nature is also recognized in Isaiah 3:9, Jeremiah 23:14, Ezekiel 16:49-50, 2 Peter 2:6-8, and Jude 1:7-8.

heard for me, in which I doe beseech thee to wash my stained and polluted soule. O, wash me throughly from myne iniquities and cleanse me from my sinnes,[446] even from those horrid ones that are against thy goodness, that thay may never more rise up against me to be either my confusion here or my condemnation for ever here after.

Amen, amen.

[196r] *Upon a little boyes reafuseing to lerne his catekism till he was frited by great claps of thonder* [447]

This untoward and disobedient childes refuseing to be instructed by its parents in the prinsepulles [principles] of religion ocasioned them not onely to threaten him to bring him to me but also forced them really to do so to try wither his great feare (which thay perseaved hee had of me) might neaseasitate [necessitate] him to learn what was for his good. But his obstinacy against doeing so appeared as well to me as it had done before to his offended parents till of a sudden, whilst he was running about and playing disregardles of the good lesson I wold have taught him, a soden and violent clapp of thunder came, which the boy no sonar heard but he ran instantly as close to me as posible hee could [196v] and lifting upe his handes with the greatest importunity imaginable cryd to me to teach him his catekism. Which I did. But as sone as the thunder was over, in one instant he againe quitted both me and what hee before was learning and fell againe to his beloved play, but did not injoy the satisfaction of doeing so long till hee againe heard a new alarameing clapp of thonder; which made him, as if that he heard had putt winges to his feete, with great swiftness draw close to me, and repeat his first request of beeing informed, and so continued very diligently to be till hee had asked me this question: whether I thought God allmighty had done thondering yet. And when I had answered him that [197r] hee had, hee instantly ran quite away from me.

Turne this, O my soule, in to a selfe condemning and humbling meditation and, seariously reflectingly, consider how oft thou hast acted this childes part to the great God of heaven when thou hast inconsiderately by som of those many thinges with which Martha was 'cumbred bene detained from Maryes imployment of sitting at Christes feete[448] and, like a good deasipull [disciple], learneing what lesson he would teach thee till thou hast bene driven to fly to him by som thondering and alarameing afliction; which has made thee with a great and expedite motion [197v] flee to the ofended deity to take out what lesson he deasigned I showld by laying his aflicting hand upon me, and there promiseing to do so, and

---

[446] Psalm 51:2.

[447] On the top of the folio Rich wrote the word "Widow," implying a dating after August 1673.

[448] Luke 10:38-42; see above, n. 90.

continuing to performe that promise till God had mersyfuly with drawne the trouble he had justly for my sinnes brought upon mee. And then I have departed to act over againe what I did before, running away from the fountaine of life to hew out to my selfe broken sisturnes [cisterns] that would hold noe water.[449]

O Lord, I do most humbly beseech thee, humble me exsideingly that ever I was so basely disingenuous as onely to fly to thy deavine majesty when I was under thy aflicting hand and that as sone as that was removed [198r] I was so, too, from thee, and lett me for time to come cleave to thee with full purpose of soule. O lett there never be in me a wicked heart of unbelefe to cause me to depart from thee, the liveing God. O give me a filiall, child like feare which may make me to stand in awe and sinn not,[450] but yett lett thy mersyes be the most powerfull and allureing motives to bring me to thee and to keep me from wandering from thee. And when I inconsiderately do so, O use what meanes thou in thy infinite wisdom seest best to bring me back to my selfe and to thee that so I may return to the shepard and bishop of my soule.[451]

[198v] *Upon wondering at an unthankefull persone*

[199r] My haveing used so many indearing wayes to oblige this friend of mine and haveing considerably presented hur without ever once receiveing thankes for all my paines and cost did make me not a little wonder at the person for hur ingratitude. But, O my soule, cease to do so onely at her disingenuity and stand confounded and amazed at thy own, who art by thy greatest and best friend seronded [surrounded] with giftes and mersyes with which he dayly loades thee and yet thou dost practise the highest straines of ingratitude, being like those lepers which did not returne glory to God.[452] O Lord, lett my condemning in my own thoughtes hur part to me exsite and stir me upe [199v] to more thankefull acknowledgments to thy divine majesty for all thy undeaserved blesinges. O, that I may have by them deepe impresions made in my heart and may study what I shall render to the Lord for all his benefittes[453] that I may practice the highest straines of gratitude for blessing me with heavenly blesinges, which canot stand with reprobation, and for by thy providence, too, bringing me to houses full of all good thinges which I filled not, to gardenes and orchards which I planted not.[454] Others labourd, and thou hast brought me to injoy the fruites of their labores.[455] O that now thou hast fed me to the full I might bless and prayse thee and [200r]

---

[449] Jeremiah 2:13; for the fountain of life see above, n. 14.
[450] Psalm 4:4.
[451] 1 Peter 2:25.
[452] Luke 17:17-18.
[453] Psalm 116:12.
[454] Joshua 24:13.
[455] John 4:38.

serve thee with chearefullness and joyfullness of heart in the plenty and abundance of all thinges; and make me to honour thee with my substance,[456] being rich in good workes ready to distribute, willing to comunicate, laying up in store for my selfe a good fondation unto eternall life.[457]

Upon a physisians cureing a most desperate disease by which he gained himselfe great store of credit and of patients that flockt to him

This exselent docters doeing a cure so very great that it was thought impossible, not onely by the persone [200v] upon whome it was acomplished but by the other skillfull physisianes, too, that ware joyned with him, has to all the world given such demonstration of his skill that it has brought to his house whole croudes of desperate patiants. Turne this, O my soule, in to a comfortable and incorageing ocasional meditation and consider that though thou art spiritually sick and hast most desperate soule diseases which many times has made thee as well as others—thy beholdares—conclude thou arte in a desperate condition, yet doe not despair of cure, but goe to the great phesitan [physician] of spirittes who has cured those who were the greatest of sinners and beg him to do so for thee.

O Lord, I humbly beseech thee that [201r] thou wouldst be pleased to doe both my impossibles and others, too, who ware my Christian friends whom I have som times called in to assist me in my cure. O Lord, blessed be thy great name; thou hast for many yeares bene pleased to give me the great blessing of a healthfull body, which has bene as the salt to all my other possest mercyes. But, O Lord, I humbly implore thy divine majesty that thou wouldst now be pleased to cure me of my spiritual sloth, and of that desperate soule disease pride, and of my hard-heartedness, and of my spiritual consumtion, and of my lethargy, and of my inpenitency. O, perfect these cures upon my soule that it may then florish and prosper; and what cure thou hast wrought by thyne allmighty powre upon [201v] me, the chiefe of sinnares,[458] may bring in many with all their desperate diseases unto thee who by faith may beleeve that thou art not onely able but willing also to do what thay need and come to thee for. O Lord, heare me when I thus call upon thee and show to me and others that thou hast been at worke upon my heart, which will both bring glory to thee and comfort to me, thy unworthy servant.

Upon a flower [the turn-sol] *that opened it selfe towards the sun*

[202r] This flowers opening it selfe towards the sun should not onely delight me to behold its doeing so but ought to instroukte [instruct] me to performe my duty

---

[456] Proverbs 3:9.
[457] 1 Timothy 6:18-19.
[458] 1 Timothy 1:15.

towards its maker and mine.[459] O my soule, consider how much it is thy priveledge as well as thy duty to dilate thy heart towards that sun of righteousness[460] whose warmeing, cherishing beames thou hast so often bene partaker of and whose reviveing, quick'ning influence thou hast to thy unexpresable comfort felt.

O Lord, I do most humbly beseech thee, make me to take notes [notice] and reflectingly to consider how thou hast made my heart narrow downewards and brode [broad] upwards, and lett it teach me this leason [lesson]: to have [202v] my heart inlarged in my desires after thinges above and straitned after the thinges of this lower world. And, Lord, too, grant that thy great mercyes which thou hast bene pleased with a liberall hand to bestow upon me may be to me as the sun was to this flower, which, feeleing the warmeth of it, made it display it selfe towards that glorious creature. O that thy bounty and goodness towards me might make me open even my very heart towards thee and then powre it out before thee in adorations and prayses continually that it may constantly be lookeing upwards towards thee, the giver and the continuer of all my reaviving mersyes.

[203r] *Upon a doors being opened to lett in a person of quality and a great many of common people then croudeing in too*

This doors being designedly opened onely for the letting in one honorable person has yett bene the reason that the rome is to the grief of those in it too much comberd with many unwellcome, troblesome, common, unruly people who canot againe easily be gott out.

O Lord, I humbly besich [beseech] thee, make me to consider how often when I have bene heareing a good sermon, and [203v] have had a soden good thought cast in to my mind, and because it was a pious one, I have entertained it. Thinkeing onely to do so to that single one, I have fond that a great number of comon, ordinary, impertenett [impertinent] thoughtes have all so before I was aware gott in which I could not putt forth againe with out much difficullty. And, O Lord! I most humbly implore that this too sadly bought experiance I have had how great an advantage my grand enemy has had of me by my being by even good thoughtes diverted in the service I was ingaged in (which made those thoughtes which were so at another time by being then unseasonable great distractores to me) be carefull for the future to keepe my heart [204r] close to what I am attending to. And when an unseasonable good thought knockes for entrance, lett me not presently give it a speedy one but say to it (as Fellix in another case did to

---

[459] Possibly *Heliotropium europaeum*, European turnsole; *heliotrope H. arborescens* is also variously tumsole and turnsole (information provided by Elsa Kramer). Craig Brough at the Royal Botanic Gardens and M. Beasley at the Natural History Museum, London, suggest this may also be a reference to the sunflower *Helianthus*.

[460] Malachi 4:2.

Paule), goe thy way for this time; when I have a more convenient season, I will heare thee.[461]

[204v] *Upon drinkeing tea*

[205r] How strangely bittar did this tea taist till I had mingled som sugar in it; which when I had don and sturd [stirr'd] it well together, what before was so displeaseing to me that I could not gett it down I afterwards did with great delight drinke a good draught of. Which did mind me of my good Godes mersyfull and wise dealeings with me, his most unworthy servant, in all the course of my life which I have heather to [hitherto] past in this vale of teares,[462] who have had it fild with checker work, haveing had both black and white, bitter and sweet. And yet by his good providence towards me he has bene pleased so to mingle the bittar draught of af[205v]fliction which he saw wholesome for me with many mersyes and some manifestations of his love to me that the cupp which my father has given me[463] I have not onely bene able to gett doune but have with dealight done so.

O Lord, I adore thee with my soule for mingling with the wormwode and the gall[464] some hony, for sweetning my bitterest crosses with a lively sense of thy unmerited spesall love, which has made me beleeveing in thee to rejoyce with joy unspeakeable and has chearefully cared [carried] me through all the smarting tryalles of my life when ellse I showld, like Issachar, have croucht under my burthen.[465] [206r] O Lord, I know that knife onely shall cutt which thou puttest an edg unto, and thou hast bene pleased not to make one gaich [gash] more then was neasisary [necessary]. And when thou hast wounded me, thou hast, like the good Samaritan, powred oyle in to my wounds and bound them up againe[466] and hast spoken peace in the midest of all my troubles; which has sweetned every condition to me and made me chearefull in the midest of all my tryalles with which thou wart pleased to exsersise me and which has made me experimentally able to say, if hee speakes pease, who can give trouble.[467]

---

[461] Marcus Antonius Felix, the procurator of Palestine from A.D. 52 to 60, heard the charges of the high priest and elders, who accused Paul of being "a pestilent fellow, and a mover of sedition among all the Jews throughout the world" (Acts 24:5). After questioning Paul, he postponed judgment. Two years later a new governor replaced Felix, leaving Paul in prison (Acts 24:1-27).

[462] See above, n. 21.

[463] John 18:11.

[464] Lamentations 3:19.

[465] Genesis 49:14; Issachar was the son of Leah and Jacob. A similar passage occurs in her diary, 5 November 1672 (3/83v).

[466] Luke 10:34.

[467] Possibly John 14:27; experimentally: see above, n. 211.

[206v] *Upon my keapeing in a rome for som time a bird and then opening the window and letting it out, and its then fluttering much about*

[207r] Whilst I have by shutting the doores and windose [windows] of this rome closely confined this pretty but flutt'ring bird, it still waited about the window to gett its desired liberty. And as sone as I had opened the casement, it instantly got out, which it no sonar had done but it did so evince its joy by flying up and doune as if madness had posest it. Which observation was usefull to mind me of some good, well meaneing peoples educateing those young ones that are under their tuition, who propose to them selves that keapeing them in from goeing abroad even to lawfull [207v] sightes and places makes them whilst thay are under this displeaseing confinement waite for liberty and looke towards it as the bird did towards the window; and when thay have got from that seavere [severe] governement, be much more wild then those who by their governors wise ordering them and giveing them liberty to doe what is lawfull are not so fond of gadding as the others and are, too, by seeing lawfull sightes disabused from those false ideas which thay have in their fancies entertained of the splendid, bewitching sightes thay heard poore deluded mortalles discourse of with so much admiration, which has made such [208r] empreasions [impressions] in their minds that thay can neaver be disabused from but by coming abroad and vewing [viewing] those very things. Which when thay have done will by frustrateing their expectations undeaseave [undeceive] them and planely discover to them that what the divell and wicked persones (which are his instruments) have made them beleeve of the gloryes of the world and of haveing liberty to injoy it was but fallacious and was much greater in the expectation then in the fruition.

O Lord, I do most humbly desire that I may be so wise in the governement of all those persones [208v] thou art pleased to commit to my charge that I may neither hold the reins of governement too hard nor lett them too loose, but may allow them all the liberty thou art pleased to allow them, and may deany them all thou art pleased to disallow them that so I may not by imprudent and unnecessary seaveretyes [severitys] make them afterwards wild and indiscrite [indiscreet] nor yet by giveing them too much liberty have that to prove destroktife [destructive] to them. O, make me call to mind my own experience how much my raised expectations have soford [suffer'd] very sensable defeates in all sublunary things and how really advantageous it has [209r] proved to me that I have by my own trying things had my esteem taken off from them; which before my ignorance of them had raised to a very great haith [height], makeing me often so besotted as to take the tinsell glittering thinges that are heare below for gold, which is more exselent and durable, and so foolish as to prefer the unsarten thinges of time before the sarten [certain] and durable thinges of eternity.[468] And lett this which I have experimented make me to allow that to them which will by viewing take

---

[468] Possibly 1 Timothy 6:17.

off their heartes and affectiones from them, and make them experimentally able to say with that great [209v] and wise experimenter of the world (who tride all things to save us the labor of doing so) that all thinges are vanity and vexation of spiritt and that the eye is not satisfied with seeing.[469]

Upon my maides makeing the fire to blaze by onely blowing it with hur moueth

[210r] How sone has my mayd by blowing the fire onely with her mouth made it blaze. Which instantly brought to my thoughts how usefull I had formerly found the breath of a pious persons mouth sodenly to make the fire of devotion that lay in my heart to breake forth and to blaze, their exsiteing warmeing and awakening discourse being instrumentall to draw out in some weake measure the strinth [strength] of my affections and by some wordes fittly spoken by a warme and lively spirituall Christian (and sett home to my heart by the great searcher of it) has, like a naile fastned in a sure place, discovered to me what worke tis possible for onely the breath of a manes mouth [210v] to make in my before cooled heart. O Lord, I do most humbly implore that the experience I have had of the power of wordes (when blest by thee upon me) either to quiett my before disturbed mind or to warme my before frozen heart may make me for the future deasireous of such inflameing breathes as may make my love blaze with more then serapheke [seraphick] heate[470] and as may make my deasires run after thee like a mighty torrent.

[211r] *Upon giveing opium to stupify the person that takes it*

This persones prescribeing his patiant opium[471] to stupefye him that so he may not be sensible of his condition mindes me how fittly inconsideration may be called the divelles opiam by which he does so stupifye them that thay are not in the least sensible of the danger that their sinnes expose them unto.

---

[469] Ecclesiastes 1:14, 2:17, 1:8.
[470] See above, n. 218.
[471] Though the eighteenth century has been characterized as "the golden age of medically-prescribed opiates" (Roy Porter and Dorothy Porter, *In Sickness and in Health: The British Experience 1650-1850* [New York: Basil Blackwell, 1989], 102), the use of opium in laudanum and paregoric was increasing common as a sedative and pain reliever.

[211v] *Upon a bucketts makeing a great noyse when it was lett doune the well by the clattring of the chaine but when it was full ascend with out hardly being heard*[472]

[212r] I have observed that whilst this buckett is descending down this well it makes with the chaine by which it is fastned a clattring noyse; but when it is filld with water, it did ascend with out being at all heard when it did so. Which sight was usefull to mind me how often persones when thay are in want of some deasired mercy do loudely proclaim to God their want of it and by their prayures make a great noyse in the eares of God to be filled with what thay are empty of. But when thay are so filled, thay doe not with a loude voyse reaturne glory to God but are silent.[473]

O Lord, I doe humbly beseech thee, lett me not be thus dome [dumb]; but as I have when under want of a mersy [212v] knaukte [knockt] so loude at heavens gate as if I meant to storm heaven by my importunate prayures,[474] so lett me when I am filld with it with a loude voyce reaturne glory to thee.

[213r] Occasional Meditationes M Warwicke 1675[475]

[214r] *Upon a frends giveing me a present and declareing she did it with this designe to make me upon sight of it to thinke of her*

This kind friend of myne giveing me this present to mind me often of her has its designed effect, for upon all occasions that it is presented to my sight it makes me thinke of hur with kind and gratefull thoughtes.

But O, my soule, with how much detestation of thy selfe may this occasional meditation make thee reflect upon thy vile ingratitude to thy God, who has so seronded [surrounded] thee with gifts as thou canest turne thy eyes no wher but thou hast a prospect of the divine bounty and yet art disingenuous as often to looke uppon [214v] sweet Lees (which I acknowledge to be to me the gifte of God) without ever remembering the giver. Nay, how frequently does it make me forgett both my selfe and him and ready som times with him mentioned in the Gospell to sing that reacum [requiem] to my soule: soule, thou hast goodes layd up for many yeares; take thyne ease, eate, drinke, and be merry.[476]

O Lord! I do beseech thee, humble me exsideingly by this consideration that thy manyfold and inumerable mersyes, which showld be like Elias charett to care

---

[472] See the quite different application in Spurstowe, "Meditation XXXIX. Vpon the Bucket and the Wheel," in *The Spiritual Chymist*, 87-90.

[473] Unlike the one leper in Luke 17:15.

[474] See above, n. 335.

[475] The occasional meditations and diary for 1674 are missing; they were never in WW's possession.

[476] Luke 12:19.

[carry] me up to heaven,⁴⁷⁷ has made me apt to senture [center] all my delightes in a dong-hill [dung hill] and to entertaine proude thoughtes in stead of gratefull ones. O, lett it now be my study what I shall render unto the Lord for all his benefittes to me⁴⁷⁸ and which way by all the actiones of my future life I may [215r] practise the highest strains of gratitude. And O, lett the sight of those sweet acomodationes with which I am (by thy bounty) possest fill me with affectionate rememberances of thee. O lett my heart by them be lifted up in the high prayses of thee, my God. And seeing I have nothing to returne thee for thy bounty to me but what thou hast demanded as an acceptable gifte (my heart), O Lord, I doe here solemnly present it to thee with this confession that I beleeve nothing deserves it but thy selfe. O, be pleased to accept it as landlordes do peper-cornes from their tenantes as acknowledgments of that homage thay owe to them;⁴⁷⁹ and though I doe give thee but a dull, cold, worldly heart, yet, Lord, be pleased to reaturne it to me an inlivened spirituall one. One touch of thyne allmightiness upon [215v] my heart, what a change wold it make! O be pleased to make in it the deepest impressions of thy mersyes that ever yet were ingraven in any that thay may neaver be by any thing efaced but may be allwayes legibly read by me to quicken me to a more diligent, constant, and universall obedience to all thy comandements.

Upon one that had offended me and confessing his fault, and by doeing so obtaineing my pardone, and afterwards repeating it againe

[216r] This persones acknowledgeing to me his conviction that he had run in to a faulte contrary to his judgment, and begging my pardon for it (which upon his promise of amendment I granted), and yet soon after repeating it, has so irritated me that I can hardly prevayle with my selfe to yield to a further tryall but am ready to cast him off as desperate because he had as much cause to forbeare doeing ill as he can have now, being clearely convinced of the crime before.⁴⁸⁰

O my soule, turne this in to an humbling meditation and reflectingly consider of thy own disingenuous acting towards the great sovereign of heaven and earth and in to an admireing one of his patience and long suffering towards thee; who, most unworthy wretch, hast in thy solemn addresses at the throne of grace confest with detestation of thy selfe thy transgressiones,⁴⁸¹ [216v] being trewly

---

⁴⁷⁷ 2 Kings 2:11.
⁴⁷⁸ Psalm 116:12.
⁴⁷⁹ Peppercorns were symbolic of land tenure. "The payment of a single Peppercorn, that *Freeholders* pay to their *Landlord*," William Spurstowe explains in his meditation "Upon the payment of a Pepper-corn," is made "not with any hope or intent to enrich him; but to acknowledge that they hold all from him" (*The Spiritual Chymist*, 84).
⁴⁸⁰ WW: "Possibly Hammond, yᵉ Baker, who would too frequently be drunk" (215v).
⁴⁸¹ Hebrews 4:16: "Let us therefore come boldly unto the throne of grace, that we may obtain mercy, and find grace to help in time of need."

satisfide of the vildnes [vileness] of them, and made vowes to God of forsakeing them, and yet hast againe taken them up and run in to the same faultes with this criminal sercomstance [circumstance] of heithnieng [heightning] aggravationes that thay ware acted in the light. But O, for ever be magnifyde that mersy that could so often pardon so disingenuous an offender. O Lord, I do admiringly acknowledge that thy wayes are not as my wayes;[482] therfore it is that I am not consumed. And, O Lord, lett me by my having so often on my selfe experimented thy clemency learn by thy unerring example to forgive my repenting fellow creature not onely seven times but unto seventy seven times.[483]

[217r] *Upon seeing a person very patient under very smarting paines*

This persones exerciseing so great patience under so very allmost intolerable paines ocasioned by the surgeones cutting and scarifying him[484] has made me with admiration behold him as it did allso his docters, who ware of opinion that it wold be neasisary for them to prescribe him opium to make him quiett, but finding him to be so with out it, admired him for it.

Which was the occasion of this meditation that patience was God allmightes opium by which he quieted with out hurting his patients and makes them with great fortitude beare with out complaineing of him though[485] thay doc to him what unhappy, impatiant persones, like wild bulles in a nett,[486] teare and intaiengell [intangle] them-selves by [217v] strieving against and yet canot avoyde feeleing the smarting sense of.

O Lord, I doe most humbly beseech thee, inable me in patiense to posses my soule[487] even under the most trying afflictiones thou arte pleased to exsersise me with that I may be dom [dumb] and hold my peace because thou doest it and say, it is the Lord; lett him doe what seames him good. O, lett me chearefully doe and patiently suffer thy blessed will, and lett this be a quieting consideration that all shall worke together for my good,[488] knowing that thou dost not willingly grife [grieve] nor afflict the children of men.[489] O Lord, I humbly besiech thee, lett this be the fruit of my punishment to take away my sinn, and then I

---

[482] Isaiah 55:8-9.
[483] Matthew 18:22.
[484] See above, n. 346.
[485] WW notes about the following: "Here I don't well understand this good Ladys meaning" (217r).
[486] Isaiah 51:20.
[487] Luke 21:19.
[488] Romans 8:28, which stresses "for good to them that love God."
[489] Lamentations 3:33.

shall be able to say with the man after thy own heart, it was good for me that I was aflicted.[490]

[218r] *Upon leaves that fell from a tree in athome* [autumn]

These ugly, discoloured leaves which fall as I walke upon the walkes have minded me of the severall ages of persons, which resemble in their youth (whilst thay are young and beautifull) the leaves when thay are first put foreth and have an actractife verdure which is very takeing to their beholders, as all so is their floriching for som time, till thay grow towards athome yellow and undelightfull. Which is like persones in their declineing age when their skins, which in their bewty resembulde [resembled] the milke, growe yellow and changed so much that the beholding them even by those that before delighted to doe so growes disagreeable to them as [218v] these decayde leaves doe now to <me>, though in the spring thay did fix my eyes often with pleasure to behold them; and their now falling on the ground mindes me of persones falling by death in to it and so turneing in to dust and rottenes.

O Lord, I doe most humbly beseech thee, lett this ocasionall meditation be so sett home that it may prove a mortifying one to me and may make me to consider that dust I am and unto dust I must returne,[491] and lett my gray hairs and my skin which has so deepe a tincture of yellow be my monitores to mind me that my crackt and tottering house of clay will not long stay here but will shortly be meat for wormes to feede on.[492] O Lord, forsake me not now I am gray headed,[493] but guide me here [219r] by thy grace and counsell, and at last receave me in to glory.

Upon beeing in a storme and on a soden seeing the sun shine cleare out, which much revived me

As I was walkeing this morneing, a sudden, surpriseing storme came, the wind blowing so exstreame boysetereously that I feared it wold have blowne doune both the treese and me; which made me hasten homewards for sheltar. But as I was doeing so, the sunn of a sudden broke out most gloriously, and so stopt my intended reaturne, and was the cause of this occasional meditation.

That the sudden storme might not very unfittly be compared to a surpriseing, unforseene affliction that som times is ready to overthrow a persone and so shakes him that he has much a[219v]doe to withstand it and is even ready to sinke under it till God is pleased most gratiously to lett the sun of righteousness

---

[490] Psalm 119:71.
[491] Genesis 3:19.
[492] Job 4:19; cf. Job 24:20, "the worm shall feed sweetly on him."
[493] Psalm 71:18.

shine forth with his astonishing luster and with healeing in his winges.[494] O Lord, I doe most humbly beseech thee, lett this meditation excite me to practise the highest straines of gratitude by bringing afresh to my rememberance how often when I have been by unexpected aflictiones shaken and ready to be overturned thou hast been so gratious to upholde me by letting me see a beame of light shineing from thy face which has both cheared me and uphelde me. And though thou hast som times but showde thy selfe through the lattiss,[495] yet but a glimpse of thee has inabled me to beare up against the most shakeing stormes thou hast yet tried me with. And when thou hast bene so gratious as to give more cleare, unclouded discoveryes of thy selfe to me, [220r] I have been able to rejoyce in a storme and to stand even against all the shakeinges of an afflicted condition. O Lord, therfore be pleased still to cause thy face to shine uppon thy servant,[496] for thou hast bene pleased hitherto to be to me a refuge in a storme,[497] and I have found thee a preasent helpe in a time of trouble.[498] And when thou hast spoken peace, noe persone nor any thing could give me so much trouble but that I could chearefully looke beyond it to thee and by sending up the respirationes of my soul gett strength to stand under it from thee, who wast never then a teror to me. Nor had I then cause to say verily thou art a God that hidest thy selfe[499] or that he that showld comforte my soule was far away, but thou wert so gratious to me as when I called to say, here am I.[500] O, be pleased to keep these experianses of thy goodness to me [220v] so freach in my memory that thay may not be efaced but may still be so many powerfull exsiteing motifes [motives] to trust still in thee at all times.

[221r] *Upon my Lord of Manchestors being at Lees and there with great delight viewing it becauze it is his future designed inheritance*

This Lords inquireing with so much exactness in to all things that belong to Lees, and with so much delight viewing his heare after deasigned inheritance, and so much pleaseing himselfe with the hopes of the possessing it may be usefull to mind me of my own fault,[501] who haveing a most glorious and eternall rest,

---

[494] Malachi 4:2.
[495] Song of Solomon 2:9.
[496] Numbers 6:25.
[497] Psalms 9:9, 46:1, 59:16.
[498] Psalm 46:1.
[499] Deuteronomy 31:17-18; Psalms 27:9, 55:1.
[500] Psalm 94:19 (God, the soul comforter); Isaiah 58:9.
[501] Robert Montagu, third Earl of Manchester (bap. 1634-d. 1683), was the son of Edward Montagu, second Earl of Manchester, and his second wife, Anne Rich, the daughter of the second Earl of Warwick, Robert Rich. He inherited the Leighs estate, which he visited from 18 September to 22 September 1675 (4/67r-v) and would legally

a purchased possession by the blood of Christ and the mersy of God in reversion after this life,[502] yet doe, too, too seldome inquire in to it and with transportes thinke of it or long to be posesor [possessor] of it.

O Lord, I humbly beseech thee, make me mindfull by this ocasionall meditation of my—not so frequently as I ought—by the eye of faith lookeing in to the future promised posession,[503] and lett this persones too much longing for an estate on earth exsite and sett me [221v] upon priseing, and esteameing, and longing for an inheritance incorruptible, and undefiled, and that fades not away reserved for me in heaven.[504]

Upon Tom Colemanes haveing sarved my lord for many yeares but at last by his negligence neaseasitateing him to cast him off, by which hee lost his deasigned annuity

[222r] This inconsiderate sarvant that had for above 20 yeares sarved his lord with som diligense has at last by an ill action so highly displeased him that he not onely flung him off but he has also lost his before designed reward.[505] Which may be usefull to caution me how I behave my selfe to the lord of lordes that I may not by any future action of my life so highly displease him that I may by doeing so pull down inevitable ruine to my selfe. O Lord, I doe most humbly beseech thee, lett this meditation exsite me to more watchfullness how I performe my serves [service] to thee that I may not justly forfet the promised recompence thou hast declared in thy God-breathed oracles thou wilt bestow upon thy ser-

---

take possession after Mary Rich's death. The third son of Robert's marriage to Anne Yelverton, Charles (c. 1662-1722), succeeded him as Earl of Manchester and became in 1719 Duke of Manchester. His son William sold Leighs to Edmund Sheffield, second Duke of Buckingham and Normanby; after his death in 1735, his half-brother Charles Herbert became the owner. He sold Leighs to the trustees of Guy's Hospital, and by the middle of the century the main buildings were demolished (Morant, *The History and Antiquities Of the County of Essex*, 2:103; Gentles, "Edward Montagu," in *ODNB*, 38:702-8; Matthew Kilburn, "Charles Montagu, first duke of Manchester," in *ODNB*, 38:696-97).

[502] "Purchased possession": Ephesians 1:14. Reversion: "A future interest in land arising by operation of law whenever an estate owner grants to another a particular estate, such as a life estate or a term of years, but does not dispose of the entire interest"—which reverts or returns to the owner (*Black's Law Dictionary*, 1320).

[503] See above, n. 284.

[504] 1 Peter 1:4. WW: "This meditation was wrote about ye 20th of Septemb^r 1675: and about this time I came from Jesus Coll Cambr. to Leez to see my Father and Mother" (221v).

[505] Tom Coleman, the footman, was one of two sick people "In great danger of death" that Rich visited on 22 March 1677 (5/94v); she "did much persuade him" to prepare for death. When she herself died a year later, Rich left his wife Ann a legacy of £70 (Fell Smith, *Mary Rich, Countess of Warwick*, 350).

vantes.⁵⁰⁶ O, make me diligent and faithfull, and lett me be allwayes abounding in the worke of the Lord; for as much as I know, my labor shall not be in vaine in the Lord and that I shall reape if I faint not.⁵⁰⁷ O lett me never be so unwise as to [222v] loose the service of 28 yeares by my negligense now or by my disobediance to thy comandes, but lett me render constant, universall, and sinseare obedience to all thy prescribed preseptes. O lett me feare to offend thee and love to obay thee; and seeing thou wert so gratious as to inable me to dedicate some of my youeth to thee and to sarve thee in the May of my life,⁵⁰⁸ O lett me not loose all the labores of the flowre of my age, those difficultyes which at my first turneing to thee I fond in my selfe deanialles, in watching against temptationes, and in resisteing them when presented to me, and in striveing against the love of this preasent world, and in laboring so to realize the things of another to my selfe that I might not prefer the unsarten things of time before the sarten things of eternety but that by an eye of faith⁵⁰⁹ seeing invisibles I might for them despise all the glittering gloryes of this world which poore deluded mortalles looke on with dazled eyes. O Lord, I [223r] beseech thee, haveing gone so far towards my intended journy to heaven, lett me not now either stand still or quit my intended purpose of goeing thiethar [thither], but lett me still serve thee and seake after eternall life that so perseavering I may at last attaine the end of my faith, the salvation of my preatious and imortall soule, and may never heare that irreversible, and sad beyond expression, sentense (depart from me).⁵¹⁰ And that I may not draw it upon my selfe, lett me now cleave to thee with full purpose of soule that in the latter part of my life I may double my diligence and so attaine the crowne of life which never fades reserved for me in heaven.⁵¹¹

[223v] *Upon observeing after a great storme some little sticks faln but the great trees stand, though thay sustained violent shakeinges*

[224r] In my walkeing this very searene morneing I could not but observe that the boysetoreous storme that had bene the night before had blowne doune a very great plenty of little sticks, which had much fouled the walkes, but that the great and strong trees stood yet firm for all the terrible shakeinges thay had from that violent wind. Which was the occasion of this meditation that the littell twigs that were down might not very unfittly be compared to young professors who ware but newly brought in to profess them selves Christes deasiples [disciples],

---

⁵⁰⁶ Proverbs 11:31, 20:22; Luke 14:14. For the characterization of the Scriptures as God-breathed see above, n. 258.
⁵⁰⁷ Galatians 6:9.
⁵⁰⁸ WW: "An. Ætatis 22. An. Do. 1647."
⁵⁰⁹ See above, n. 284.
⁵¹⁰ Matthew 25:41, Luke 13:27.
⁵¹¹ 1 Peter 5:4.

and had some convictions of the neaseasity [necessity] of their being so, but had never yet tasted of the excellency of their being so. And upon their first coming in of a sudden meet with tryalles and affliction for their profession, and upon seeing that thay canot have Christ [224v] but thay must have his cross too, thay fall from him rather then suffer persecution.[512] But the old deasipulles that have bene long trained up in his skole [school] and know that though in the world thay must suffer persecution,[513] yet in him thay shall have peace; and have experiansed that if he speake pease, thay may rejoyce with joy unspeakeable and full of glory, even under all the most sensible troubles that can be inflicted by the males [malice] of men; stand firm and undauntedly even under the greatest stormes that are raised by the divell and his instruments to overthrow them.

O Lord, I doe most humbly beseech thee, lett me call my own experiances to mind, and lett them make me rather suffer aflictiones with the people of God then to injoy the pleasures of sinn, which are but for a moment,[514] knowing that thou hast particular cordialles for an afflicted condition and that I have fond the warme and lively comfortes of the Holy Ghost has given me new strinth [strength] and spirits when I have bene ready to sinke under [225r] my otherwise insupportable troubles. O, lett me be kept by the power of God through faith unto salvation.

Upon a great mist that was abroad when I went to my prayures, and when I had finished them, seeing it dispelled by the sunnes shineing out

As I was goeing to make my solemn address to the author of my being and to offer up my sacrifice of prayse,[515] which I would fain have had ascend up in the respirationes of my soule as all incense for those mersyes which are as numberless as the stars in the firmament, I perseaved [perceived] so great a mist that though I looked in to the garden I could for its thiknes perceive hardly what was there. But when I had finished my morneing prayur, I was noe sooner risen off from my knees but I perceived the glorious light of heaven had broke out, by which I was not onely inabled to [225v] view the thinges I did before so very obscurely doe but also by that glorious creatures shineing on them I did see them manyfested to me with such a vareniech [varnish] on them as made it most delightfull to me to gase upon them. This ocasionale meditation may be usefull to me in bringing againe afresh in to my memory the great and good Godes mersyfull dealings with me in relation to my spirituall concernes. Who, when I have turned my eyes inward to looke in to the cloysetor [cloister] of my own heart to search for some of the graces of the blesed spiritt, have seene by reason of my cloudeing sinnes

---

[512] See Galatians 6:12.
[513] 2 Timothy 3:12.
[514] Hebrews 11:25.
[515] Hebrews 13:15; cf. Jeremiah 33:11.

nothing but thicke mistes and darkeness. But when I have poured out in prayer my soule to God in strong deasires for light from heaven to discover [226r] what was there, I have afterwards had such a beame of light from heaven darted in to me as has in som good measure dispelled the thickness and has shown me som of the graces of the blessed doves infuseing in to me, which after that light had evinced to me did prove a most ravishingly agreeable prospecte to me to beholde.[516] O Lord, lett the often times I have experianced—that though I have gone sad to my prayers yet I have come away (as Hannah did) with my countenance no more so[517]—make me, as the sweet psalmist of Israell sayd he did, give my selfe to prayur and with him allso prayse thee seven times a day[518] till I come to that sweet and desired reste where I shall everlastingly sound forth thy prayses.

[226v] *Upon a great housekeeper who, though he provides most liberally for all his family, yet reserves some peculiar daintyes for his children*

[227r] Though this generous housekeeper does evince to all his beholders how plentifully he provides for all his family, yet he does reserve for his children some peculiar and more choyse provisiones then he voutesafes to confer upon the otheres. Which observation may be usefull to mind me of the great providor for all the world, who does with a munificent hand scatter abroad to all his creatures many temporall benefittes by his generall providence, yet he does reserve som spirituall ones for his chosen ones.

O Lord, I beseech thee, therfore remember me with the favor which thou bearest unto thy people. O lett me not onely have thy left hand blessings but those also of thy right, those soule mersyes which cannot stand with reprobation.[519] Lett me experience some of those warme and lively comforts of the Holy Ghost which are the soules sweet-meates and [227v] which none taste of but those renewed soules which shall here after be feasted with the lambes maredge supper.[520] O lett me have some of those elixirs of pleasures which the world are

---

[516] At Christ's baptism the "Spirit of God descending like a dove" (Matthew 3:16) and the "Holy Ghost descended in a bodily shape like a dove" (Luke 3:22). "Holy Ghost's" is written above "blessed doves."

[517] 1 Samuel 1:10-18; see Hannah above, n. 297.

[518] Psalm 119:164.

[519] Proverbs 3:16 states that in the right hand of wisdom is "Length of days . . . and in her left hand riches and honor," which in Samuel Rutherford's reading "Eternity hath the honour, and the right hand. Riches is of the left hand blessing of wisdome" (*Christ Dying and Drawing Sinners to Himselfe* [London, 1647], 296). The right hand of God "savest" in the Psalms and offers "pleasures for evermore" (17:7, 16:11), a salvation promised in the New Testament through the mercy of Christ, who sits at the right hand of God (for example, Matthew 25:33-34).

[520] John 14:26, Acts 9:31; Revelation 19:9.

unaquainted with, which are a stilling of the desires, a quieting of the wishes, and a beleeveing in thee. Lett me rejoyce with joy unspeakable, and give me that inward peace, which as the world cannot give,[521] so it cannot take from me. But, O Lord, keepe me from mistakeing the silence of conchance [conscience] for the peace of conchance. O give me a childes portion. O lett me upon undeaseavable [undeceivable] grounds know that I have some distinguishing inward and spirituall delights which the carnall world are great strangers unto, and lett me prize them above all their dung-hill and carnall dealightes. O lett me see that one beame of light shineing from thy [228r] face is enough to eclipse all the glory and beauty of this world in its highest lustor.[522]

Upon seeing as sone as I waked in the morneing upon my beds testor just over my head a fine imbroydered crown

After I had by the mersy of God to me had the refreshment of an uninterrupted nights rest and by sleep (which is the nurse of nature, the parenthesis to all my cares and griefs)[523] been composed, at my first opening of my eyes thay ware entertained with the sight of a crowne which by the apolsteror [upholsterer] was imbroydered at the testor of my bed[524] just over my head, [228v] and by the light of a great blasing fire was made in my chamber, and which through my drawne curtanes gave so great a light that it showde me this crowne (which before I had not taken notice of) and made it allso apeare very bright and fine. As this sight was the first I viewed, so these thoughtes ware the first I thought: that my awakeing from this naturall rest may be usefull to mind me of my wakeing from the sleep of death and this crowne may doe so of the unwithring one that fades not away[525] reserved for me (I hope) by the mersy of God and through the merites of Christ in heaven. O Lord, I doe most humbly beseech [229r] thee, my good and gratious God, so to sett home and to saintefye unto me this occasional meditation that I may never more either be afraide to dye or be unwilling to doe so. O make me to remember that nothing dyes finally and totally in a child of God but sinn;[526] and therfore lett me not be unwilling to sleep in Jesus,[527] though when I do so in my bed of dust, wormes will make possibly their houses in my eye holes,

---

[521] John 14:27 and the second collect at Evening Prayer, "Give unto thy servants that peace which the world cannot give," in *The Book of Common Prayer*, B1v.

[522] See 2 Corinthians 4:6; though the light does not eclipse the beauty of the world.

[523] William Shakespeare, *Henry IV, Part Two*, 3:1, 5-6: "gentle sleep, / Nature's soft nurse."

[524] Tester: canopy over bed.

[525] 1 Peter 5:4.

[526] She seems to have in mind Luke 20:36.

[527] 1 Thessalonians 4:14.

and eate away the balls of my cheekes, and feed upon my vile body.[528] Yet at the resurrection when I am summoned from my cold bed, I shalt then, not as now onely see a crowne, but solemnly have one putt upon [229v] my head, not a pitifull imbroidered one which will decay with time but one in comparison of which all those that were ever yet worn by a Ceasor or an Alexsander come as far short as the most base, sordid, despicable thinges we can imagine doe of that crowne above, which is as farr above our most raised fansy of it as our deasertes of it. O make me long for this coronation day, and lett the previous thoughtes of it—my haveing my eye upon this recompense of reward (a reward of free grace, not of meritt)—make me be not onely contente but willing to be dissolved and to be with Christ.[529]

[230r] *Upon a stand in the parke which is in a tree I use often to retire to*

This tree which I use to gett alone in to that I might be rid of all out ward distractiones that so I might undisturbedly convers with God and my selfe[530] mindes me of Zakeaus tree, which he climbed up in to that he might from that have a sight of Christ.[531] O Lord, I doe most humbly beseech thee, by this thought lett me be excited to practise gratitude and to returne glory to thee, my God, for letting me often from hence (though not with my bodily eyes, yet with those of my faith) see my deare and lovely Jesus so clearly as to be able to say, I have seene the Lord. He has indeed appeared unto Mary.[532] O, for ever blessed be thy great and [230v] condescending goodness that would not lett me goe seekeing for Jeasus without finding thee whome my soule loves[533] and then injoying most sweet soule ravishing dealightes in beholding that perfect beauty that even glorious angelles with vailed faces stand in raptures to admire.[534] O, for ever blesed be that goodness that has made thee to manyfest thy selfe so unto me as thou hast not manyfested thy selfe unto the unregenerate world who are therfore ready to say, what beauty is there in him that we showld desire him.[535] O, as I have had

---

[528] Rich has in mind Job 7:21, 21:26, 24:20; see also above, n. 6.

[529] Philippians 1:23 and above, n. 253.

[530] The place of retirement mentioned in the diary (22 May 1671, 2/182r; 9 May 1673, 3/170v) may have been an old pollard tree in which, Fell Smith claims, Mary Rich "had had fixed a wooden gallery, ascended by steps" (*Mary Rich, Countess of Warwick*, 251). See also above, n. 206.

[531] Zaccheus, the rich, but short, publican who climbed into a sycamore tree for a better view (Luke 19:4). A similar allusion occurs in the diary, 15 July 1677, 5/154v. George Swinnock urges his soul to imitate Zaccheus, "climb up into the *Sycamore* of meditation, and obtain a sight of thy Saviour" (*The Christian-Mans Calling*, 443).

[532] Mark 16:9, John 20:11-18.

[533] Song of Solomon 3:4.

[534] Possibly Isaiah 6:2.

[535] Isaiah 53:2.

clearer and more unclouded discoveries made to me of thy selfe by thy selfe than thay have had, so make me admire thee more and conclude with the spouse in the Canticles that he whom my soule loveth is all together lovely.[536]

[231r] *Upon woundes that have been stanched and yet of a sudden bleeding againe*

This soden breakeing out of a wound that was stanched mindes me of some great griefes that have bene thought cured and seameingly apeared to be so to the person aflicted and to their beholdares, too, till of a soden some eruption of pasion occasioned upon som new object has made that wound by grief made in the heart to bleed as fresh as at the first and made the persone shed as many teares as if the beloved persone thay shed them for was but newly dead.

O Lord, I beseech thee, lett this caution me carefully to avoyde what ever I have already experiensed or have cause to suspect may heare after make my grife breake out againe. O lett me not be disquieted by veiwing new persones [231v] or nearly related persones to him whose removall from me by death has so often made me against all my resolutiones breake forth in to disquieting pationes. O lett me seariously consider that the great quieting consideration that is indeed soporteing [supporting] is that it is the will of thee, my God, it should be so, and therefore give me that perfect subjektion of soule to thy will that it may make me to be dumb and holde my peace at all times and upon all occasiones. O, that there may neaver be a repineing thought at what thou hast done, but that I may poses [possess] my soule in patience[537] by the exersise of which vertue I may be kept in the possession of my selfe and may not any more breake out to the dishonor of my profession and to the wounding of my own conchanse [conscience].

[232r] *Upon being with a persone that was in labor*

With how much simpathyseing [simpathizing] compation have I seene the paines this beloved friend of mine has undergone and heard hur dolorous complaintes ocasioned by hur haveing so many strong throwes before there was a birth.[538]

But O, my soule, lett not all thy compasion go to this friend, who will for joy she is dealivored sone after forgett all she has sufferd,[539] but extend it further to those that are under the panges of the new birth and whilst they are so sus-

---

[536] Song of Solomon 5:16.

[537] Luke 21:19.

[538] Rich was with Essex Finch on 18 April 1675 during the labor and birth of a girl, born the next morning—"a munday" (4/10v). Extracts from an old prayer book state, however, that Essex's first child was born "On Monday ye 16 April, 1675" [the sixteenth was, in fact, a Friday], a godmother was Mary Rich, and the infant died the next year on January 28 (Finch, *History of Burley-on-the-Hill, Rutland*, 1:181).

[539] John 16:21.

taine many throwes and throbs before ther is a birth, their conchanses giveing them many a sensible trouble for the miscaredges of their unregenerate forepast life; which they are so vile as many times to stifle and [232v] not harken unto, but goe to seake realife from it from any thing that dos but approach them under the name of a diversion, but find it not though thay pershew [persue] it in all objectes and plases. Where as if thay wold heare that home preachar with in them, which is as the candell of the Lord searching in to their inward partes,[540] those throwes wold bring forth to them the blessed fruites of a sincere convertion which wold give them more cause of trew rejoyceing then ever any mother had for joy that a man child was borne in to the world.[541] Christ then wold not onely be borne for them but in them.

O Lord, I doe most humbly beseech thee, lett me never be guilty of that folly to practise my selfe what I doe pitty them for and condemne [233r] them for; but O, make me harkene unto my domestike-chaplain, who is neaver silent though he has bene too often silensed by me. And when he puttes me next upon that hard but very neasisary worke of self examynation, grant I may try wither I have had this new bearth, knowing that ther are false conceptiones in the spirituall birth as well as in the naturall one. O Lord, be pleased to grant I may not be mistaken in that which is of eternall consernement unto me, but lett me know unto my everlasting comforte that I am regenerate and borne againe[542] and that all the throwes I have formarly felt was in order to my being so. And then, though I am childeless, I shall have [233v] more ground for lasting joy then if my children ware like olive branches rond aboute my table.[543]

Upon my Lady Cranbornes haveing one side of hur strouke by the dead pallsy

[234r] This ladyes haveing had so loude a somones [summons] from heaven to prepare for her dissolution as hur being by the palsy halfe dead, and yet being so very vaine as to play at dice and cardes and dress hur selfe in all the most gay and fine vaine, new fashiones, was not onely very amaseing unto me but was so allso to all hur beholdares for whom hur actiones gave them both great pitty for hur and amasement at hur, knowing she was onely so happy as hur sottish inconsideration could make hur.[544] O Lord, I doe most humbly beseech thee, make me by this be minded how much I ought to be humbled by considering how little I

---

[540] Proverbs 20:27.
[541] John 16:21.
[542] John 3:3, 7; 1 Peter 1:23.
[543] Psalm 128:3.
[544] Lady Diana Cranborne (c. 1623-1675), the daughter of James Maxwell, Earl of Dirletoun, and his wife, Elizabeth Besyne, was the widow of Charles Cecil, Viscount Cranborne (bap. July 1619-d. 1660). Their son James, third Earl of Salisbury (1646?-1683), married Margaret Manners, daughter of the eighth Earl of Rutland: George E. Co-

have bene minded of my own mortality by what thy providence intended to call me to consider it by who hast not onely [234v] brought death in to my house but in to my bed, and by takeing by it from me my husband hast made me, as it ware, halfe dead. For as thy God breathed oracles telles me we ware not two but one,[545] and haveing so loude a summons to prepare my selfe to leave the world and to goe out of my house of clay,[546] O lett me not be vaine or spend my time in recreationes; but lett now vaine delights be gone, and lett me now spend my inch of my preatious time that is yet lent me to those great endes for which it was given me, even to worke out my salvation with feare and trembling.[547] And lett me now in the day of adversity consider that I may not for want of doeing so goe doune merely [merrily] to hell.

[235r-v] [Blank]

[236r] Ocasionale Meditationes made by M Warwicke 1676

[237r] *Upon a journy from Lees to Londone*

At my first setting out from Lees the weather was very misty and stormy, and so it continued to be till neare the sun setting, and then it proved a most sweet and delightfull evening, the sunn apeareing and all the mist disapeareing.[548]

This journy may be usefull to mind me of my great one which I am travelling from earth to heaven, in which I have met with many stormes, both at my first treading in that straite path that leades to that city that has a foundation whose maker and builder is God[549] and also in my journeying towardes it with cloudeing miste<s>. [237v] But, O Lord, I most humbly implore (if good in thy sight) that though I have in the formar part of my life had some fowle dayes, yet that in the evening of it (towardes which by thy long suffering towardes me I am now drawing) I may have the most serene and quiett that so my last dayes may be my best dayes, that the sun of righteousness shineing upon me[550] may make me take more delight and trew solace than in all my former dayes that so I may undisturbedly prepare for my change. And, O Lord, grant that my sun may not sett in a cloude but that I may by thy mersy towardes me goe triumpingly to heaven,

---

kayne et al., *The Complete Peerage*, 12 vols. (London: St. Catherine Press, 1910-1959), 11:406-8.

[545] Matthew 19:6, Ephesians 5:31. For God-breathed see above, n. 258.

[546] Job 4:19.

[547] Philippians 2:12.

[548] Rich went to Warwick House on 11 October 1675, returning on 25 March 1676 (4/74v, 133v); she left again for London on 8 April 1676 and remained until 3 August 1676 (4/140v, 179r). Her last stay in London was from 7 to 24 February 1677.

[549] Hebrews 11:10.

[550] Malachi 4:2.

haveing had a preavious gust of it as an earnest of that purchased possession[551] which may make me long to be at my eternall rest, where I shall be hapy in the injoyment of thee, my God, to all eternity.

[238r] *Upon the consideration of the different esteem that is put upon an estate onely for life and that which is an inheritance*

How inconsiderably do we value an estate for life in comparison of that estimate we putt upon that which is an inheritance,[552] and yet how foolishly besotted are we in our valewing the thinges of eternall consernement less then that which is to end with our lives.

O Lord, I beseech thee, sett home to me this occasionall meditation that I may not be over solicitous for the things which I must leave when my life does, but make me much highlier to prize an eternall inheritance, and make me to seek after it and to use my utmost diligense to attaine it, remembering that the things which are seen are temporall and of noe long continuance but that the thinges which are not seen are eternall.[553]

[239r] *Upon the weeders sweeping in athome* [autumn] *of the walkes*

I have observed in my morneing walkeing this authome[554] that though the weeders of the garden do frequently sweep the walkes so cleane that there is hardly any durt ocasioned by the fall of the leaves to be seen after their haveing cleansed it, yet that by the next day there is occasion for their doeing so againe, the same place being full of that which ought to be flung out. And I have taken notice, too, that when either through carelesness or weariness to be every day repeating the same business thay have left what should have been removed out dayly to be the worke togeather of 3 or 4 dayes, the burthen which thay car'ed out was so heavy for them that it made it both very difficult [239v] and laborious to them because of the waight. This observation may be usefull to me first to mind me of the frequent need I have to be lookeing to my own heart by my daily inspection in to it to be sure that it be kept so clean that the durt and pollution of sin which defiles it be flung out and, secondly, that I do not leave the weeds of sin or any old custome remaineing in the garden of my heart for any long space of time together, but that I doe by unfained [unfeigned] repentance gett rid of it before it take such deep rooting in me by either custome or inadvertency that I shall find it much harder than I should do if I every 24 howres flung it out.

---

[551] Ephesians 1:14.

[552] Also called a life estate and life tenancy, "An estate held only for the duration of a specified person's life" (*Black's Law Dictionary*, 568).

[553] Cf. 2 Corinthians 4:18 and above, n. 100.

[554] She returned from London 3 August 1676.

O Lord, I doe most humbly implore that thou wouldest be pleased to make me by this observation more than [240r] ever watchfull over my treacherous and desaitefull [deceitfull] heart that no sin may make its abode there, but that I may resist the very first approaches of it and cast them out with a hearty desire thay may never more come near me. And lett this, I doe beseech thee, be a constant warfare vigeorously [vigorously] maintained by me that I may not yield that any coruption be an indweller, for fear I should then find more difficullty to disposes [dispossess] it then I should doe in first flinging it out. And O, thou my good and my gratious God who hast an absolute sovereignty, and canst doe what so ever thou wilt, and nothing can withstand thee, and whose prerogative it is to subdue iniquities, subdue myne. These sones of Zeruiah are too strong for me, but not for thee.[555] And if this indwelling coruption canot be quite in [240v] this life be destroyed, yet lett it never be in me as a king to raine [reign] and rule, but lett me sett thee upon the throne of my heart, and then lett all my sinnes fall doun before thee as Dagon fell before thine ark and never rise more.[556]

Upon goeing to prayers as sone as by the ringing of a bell I was called to doe so

[241r] As sone as the bell is rung to prayures, we presently assemble our selves to make our solemn addresses at the throne of grace[557] and to the author of our beings doe send up the respirationes of our soules for such mercies as we stand in need of either for our soules or our bodyes.[558]

Which mindes me of God allmightyes some times approaches to the soule by the saintefyeng [sanctifying] motiones of his most blessed spirit, in a more than usuall maner exciteing us to pray; by which exstraordinary instigationes of his to come to the performance of our devotiones to him, he does, as it ware, ring himselfe the bell to prayers. O Lord, I doe most humbly beseech thee so to sanctify to me this occasionall meditation that I may never [241v] more dare to stifull [stifle] the constraineing motions of thy sweet and blessed dove [spirit], but may, when it does next call me to that high and never to be anufe [enough] prized priveledge of falling downe at the throne of thy grace[559] to powre out there

---

[555] Joab, Abishai, and Asahel were "the sons of Zeruiah" (1 Chronicles 2:16), the sister of David; her husband remains unnamed in the Bible. They both served and troubled David, who exclaimed, "the sons of Zeruiah be too hard for me" (2 Samuel 3:39) and "What have I to do with you, ye sons of Zeruiah, that ye should this day be adversaries unto me?" (2 Samuel 19:22).

[556] 1 Samuel 5:2-5. The image of Dagon, the patron deity of the Philistines, fell twice before the ark of God, the second time losing its head and palms.

[557] Hebrews 4:16; see above, n. 481.

[558] Recalling collects from *The Book of Common Prayer*, such as those for the Fourth Sunday in Advent and the Second Sunday in Lent.

[559] Perhaps Revelation 7:11.

my requests unto thee, I may instantly come at thy ringing, and may never be so impudently bold as to stay then away, but may by the most expedite motiones of my soule fly up to thee. And, O Lord, I doe most humbly implore that when thou doest, as it ware, bespeak a prayer, thou woldst inable me to pray with faith and fervency that in it my desires may run after thee as a mighty torrent, that in the duty my prayer may be like faith flaming. And, O Lord, lett me not then onely have the pre[242r]sence of an ordinance[560] but also the presence of thee, my God, in it that so I may have cause to say, it is good for me to draw near unto thee, my God.[561]

[242v] *Upon an ill tenante that though he were so at my will, haveing noe lease, yet expected to be continued in my farme still, though he kept back my rent*

[243r] How much displeased did I find my selfe with my ill tenante for his injustice in detaineing my rent and with his unresonablenes, too, in reaquesting me still to be continued in my farme, though but a tenant at will, without paying me any thing for it.[562] O my soule, reflectingly consider by this thy own guiltyness to thy great landlord under whom thou art a holder both of thy rotten claye house[563] and all so, too, of all the land thou arte mistress of and art a tenant so perfectly at his will that he can turne thee when he pleases out of all. And yet thou art so disingenuously unjust and bold as to detaine from him his chief rent of prayse and therfore art but censuring thy own fault in anotheres persone. [243v] O Lord, I doe most humbly besich [beseech] thee, lett me not any longer dare to detaine my rent from thee, but make me now be thy constant pay master and every day to bless thee and to sing prayses to thee, my God, whilst I have my breath; and when I cease to have it, I shall (I hope) doe it bettar.

Upon some poore persones waiting without the gate and receiving there with joy and thankefullness some of the broken meat that came from the feast that was kept with in the house[564]

[244r] How thankefull are these poore neaseasitos [necessitous] persones that are kept without the gate there waiting for some of the broken meat which is brought

---

[560] See above, n. 31.

[561] James 4:8.

[562] Tenants at will had possession at the consent of the landlord. The length or rent of the tenancy was not fixed, and either the tenant or landlord could end the tenancy "upon fair notice" (*Black's Law Dictionary*, 1477).

[563] Job 4:19.

[564] A variation of this meditation, similar in substance though at times somewhat different in expression, is included among the occasional meditations in Walker, *Eureka, Eureka*, "Meditation III," 152–53.

them from the feast that was with in the house. Turne this, O my soule, in to a usefull occasional meditation by considering the happy and the different state of the Church Triumphant above that of the Church Militant; the first of which, who are in the possession of eternall bliss, and are there happy in the vision of God, and in the fruition of him injoying him in his fullest love, are every day feasted with some of the lambes maredge suppar;[565] whilst the others are waiting yet without and are glad of some cromes [crums] and pareinges,[566] as it were, of glory, which thay rejoyce at and are gratefull for. O Lord, I doe most humbly beseech thee to saintefy [sanctify] unto me this occasional meditation that whilst I am present in the body and therfore absent from thee, my Lord, I may pay thee my thankes for some times giveing [244v] me some previous gustes of heaven which are very refreshing. But O, doe thou be pleased to give me some larger earnest of heaven than ever yet I had. O, though in this vally of teares,[567] whilst I am but at the gate of that pallace where the divine soules are everlastingly feasted with their heavenly bainketes [banquets], I can have none of their elixirs; yet be pleased to skater [scatter] some of their full and delicious feastes to me, who am waiting at the porch of glory to receive some fragments. O, entertaine me with some of those joyes with which thou dost solace those who are ever with thee that so I may be able to say that Christ possest by faith here is young heaven, glory in the bud.[568]

Upon a fathers different caredge in the education of his children

[245r] I have observed that a very wise, kind, and indulgent father has bene neaseasitated in the educateing of his children to use severall wayes in the traineing of them up to effect his great designe of making them all good. Some he findes so very tractable to his commandes that thay show a ready obedience to them upon the acounpt of that awefull and filiall feare thay have of him with out his useing any correction to make them to doe so. But some otheres he findes so very stubborn and untractable that he is fain to use correctiones to them to breake their untamed willes and to make them plyable by his discipline, which he uses for their good and with out which they wold be lost. Turn this, O my soul, in to an humbling consideration and think how much undutyfullness thou hast been

---

[565] Revelation 19:9.
[566] Cf. Matthew 15:27, Mark 7:28, Luke 16:21.
[567] See above, n. 21.
[568] This line appears in Samuel Rutherford, *Joshua Redivivus, Or Mr Rutherfoord's Letters, Divided in two Parts* (Rotterdam[?], 1664), 102, a book Rich notes she often read in 1666 and 1667 (1/11v, 16r, 32r, 60r, 103v, 122r). The diary also quotes the line (26 August 1668, 1/227v; 21 January 1669, 1/285r; 27 November 1669, 2/6v). Variations include Flavel, "The choicest Wheat," in *Husbandry Spiritualized*, 75; Charles Owen, "Hymn I," in *Hymns Sacred to the Lord's-Table, Collected and Methodiz'd* (Liverpool, 1712), 1.

guilty of to thy great father in heaven by thy not heareing the rod and considering who has appoynted it.[569] [245v] When he whipt thee by it first, thou hast drawne from him by that unteachableness very frequent and sharpe chastisements to effect his kind designe of makeing thee holy here that thou mayst be for ever here after happy.

O Lord, I doe most humbly and thankefully acknowledge that there is not one correction I could have bene without. I know, O Lord, that thou dost not willingly grieve nor afflict the children of men;[570] but that when thou dost chastise us here, it is for our prophit [profit] that we may by these temporall punishments be minded to fly from wrath to come. O Lord, thou hast skorged [scourged] me onely with rods, but thou mightest have done so with scorpions.[571] And though thy rods have, as it ware, drawne blood and made my very heart to tremble and my heart strings to be even ready to crack, yet thou hast still inabled me to bear up and to be better'd under thy correcting hand. And though noe afliction for the preasent is joyous but [246r] grievous, yet afterwards by thy sanctifying them to me I have experienced that it was of very faithfullness that thou didst correct me. And O, that this might now at last be the blessed fruit of my punishment to take away my sinn that so I may come out of the furnace of affliction as gold tryed and purify'd from my dross[572] and that I may for the time to come have a perfect sobmission unto the will of thee, my God, both in doeing what thou commandest and in suffering what thou inflictest that I may never more force from thee new sharp afflictiones. O Lord, I doe acknowledge that if I had been to chuse what rod I showld have bene whipt by, there would have but littell dust been beaten out. O lett me therefore never more dare to be so unwise as to think I know what is best for me; but the cup which thou, my heavenly father, givest me,[573] lett me drinke it, knowing that though it may be bitter, yet it will prove wholesom for me. And in all thou laiest upon me lett me be dumb, and hold my peace because thou dost it, and say, it is the Lord, lett him doe what seames him good.[574]

[246v] *Upon a disease called the tarantula, which proves mortall by causeing exseasife* [excessive] *laughing*

[247r] Those persones that doe not know the deadlynes that exsesife laughing occasiones and see the persons, as thay thinke, onely meary [merry] conclude

---

[569] Micah 6:9.
[570] Lamentations 3:33.
[571] 1 Kings 12:11, 2 Chronicles 10:11.
[572] Isaiah 48:10; Proverbs 17:3.
[573] John 18:11.
[574] 1 Samuel 3:18.

thay are very happy and are ready to applaud their condition.⁵⁷⁵ But som more knowing observers that see their danger and that their mirth will kill them both pitty them and indeavour to cure them before thay have laught them selves dead. Which mindes me of some unregenerate persones who are the great mirth-mongers of the world and doe entertaine with greediness any thinge that will cause laughter, though by doeing so thay evince themselves to be one of those fooles mentioned in the God-breathed oracles who make a mock at sin and so laugh at that which will kill them.⁵⁷⁶ And all the while their unknowing companiones think them happy because thay are as much so as their inconsideration [247v] of their danger can make them; but their more knowing, skillfull, regenerate friends have so much insight in to their desperate condition that thay seek to cure them before it be too late, and heartily compassionate them under their great danger, and therefore would be glad to see them in order to their cure to have their laughter turned in to weeping,⁵⁷⁷ which penitentiall teares might prove healthfull to them. O Lord, I doe most humbly beseech thee, lett this ocasionall meditation doe me good and lett me not chuse to laugh here at sinn, which will onely make me goe merrily to hell and so prove deadly to me, but rather chuse to mourn here and to rejoyce to eternity⁵⁷⁸ than to joyne with the wicked world in their mirth, which will, without repentance, occasion my eternall death.

---

⁵⁷⁵ Compare the reaction against laughter and mirth the tarantula prompts in the anonymous *The Spiritual Bee, or a Miscellaney Of Scriptural, Historical, Natural Observations, and Occasional occurrencyes, Applyed in Divine MEDITATIONS* (Oxford, 1662), second part, 92-97. The bite of the tarantula could, it was thought, cause "a frensie of madness and laughter" cured by music (John Playford, *An Introduction to the Skill of Musick* [London, 1674], A5r); see also John Swan, *Specvlvm Mundi: Or A Glasse Representing the Face of the World* (Cambridge, 1635), 425. Music lessened the pain and caused dancing, some thought, which shook off the poison; others believed the poison prompted fits of dancing lessened by music: Thomas Willis, *An Essay of the Pathology of the Brain and Nervous Stock* (London, 1684), 43; Walter Charleton, *Physiologia Epicuro-Gassendo-Charltoniana: Or A Fabrick of Science Natural, Upon the Hypothesis of Atoms* (London, 1654), 368-69. The modern medical term for this affliction is tarentism or choreomania (*International Dictionary of Medicine and Biology*, 3:2850, 1:547-48).

⁵⁷⁶ Proverbs 14:9. For the characterization of Scripture as God-breathed see above, n. 258.

⁵⁷⁷ James 4:9.

⁵⁷⁸ Rich may intend the mourners in the Beatitudes, Matthew 5:4.

[248r] Occasional Meditationes made by M Warwicke 1677

[249r] *Upon my lookeing out of my window at Chellsy upon the Theames*[579]

This sweet rivar of Thames that out of my window at Chelssy I looked upon with so much pleasure and delighted to do so for a long time together whilst it was smooth and that there was noe windes to make it rough, yet afterwards when a sudden and a violent unexpected storme arose, what was before so allureing to me to veiw whilst it was serene and [249v] calme did afterwards when the waves were rough prove rather fritefull to me then delightfull and made me shut my window to keap me from longer seeing it.

This may be usefull to mind me of the great allureing and attractiveness there is in seeing a persone that is patiante and calme and is freed for boysetereous and turbulent disorderes from passion, who whilst thay continue to be so, delightfully entertaine the eyes of all their beholderes. But if onse that admired gentellnes does by a soden eruption of their pation turne into fury, by which unbe[250r]coming patione the very forme of their visage for the present seames to be so changed that it lookes frightfull to the beholderes, thay cease to looke upon them, though thay desired to do so whilst by the inward pease and calmenes of their breastes their faces apeared very sweet and beautifull but are now by the storme that is with in them very unallureing.

O Lord, I doe most humbly beseech thee, by this meditation make me more then ever yet I have done study to practise those Christian adorneing graces of meekenes and patiance[580] by which I shall evinse to otheres who are my beholderes the great beauty there is in [250v] being calme and being freed from unbeseeming and violent pationes. I may not forse my beholderes so to dislike me as to be dissatisfied with coming neare me but may by sweetness and gentellnes adorne my holy profession and exsite otheres to be imitators of those graces that thay beholde by thy holy spiritt to be planted in me.

Upon workeing

[251r] This needles makeing way for the thread whilst I am working mindes me of legal and evangelical repentance. Legal repentance makes way for evangelical as the needell makes way for the thread. But though the needle makes way for the

---

[579] Printed with some rearrangement of syntax among the occasional meditations in Walker, *Eureka, Eureka*, "Meditation V," 159-60.

[580] 1 Timothy 6:11 as well as meekness: Matthew 5:5, Colossians 3:12; patience: Luke 21:19, 2 Timothy 3:10, Hebrews 6:12 and 10:36, James 1:4, 2 Peter 1:6, Revelation 14:12.

thread, yet the needell it selfe dos not sow. It onely makes way. So the law makes way for the Gospell, which is the way of our salvation.[581]

O Lord, I do most humbly and earnestly implore that I may by this meditation be putt upon examining my selfe more than ever yet I have done the trueth of my repentance [251v] that I may not satisfy my selfe with a false repentance but may have a true evangelical one. O lett me not onely have an Ahabs outside repentance, which was onely in apeareing humble but yet was neaver truly inwardly humbled,[582] and so might be compared to a plome [plum] that may seame to be saft [soft] with out but yet with in it has a hard stone. O Lord, as I have formerly had legal sorrow and the flaiches [flashes], as it ware, of hell flames in my conchance [conscience], so lett me now have the comfortes of the Gospell, which those legall sorrowes ware the forerunners of. O grant me a repentance unto life neaver to be repented of.

[252r] *Upon a very dusty table that had a very fine carpett over it*[583]

Whilst this fine carpett was layde over this table, it appeared very fine and cleane. But when that adorenieng cover was taken off, the table was discovered to be under it very dusty.

---

[581] Henry Wilkinson's 4 September 1677 sermon at Leighs is the source of her meditation and its analogy. "He sayd that legall repentance makes way for evangelicale repentancy as the neadell makes way for the thread, but though the neadell makes way the neadell It selfe dos not sow: It onely makes way. So the law makes way for the Gospell but it is the Gospell that Is the way for our salvation" (5/182v). After the Restoration Wilkinson (1616/17-1690) lost his academic affiliation with Oxford University; the 1662 Act of Uniformity then deprived him of his livings. Wilkinson sought clerical positions in the Essex parishes of Gosfield and Sible Hedingham. Before he moved to Suffolk he was one of the ejected ministers Rich aided; the diary notes his Leighs sermons. (See Jim Spivey, "Henry Wilkinson," in *ODNB*, 58:1004-5.)

[582] Ahab, the king of Israel and husband of Jezebel, incurred God's wrath for, among other evils, the death of Naboth and the worship of Baal. Moved by Elijah's dire warning of God's vengeance, he donned sackcloth and fasted (1 Kings 21:27-29); biblical commentators, however, deem his repentance hypocritical. Thus Rich's summary of Wilkinson's 4 September sermon recalls, "As Ahab went a great way and pretended to the out side of repentance for he went softly and wore sack cloath, yet his repentance was not right, for he may rather be sayde to be humbled then to be humble" (5/182v). See also, for example, John Lesly, *An Epithrene: Or Voice of Weeping: Bewailing The want of Weeping. A Meditation* (London, 1631), 287; Blackwood, *A Treatise Concerning Repentance*: "*Ahab* humbled himself in sackcloth, but his heart was not humbled. One teare flowing from a broken heart, is more accepted then many such sackcloths" (13).

[583] Among the occasional meditations in Walker, *Eureka, Eureka*, "Meditation VI," 161-62.

Which mindes me of a formall professor that puttes all his devotion in formality of dutyes and in out ward gestures which to the beholders of him makes him appeare decently but all this while under that outside and the apearance of a trew devotion his heart is durty and nasty, he onely takeing care, like a painted sepulcher, to apeare [252v] beautyfull with out whilst with in there is all uncleanness,[584] and so thinkes by putting on an hypocriticall out side to cover all inwarde faultes and so sarve the divell in Christes livery.[585]

O Lord, I humbly beseech thee, make me not to satisfy my selfe with onely the out ward formality of dutyes which may seem well to my lookers on, but make me look to the inward and spirituall performance of them how my heart is affected in them. And lett me looke to heart-cleanseing, knowing that thou, my great God, lookest in to the heart and that though I [253r] may by covering over my durty heart with a fine out ward formality deseave [deceive] men, yet I canot deaseave thee, the great heart-searchar before whome all thinges are naked and open.[586]

[253v] *Upon childrenes being at play in the streetes and falling there afighting and one coming and takeing away one of them and correcting of him, which made the lookers on to conclude that he that did it was the father of the childe*[587]

[254r] These children that are at play in the stretes, and by their dealighting to do so are drawne to forgett the time was alotted them to take their recreation in and to out slip their prescribed houre to reaturne to lerne their leasones in, have not onely by their so doeing ventured a whipping, but have allso falne out amongest them selves, and by fighting have falne ateareing one anothers faces. Which one of their ofended fatheres seeing, run presently out, and snatcht away in his armes his sonn, and instantly seveerly corected him for it. Which othere persones that ware the beholderes of in the strete observeing, though thay neither knew the boy nor the [254v] persone that ended the fray by takeing away the fightar, yet by perseaveing what he had done concluded by the seasonable correction hee gave him that he was the carefull father of the child that to prevent by his fighting it may be the loss of an eye had used his rod.

---

[584] Matthew 23:27.

[585] See, for example, those who "have only a show of godliness," "he who is a pretender to Saint-ship." "What is this but to abuse God to his face, and to serve the Devil in Christs Livery?" (Thomas Watson, *The Godly Mans Picture, Drawn with a Scripture-Pensil* [London, 1666], 10).

[586] Implicitly or explicitly in Hebrews 4:13, 1 Chronicles 28:9, Psalm 44:21, and Romans 8:27.

[587] Printed among the occasional meditations in Walker, *Eureka, Eureka*, "Meditation VII," 163-65; compare Fuller, "Love and Anger," in *Good Thoughts in Bad Times. Together with Good Thoughts in Worse Times*, part two, 94-95.

This may be usefull to mind me of the great father of all the familyes of the earths wise proceedings with his children when he sees them forgettfull of their time, and wasteing that part of it about thinges of no consernement that ought to be imployde in learneing what is for their everlasting consernement, and are allso quarrelling and fighting [255r] not against their lustes but one against another. He does, to prevent the mischife thay might do one another, corect them seasonably, by which he dos shew his fatherly care of their not afterwards falling in to greator mischiefs if thay ware left wholly uncorrected.

O Lord, I do most humbly beseech thee, saintefye this occasional meditation so to me that I may remember that though there is no knowledge of either love or hatred by all that is before us, and that as to thy outward dispensationes thay are many times in the darke to us, yet that it is a signe of sonship that thou correctest a careless, disobediante child; and therfore lett me not in an afflicted condition (if thou by thy [255v] providence shalte againe bring me in to it) thinke that thou therefore hatest me, but that thou arte a most gratious father who, to prevent in me what thou foreseest and I do not would mischife me, doest corect me.[588]

Upon drawing of a curtaine to keep the sunn from putting out the fire[589]

[256r] As sone as I perseaved that the sunes shineing in to the rome wold putt out the fire, to prevent its doing so I instantly drew the window curtanes. Which mindes me of the neaseasety [necessity] there is that God showld somtimes, when he sees the fire of celestiall love that is in the heartes of his own people neare being putt out by earthly flames that are kindled in their heartes for creatures, to take that away from us which would else take us from him. And if he dos not doe that by death, yet to prevent our cooleing in our affections to him he dos, as it ware, by som darke providence draw a [256v] curtaine betwene us and what we do dote so upon. By which he does discover that it is necessary to have some interposeing thing to keape in the heavenly fire that it may not be putt out by the over loveing of those creatures that are but moulds of clay.

O Lord! I doe beseech thee, when thou seest me ready to have the fire of thy love putt out of my heart by any thing, be so mersyfull unto me as to draw what obscureing curtain thou pleasest to hinder it that my love unto thy divine majesty may be like the fire upon the alltar that never went out.[590] O lett it neaver [257r] be putt out by any earthly object, but lett the love I beare unto thee, my God, drown and swallow up all creature loves. O blott out every name from my corrupted heart that

---

[588] More generally, the counsel in Proverbs 29:17.
[589] Printed among the occasional meditations in Walker, *Eureka, Eureka,* "Meditation IX," 169-70. The folk belief about the sun's effect upon fire has not been established. Among the meditations Rich was rereading on 1 November 1667 was "one aboute the sunes shineing so brite that it put out the fire" (1/133r), perhaps an earlier version.
[590] Leviticus 6:13.

hinders the deeper ingraveing of thy name, and remove me from what and whom thou willt so thou wilt by it bring me nearer unto thee. O, though I have sparkes for creatures, yet lett my greatest blase blase towardes heaven.

[257v] *Upon deasireing a friend to preserve safe for me some pretious things, which were kept so till I neaded them and then were seasonably produced to help me*[591]

[258r] How earnestly have I petitioned my friend to lay up safe for me some things I esteamed as preatious till I have need of them, and thay have faithfully by them bene preserved till thay were usefull for me, and then thay ware seasonably produced to helpe me. This may be usefull to excite me to practise gratitude to my best and highest friend, whom I have oft sent up unto the respirationes of my soul to keepe for me both those truthes I have learnt out of his sacred word and those experiences, too, I have had of his goodness and soportes [supports] to me [258v] under afflicting providences, not dareing to trust onely to my memory those ingageing mersyes I have formerly had voutsafed unto me lest his word and benefitts should slip out of my mind. And I have, too, petitioned him that he wold bring afresh in to my mind those truthes when I needed them most.

O Lord, I doe adore thee for bringing againe afresh in to memory those supporting promises to strengthen my weake faith when I most neaded them, which thou didest there preaserve for me till the times of my greatest exsigensyes [exigencies] and didest then comforte me by them. And, O Lord, I do, too, thankefully acknowledge that [259r] when thou didest as a gratious father chastise me by aflictiones for my enormityes and I was even ready to faint in the takeing of that wholesom soule-physick of thy prescribeing, that thou warte then pleased by my considering the benefittes had formerly acrude [accrew'd] unto my bettar part by saintefyde [sanctified] aflictiones to make me not onely in some good measure patiant under them, but didest also make me to beleeve thay wold be for my spirituall good, and so didst make my memory a cabinett to keap my own experianses, and seasonably to produce them to keap me from doeing, as Issachar did, crouech under my burthen.[592]

[259v] *Upon my often wakeing in a night and presently falling asleepe againe*[593]

How often have I this night waked, and yet I have instantly falne asleepe againe, being so drowsy that I could not long keape my selfe from slumbering or sleepeing. This may be usefull to mind me of my spirituall condition, haveing often

---

[591] Printed among the occasional meditations in Walker, *Eureka, Eureka*, "Meditation XII," 178–80.

[592] Genesis 49:14; see above, n. 465.

[593] Printed among the occasional meditations in Walker, *Eureka, Eureka*, "Meditation XIII," 181–83.

been in an awakened frame in which I have been putt upon seeking after the great thinges of my eternall consernement, which have then bene so realised unto me as to make deepe impres[260r]siones upon my heart and have made my soule to follow hard after God[594] for mersy and for power to sarve him bettar. But alas! how soon have I by carnall security bene drowsy againe and faln asleep; and though in the divine recordes of Godes reavealed will unto us he has bid that we showld not sleep as doe others but that we should be watchfull,[595] yet I have bene often apt to forgett that precept and to say unto my selfe in a spirituall sense what was sayde of naturall rest (which is a shutting up of the senses) of Laseros, that if he slept he should do well.[596] But, O Lord, I do most humbly beseech thee, do thou do unto me as thou saydest thou wouldest do unto him: [260v] come and awaken me out of sleepe.[597] O lett me no longer be so unequall in my devotiones as to have my goodness like a morneing dew which soone passes away,[598] and to be some times awake and some times asleepe, but lett me be kept watchfull by the serious sense of my mortality and of the strickt acconpte I must give unto thee of all I have done in the flesh, wither it be good or evill. And when thou seest me falling againe in to my spirituall lethargy, do thou say unto me as the mariners in the storme did unto Jonagh, arise thou slougard and call upon thy God.[599]

Upon perswadeing one to take care not to loose their stomake to their meat

[261r] With how much care did I press this person (who began to loose hur stomack to her meat) to strive to eate to preserve it; and if she fond she did not by atempting to eate recover it, then bid hur send to hur docter for some wholesom physick and not delay to take it least hur not doeing so should prove dangereous to her health.[600]

Turne this, O my soul, in to a usefull occasionall meditation and consider how dangerous it may prove to thee, my soule, to loose thy spirituall apetite to the ordinances of God,[601] which are the soules food appoynted to nourish it and to be instrumentall to preserve it unto eternall life.

O Lord, I therfore most humbly beseech thee to make me observe and be watchfull that I do not loose my [261v] stomak and a spirituall apetite unto the nourishment apoynted for my bettar part; and when I find the least nauseateing

---

[594] Psalm 63:8.
[595] 1 Thessalonians 5:6; see also Christ's rebuke of Peter, Matthew 26:40.
[596] John 11:12.
[597] John 11:11.
[598] Hosea 13:3.
[599] Jonah 1:6.
[600] WW: "Perhaps her own woman Mrs English, who was much out of order ab^t. this time" (261r).
[601] See above, n. 31.

to thine ordinances, O make me instantly apply my self by prayur unto thee, my great and good physitian, and not to be unwilling to take the remedy for spirituall distemperes of repentance, knowing that somthing is amiss when I do not find that divine gustow in thy ordinanses as formerly I have done. And, O Lord, lett me never leave till by the use of meanes I have againe recovered that quick apetite I have had to those cundeute [conduit] pipes of grace, but O be pleased to make me so constant a frequentor of the mea[262r]nes of nourishing my soule that at last by them my soule may prosper, and thrive, and not be in a languishing condition for want of my makeing use of my foode and so starve my soule.

Upon a persone that had great knowledge and very quick but unsaintifyed parts[602]

[262v] This persone that is in this very profane age celebrated for a great witt and is very acceptable to all his companions upon the accounpt of his being so does yet make so very ill use of those acute partes God has bene pleased to bestow upon him that he onely makes use of them to laufe [laugh] at all that is either serious or sacred, indeavoring as much as in him lyes to make all devotion be turned in to ridicule; and so uses all that knowledge God has bestowed upon him to so ill use that in stead of useing it for the great design it was bestowde upon him for to glorify his great creator with it, he does onely turne [263r] it againest him; and therfore makes use of his knowledge to his own finall destrouktion with out repentance, it being onely made use of by him as a torch to light him to hell by.[603]

O Lord! I do most humbly beseech thee, lett this meditation make me rather to chuse to have a little saintefyde knowledge then the most raised and quick partes unsaintefyed, and lett me make use of those partes thou art pleased to bestow upon me to thy honnor that so I may never fight againest thee with thy own weapons but may bring some glory to thee with them. O, be pleased to give me light in my head and fire in my heart.[604] O, be pleased to send the fire [263v] from heaven that may make me inflame others with trew zeale for thy glory that so useing those weake partes for thee thou hast voutsafed me I may at last by the knowledge I have make such use of it as to be lighted to the region of bliss, whilst otheres with greattor knowledge with out grace goe in to utter darkeness.

---

[602] Printed among the occasional meditations in Walker, *Eureka, Eureka,* "Meditation X," 171-72.

[603] Among the Restoration wits notorious for their debauchery and irreverence, John Wilmot, second Earl of Rochester (1647-1680), was foremost. The metaphor in the seventeenth and eighteenth centuries is linked with reason and knowledge, e.g., "Many a Mans knowledge is a torch to light him to Hell. Thou who hast knowledge of Gods Will but dost not do it, wherein dost thou excel an Hypocrite? Nay, wherein dost thou excel the Devil?" (Watson, *A Body of Practical Divinity*, 512; Samuel Bourn, *The Believer's Hope of the Transforming Vision of Christ* [London, 1721], 50).

[604] Psalm 39:3; Jeremiah 20:9.

Upon seeing a silke worme spin[605]

[264r] This silke worme has for a long time entertained my eyes with observeing how busily it was imployed in spinning its curious thread of silke; and that when it had made its purse of silke in to which it has confined it selfe, if the lookeres to it do not wind what it has spone off, rather then it will keape that waite of silke upon its backe, it will make a way to gett from under it by eateing a hole at the top of it and so flings it off. Which mindes me of those very vaine persones that are puft up with their being adorned with fine close [clothes], which is being proud of putting on of that which the [264v] silke worme puttes off.

This may be usefull to caution me against loveing and delighting in fine silkes when I do consider that all the finest and best mingled ones that can be putt to adorne me with are all spun by a poore worme and that to be proud of fine closes is to be so of that which is the monument of our sinn, for if Adam had not sinned, we showld have had no need of cloathing to have hid our shame;[606] and that even pearles which are by many purchased at so deare a rate that thay may adorne them selves with them are but the sickness of the fish; and that crimson [265r] with which crowned heads are often cloathed is dyed with the blood of a fish;[607] and that even gold and silver for which many persones venture their immortall parte is dig'd out of the entrails of the earth. And it is in the inspired volume told us that he that loves silver shall not be satisfy'd with silver,[608] nor is all the gold that is in all the mines in the whole world worth one immortall soul.

O Lord, I do most humbly implore that thou wouldest by these considerationes of the inconsiderablenes that is in all these glittering adorenements which poore, deluded, proud persones looke on with eyes of [265v] admiration humble me exsidingly [exceedingly] for haveing in my youth bene too guilty of this sin of too much loveing and delighting in fine closes, being then too much taken up with the adorneing of my vile body and too little so with the adorneing of my bettar parte. O Lord, make me for the time to come to watch against this sin which did so easily besett me, and lett me never more lift up my soule to this

---

[605] Printed among the occasional meditations in Walker, *Eureka, Eureka*, "Meditation XI," 173-77.

[606] Genesis 3:7.

[607] The source is George Gifford's 19 December 1675 sermon at St Andrews, Holborn (4/93r). Rich's summary of the sermon in her diary contains passages very close to those in the meditation: "If Adam had not sined we showld have no neade of cloathing to hide our shame; . . . pearles ware but the sickness of a fish, and that crimsone was but dyde with the blood of a fish, and that all the fine silkes ware but what was wrought by a little worme" (4/93r). Gifford (1624[?]-1686), the son of George Gifford, Malden, Essex, was Gresham professor of divinity and rector of St Dunstan's-in-the-East; he became president of Sion College in 1677 (*Alumni Oxonienses*, ed. Joseph Foster, 4 vols. [Oxford: Parker and Co., 1891-1892], 1:563).

[608] Ecclesiastes 5:10.

tinsell and pageantry vanity, but make me study to be like the kings daughter all glorious with in.⁶⁰⁹ And though thou, my God, hast tolde us that those that ware gay [266r] apparell are in kinges houses;⁶¹⁰ and that in thy inspired volume the vertuous woman is sayde to have all her household cloathed with scarlett and that hur own cloathing is silke and purple,⁶¹¹ which seems to intimate that it is not unlawfull to weare silke, scarlett, and purple; and that the silke worme was not made onely to spin for the proud; yet, O Lord, I doe beseech thee, lett me never more yield to that pitifull temptation of being drawn to esteeme either otheres or my selfe upon the acounpt of being sett out with much bravery, but lett me valew more others—my fellow Christianes—and prise more in my selfe the adorneing of a sweet, meek, quiett, contented spiritt which is in [266v] thy sight of great valew.⁶¹² And if I be adorned with the graces of thy holy spiritt, help me to consider thay will make me fine to all eternity; where as all my bodily adornments are pulld off at night when I goe to rest and must be all for ever parted with at the night of death. O Lord, therfore be pleased to make me often call to my rememberance the very great and sensible pleasure I have often experienced in cloathing naked backs⁶¹³ when thou hast lett me have the honor of being thy allmenore [almoner] and disperse thy charity through my handes to thy [267r] neasestos [necessitous] poor. And lett that make me rather to chuse to cloath naked backes then to please idle eyes and rather chuse to see many of my fellow creatures kept warme, being covered with my charity in plain but warme apparell, then to starve my charity by putting upon my selfe one rich, laiste gonde [laced gown] which wold, if sold and distributed unto the poor, make many deasent [decent] and convenient gondes for seaverall indigent persones.

[267v] *Upon my dogs care when hee was a hunting not to loose me, and when I called him instantly forsakeing his hunting to follow me in*⁶¹⁴

[268r] This poore brute creature is so watchfull to observe all my motiones that his eyes are selldome off a me for feare I showld leave him behinde when I goe to walke. Which when I did, he attended me to the Willdernesse and then left me to pershew [persue] a rabett. Which whilst he was hunting and in his most eager

---

⁶⁰⁹ Psalm 45:13.
⁶¹⁰ Luke 7:25.
⁶¹¹ Proverbs 31:21-22.
⁶¹² 1 Peter 3:4.
⁶¹³ The charity praised in Matthew 25:36, 38, 40.
⁶¹⁴ Compare Boyle, "Reflection III. Upon my Spaniel's Carefulness not to lose me in a strange place," in *Occasional Reflections*, 5:85-86; Flavel, "Upon the love of a Dog to his Master," in *Husbandry Spiritualized*, 248-49.

persute of it, I did observe that he would now and then desist from his game so long as to come in to the walk I use to frequent to see if I ware still there. And when he saw I was, he ran presently back againe to his beloved pleasure of hunting. But as soon as I was returneing home and gave him a call, he quitted what he was so vigorous in persuing rather then forsake [268v] me. This caredge of this diligent, loveing, brute creature to me may be usefull to humble me under the consideration of my disingenuous behaviour to my great Lord, being too apt in the midst of my pleasures to forgett to looke after my God and to be too much pleased in the injoyment of them to be soon called off from them to come home unto my God when he bids me to doe so either by the secret whispers of his holy and blessed spiritt, or by his sacred word, or by his imbassadores, being too ready to linger and stay from him that I may still a little longer taste my sensuall delights.

O Blessed Lord! I do beseech thee, lett [269r] me be taught diligense and obedience from this dumb creatures behaviour to me that I may never more be so taken up with my lawfull pleasures as not to have frequent returnes to thee that I may not loose thee by persuing senshuall delights, but may be more weaned from them, and may when ever thou callest me off from them quit them all to follow thee. O lett vayne delightes be gone, and lett me be every day more and more weaned from them, remembering that pleasures dye in the birth and therfore are not worthy to come in to the bill of mortality, and that none of them has eternity stampt upon them, but that the pleasures of sinn are but for a season.[615] O Lord, I therefore most humbly and earnestly implore that when I am too eager in my persutes of them, do thou call me off and make me, when thou dost so, instantly run from them to thee.

[269v] *Upon a boy that was selldome obedient to his fathers comandes longer then by corectiones he was made to be so, he being still worst when his father was kindest unto him*

This untoward child that is onely dutyfull to the comandes of his father when he is kept so by seavere correctiones, but when he is treated with gentleness and his kind parent uses him so very oblidgeingly that he is resolved to try to concure [conquer] his untractableness by all the kind and gentle usage imaginable, does instantly grow worse and more disobedient to his comandes for all his kindnes and does by his doeing so discover so ill and disingenuous a nature [270r] that I canot heare of his ill caredge without disdayneing him for it, seeing he is like one of the tops he often uses to reacreate himselfe with which never goes longer then it is whipt to make it do so.

This action I am with so much severity passing my censure upon of this boyes behaviour may be usefull to make me, as Pharaohs bottelor did, call my own

---

[615] Hebrews 11:25.

faultes to rememberance this day;[616] for not unresemblingly have I delt with my father in heaven who, when he has (as a most indulgent father) corrected me for my disobedience unto his commandes, I have then in my afflicted condition powred out a prayur to God and, as it ware, [270v] knockt loud at the gate of heaven for mersy and support under my otherwise insuportable burdens,[617] and have then obeyed those excellent comandes of the great Gods, and done so, too, as knowing thay ware imposed upon me for my good and as haveing experienced thay ware for my own advantage, haveing fond that in the keeping of them there is great reward. But when God has been pleased to take off for som time his fatherly chastisements and to draw me to him with the cordes of a man,[618] with loveing kindness and gentleness, I have been [271r] so basely disingenuous as to grow worse by his love and to follow him afore [far] off then when my soule before followed hard after him[619] and I did then cleave to him with full purpose of soule.

 O Lord, I do most humbly beseech thee, humble me exsidingly [exceedingly] under the sense of my base and vile caredge to thee, my God, who have requited thee evill for good[620] and have been more disobedient to thy inspired preceptes when thou hast bene most gratious unto me. O Lord, I do most humbly and earnestly implore that thou wouldest in an espesall maner humble me for my crying crimsone sines[621] againest thy love and indeareing mersyes. O Lord, I do [271v] acknowledge that out of my own mouth thou maiest justly condemn me,[622] haveing often declared that I could never be brought to any obedience by any thinge but love in my transactiones with creatures, but that I was not proof against their kindness but was drawne and overcome by it. And yet, wretched creature that I am, I have bene proof againest thy ineffable love and have not bene, as I ought, melted and allured by it, though thou hast followed me with loveing kindness all my dayes.[623] O, be pleased now at last to lett thy mersyes make me in earnest to give up my selfe, my whole selfe, a liveing sacrifice unto thee holy and acseptable, which is but my reasonable servise of thee.[624]

---

[616] Genesis 41:9.
[617] See above, 144 and n. 335.
[618] Hosea 11:4; see also above, n. 88.
[619] Psalm 63:8.
[620] Cf. 1 Samuel 25:21.
[621] Isaiah 1:18; see above, n. 444.
[622] Cf. Job 9:20, 15:6.
[623] In Psalm 23:6 "goodness and mercy."
[624] Romans 12:1; see above, n. 43.

Occasional Meditations upon Sundry Subjects: With Pious Reflections upon Several Scriptures By the Right Honourable Mary, late Countess Dowager of Warwick. London, Printed for Nathanael Ranew, at the King's Arms in S. Paul's Church-Yard. 1678.[625]

Meditation I. *Upon a Damm made to stop the Water*

This Damm that is put up purposely by this person to keep to himself the water, declares him to be no good natured man. Because, though he is supplyed by Neighbouring Springs with more water than he needs for his necessary uses; yet stops the Current of it from [146] his Neighbours, who want it, desiring to keep all for himself.

Turn this, O my Soul, into an Occasional Meditation, which may be useful to thee. By considering that this may not very improperly be compared to rich persons, to whom God hath given with a liberal hand great plenty of this worlds wealth, by which he designs that they should not only be watered themselves, but water others also.[626] But they instead of *distributing to the necessitous poor,*[627] inclose to themselves all that God hath bestowed upon them, to bestow it upon their *excesses* in rich Cloaths and Furniture, with which they adorn their persons and walls, which expences are the *Damm* which stops the current of their charity, and keeps it back from the poor and indigent, whose wants would be comfortably supplied by their superfluities.

O Lord, I beseech thee to humble me exceedingly under the remembrance of my former guiltiness in this kind: and make me for the future, [147] when thou art pleased to pour thy benefits upon me, to consider thou designest I should be thy *Almoner* to conveigh, as through a Conduit-Pipe, thy *Alms* to thy necessitous poor, and let me never more dare to stop and damm up what I ought with a liberal hand to sow for the refreshing of others. O let me willingly *starve* a lust to *feed*

---

[625] This collection of thirteen occasional meditations and twelve scriptural reflections was published with Walker's *Eureka, Eureka*. The following four meditations do not appear in the British Library manuscript; some of the other meditations contain alterations not found in the original and are presumably those of Walker, if not Ranew. Variations in two of them, Meditations III and V, suggest the possibility of texts other than those in the manuscript.
[626] Proverbs 11:25.
[627] Luke 18:22.

a Saint. And let me remember that he that *sows sparingly, shall reap sparingly.*[628] And let me not only now and then drop a little for charity; but make me one of those persons mentioned in thy word, who being liberal, *devise liberal things, and by so doing be established.*[629]

Oh, make me, as it were, an open Flood-gate to water my Neighbours Necessities, that so I may, as much as in me lies, be an Imitater of thy Divine Bounty, *who dost good to all.* Oh make me to do so as far as I am able, but especially make me remember *the hooshold of faith*;[630] that so I may shew my love to him that *begetteth by loving him that is begotten.*[631] And seeing my goodness extendeth not to thee; let it do so to thine. Make me to feed hun[148]gry mouths, and cloath naked Backs, that at the last day I may be amongst those to whom thou wilt say, *Come ye blessed of my father, inherit the kingdom prepared for you from the foundation of the world. For I was hungry,* &c.[632]

Meditation II. *Upon the Consideration of the different manner of the working of a Bee and a Spider*

While I am minding this despicable Spider, which for all its being so, hath some of its kind that have the honour to inhabit the Courts of the most glorious Potentates, (for the inspired Volumes tell us, they are in *Kings Palaces*).[633] It makes me consider, that the work they are so busily employed in, while they spin their Webs, (which is all spun out of their own Bowels, without having any help from any thing without them) is when it is finished good for nothing; but is soon brush'd down and flung away: Whilst the industrious Bees, that are busily employed in making of their useful Combs, do daily fly abroad to enable themselves to do so: And flying from one Flower to another, gather from every of [150] them, that which both renews their own strength, and yields others sweetness.

By the Spiders work I am minded of a Formalist or proud Professor, who works all from himself and his own strength, and never goes out of himself to a Promise to get strength for his performances, or to work by: And therefore his thin-spun Righteousness is good for nothing, and will be flung away.

The Bees going out, minds me of the Real Christian, who is renewed in the Spirit of his mind,[634] and that he may be enabled to work the great work, he he [*sic*] came into the World for, he goes out to an Ordinance,[635] and to Christ in a

---

[628] 2 Corinthians 9:6.
[629] Isaiah 32:8.
[630] Galatians 6:10.
[631] 1 John 5:1.
[632] Matthew 25:34-36.
[633] Proverbs 30:28.
[634] Ephesians 4:23.
[635] See above, n. 31.

promise for strength to work by, and by them obtains it, and this makes his work give hony, and become good for something.

O Lord, I do most humbly beseech thee, let me not dare to work from my self, but to go out daily to thee, for ability to work my great and indispensable work with: That I may deny my [151] own Righteousness, and make mention of thine only. And may thereby find such sweetness from every Ordinance and Promise, that my Soul may be like a Garden which the Lord hath blessed;[636] and may prosper and thrive exceedingly.

Meditation IV. *Of my Gardeners chusing fine young thriving Stocks to graft on, and rejecting old and withered ones*

My Gardiners care now he is grafting, in chusing young and flourishing Stocks, and passing by those which are old or withered; minds me of Gods dealings with his Creatures in grafting his Grace upon their hearts. He seldom doing it upon old decrepid withered sinners, those old Stocks being oft neglected by him, because they willingly forgat their Creator in the days of their youth,[637] (when they had an inspired Precept to remember him) and would go on in ways of sin, and live so wholly without God in the world, that he was but seldom in their thoughts, they resolving to indulge themselves in all forbidden pleasures, thinking that [155] at last a death bed Repentance and crying of God mercy, and saying *Lord, Lord*, would be enough to fit them for those eternal mansions whereinto no unholy thing shall enter:[638] And so boldly go on to add sin to sin, (upon presumption of mercy) while death is ready to close their eyes, not considering that there is not in the God-breathed Oracles,[639] one example (that I remember) of sick-bed saving Repentance. And though there is one of the Thief upon the Cross kept upon record, to keep real penitents from despairing of mercy at the close of their days;[640] yet there is but one to prevent bold impenitent sinners from presuming of mercy.

And though the mercy of God ought not to be confined to any Age, yet we may observe he doth not frequently work saving Grace in old and withering Creatures, but chuses young Disciples, and loves and delights to graft his Grace on such, that they may go on to bring forth more fruit in their Age, having given God the Spring and May of their lives, by a solemn Act of an early self-dedication to him, and chusing to work in all his ways. And who by setting [156] forth betimes in their journey to Heaven, have a long time to glorifie God in: and to be examples and encouragers to others to come in, to serve God, by assuring them

---

[636] Rich may have in mind Jeremiah 31:12 and perhaps Isaiah 58:11.
[637] Ecclesiastes 12:1.
[638] Matthew 7:21.
[639] See above, n. 258.
[640] Luke 23:39-43.

that *all his ways are pleasantness, and his paths peace.*⁶⁴¹ And that his *yoak is easie,*⁶⁴² to those who take it on them, though it may gall their Necks that struggle at it, and are unwilling to bear it.

O Lord, I do most humbly beseech thee by this occasional Meditation, let my heart be lifted up in the high praises of thee my great and good God, for not suffering me to continue so long under the reigning power of sin, as to be cast off as an old and too withered a stock to graft Grace upon, but that thou wert pleased to shew me the Beauties of Holiness betimes,⁶⁴³ before the Autumn of my age. Though, Lord, I do confess, with S. *Augustin,* that too late, Lord, too late I knew and lov'd thee,⁶⁴⁴ and do heartily grieve that I did not, as I should, devote all the spring of my years to thee, but did give some of my green time to vanity and folly, being then too comformable to the wicked world, and too little conformable to thy blessed Will.

[157] But oh for ever admired be thy mercy that did pluck me as a Firebrand out of the Fire,⁶⁴⁵ and left me not to be fuel for everlasting Burnings. Thou mightest then Lord, justly have said to me; *Thou that art filthy, be filthy still:*⁶⁴⁶ and mightest have punished my former sins with leaving me to die in my sins. But blessed be thy name, that thou didst implant in me some of the Graces of thy sweet and holy Spirit, before my old age, by which thou hast been pleased to give me more time to serve thee, and taste the pleasures which are to be found in doing so. And hast thereby enabled me to declare to others what I have my self long experimented, that *thou art good to the Soul that seeks thee:*⁶⁴⁷ and the purest, most satisfying and lasting pleasures are to be found in an holy and strict walking with thee, and that, *in keeping thy Commandments there is great reward.*⁶⁴⁸ And that religious persons have their joys, though the blind *Sodomites* of the world want eyes to see them. O Lord, make me now in my old age bring forth more fruit, that so thou mayst not say of me, as [158] as [sic] justly thou didst of the fruitless Figtree, *Cut it down, why cumberst thus the ground.*⁶⁴⁹

Meditation VIII. *Upon the lighting many Candles at one*

This Candle that hath lighted so many, still gives as much light as it did before, and hath lost nothing by what it hath imparted unto them.

---

⁶⁴¹ Proverbs 3:17.
⁶⁴² Matthew 11:30.
⁶⁴³ Psalm 29:2.
⁶⁴⁴ Augustine, *Confessions*, Book X, chapter 27.
⁶⁴⁵ Zechariah 3:2.
⁶⁴⁶ Revelation 22:11.
⁶⁴⁷ Lamentations 3:25.
⁶⁴⁸ Psalm 19:11 and perhaps Proverbs 13:13.
⁶⁴⁹ Luke 13:7.

Improve this, oh my Soul, by considering, that some excellent Christians (who as the inspired Volumes tell us of that admirable person S. *John Baptist*, who was a burning and a shining Light)[650] are so conspicuous, that all Beholders take notice of their well ordered conversation, their Light so shining before men, that others seeing their good works are thereby excited to glorifie God,[651] and are also so communicative of that light wherewith God hath vouchsafed to enlighten their understandings, that they are in a spiritual sense, what *Job* said he was in a[167]nother, eyes to the blind:[652] and are still teaching young Disciples what they who are old have been taught of God; and so train them up in the School of Christianity. And yet by imparting their knowledge of God, know him not the less themselves, but many times the more, and by informing them of the pleasures of Religion, bring them into the holy path which leads to eternal life, yet hinder not their own progress toward Heaven.

O Lord, I most humbly beseech thee, let this Meditation provoke me, more than ever yet I have done, to impart to my Fellow Christians, (especially my Family, under my authority) what I know of thee, that by my declaring how good a God thou art, I may bring many others to know thee, not only with a general, but an experimental knowledge; which will make them say as I do, *That thou art good, and dost good.*[653] O let me by declaring what thou hast done for my Soul, cause others to joyn with me in adoring thee for thy greatness, and loving thee for [168] thy goodness; that so we may magnifie thy name together. And I may be instrumental to impart light to others, and be made a burning and a shining Light my self.

---

[650] John 5:35.
[651] Matthew 5:16.
[652] Job 29:15.
[653] Psalm 119:68.

Textual Notes:
Additions and Deletions

The revised entry precedes the original.

3r.	deadly sike — allmost deadly sike
5r.	I will drinke — I will swalow
6r.	thy patiante (sike of sinn) — thy sike patiante (of sinn)
8r.	did deasire — could deasire
	gronde of this — ocasion of this
9r.	returne to the world — reatire to the world
10r.	and though I cannot comand — though I cannot comand
11r.	find the fire to glow — find the fire to smother
12r.	who to show their gratitude — to show their gratitude
	this observation showld — this showld
	gratitude to that God — gratitude to him
13r.	a littell water onely — a littell water
	by telling me that who so offereth it — by telling us that who so offereth praise
14r.	provision by which — provision which
	lesson allso: to be thankfull as — lesson allso from these prity creatures to be thankfull
15r.	Upon walkeing — Upon goeing
	and presently — and then presently
16r.	bring to my mind — bring to mind
	I am often content — I am often deasireous
	the sweet and spirituall part of it — the spirituall part of it, the swetnes of it
17r.	indeavered to be filled — indeavered a while to be filled
	I might have perfumed — I might by it have perfumed
18r.	surprised with joy to see — surprised to see
	I aprehended — I feared
	which I expected wolde — which I feared wolde
	gloriously shine out — gloriously out shine
19r.	gase upon that object — gase againe upon that glorious object
	that light — that glorious light
20r.	comparison for a child — comparison betuine a child

21r.	which seemed a glimse of heaven on earth—which was it ware a glimse of heaven
	those ware the soules—those comfortes ware the soules
	a littell glimering—a littell lifting
22r.	as bright as ever—as gloriously as ever
	Lord, doe thou againe restore to me the light of thy countenance—and restore to me the light of this countenance
23r.	my own ofense—my own action
24r.	in the Gospell who was—in the Gospell was
	abundantly from thee—abundantly from
	to acknowledge that it is—to say it is
26r.	for feare of being presently chill and takeing some—for feare of keaching some
	I not more indeaver—I not indeaver
27r.	by the duty I have—by the duty have
28r.	and though she—and yet though she
	and fawning that—and fawning upon me that
29r.	upon my own and—upon my selfe and
	been at my ease—been lase and at my ease
	to rise and with the spouse—to rise and to say with the spouse
	to make excuses—I have to make excuses
30r.	what a transport of joy was I in at—how transportes was I in of joy at
	cause any more to make—cause to make
31r.	may not unfitly—may be not exstreamely unfitly
	the law and the Gospell worke upon the heart—the law and the Gospell
	God has threatned—God has pronounest
33r.	give up my self—give my self
	my reasonable servise—my reasonable servise of thee
33v.	instantly to goe out—instantly goe out
34r.	observation was more convinced—observation convinced
35r.	one another to provoke unto love—one another to love
	separated asunder—separated far asunder
	was so exstinguished as to their present sens of it that—was so exstinguished that
	best way to preserve—best to preserve
36r.	bring it into the—bring it to the
	bringing his liveing body to it, was revived—bringing his liveing body to revived
36v.	Upon seeing a childe—Upon a childe
37r.	to take the paines—to take paines
	much greater fault, who—much greater who
38r.	now I perceive—when I perceive
	if I touch it—sartenly if I touch it

39r.	summones to come—sommones that my frende gave me to come
39v.	howres have I then injoyed—howres have I injoyed
40v.	as sone as another had—as sone as he had
	presently reflect and think—presently think
	that tears presently flow foreth—that thay presently flow with ease
41r.	and inable me to offer—and to offer
41v.	I have observed—How have I with patiance observed
	brought and sett under—brought under
	it was dirty—it was so durty
42r.	has a purifying, cleanseing vertue.—has a purifying cleanseing vertue and is able to clense a manes wayes by takeing heade ther unto and is as fire to purefy and consume all the drasse.
42v.	may fitly be compared—may fitly eno' be compared
	clouded and dos not shine—clouded and not shine
45r.	will prove as—will apeare as
	how fitly it might be compared—how fitly compared
46r.	that he has by the beholdares bene taken for that which he was—that thay have by the beholdares taken for that which thay ware
	carefull onely to seame—carefull to seame
47r.	take some of them—take some of them from her
48v.	neare any stair—neare any stepe
49r.	to catch a fall—to falle
	Thus deales my—Not unresemblingly my
51r.	How beawtifull—how lovely and beawtifull
	and how much more is it taken—and much more is taken
	I was considering upon it was—I was considering was
	but to deride them—but discover them and to deride them
52v.	blurde by the—bene blurde of by the
54r.	and to indolge—and was resolved to indolge
55r.	God has sent—God sent
	and that he was throune upon—and that siknes has throune him upon
	skreames prosideing from—skreames out of
56r.	with out any noyse but cries for mersy—with out any noyse
57r.	bateing it very well—bateing very well
58r.	showld doe harme—showld doe harme amongest them
	with the strongest—with the most strongest
59r.	proved their ruine—proved their death
59v.	powre of thee, my God—powre of God
60r.	this morneing—in the morneing
61r.	adorne the one then the other—adorne the one more then the body
	have on the ornament—have the ornament
	in thy sight of great valew—in the sight of God of great valew

62r.	sunes shineing—sunes shineing out
	cloudes gathering threatned—cloudes threatned
63r.	compared to the changes—compared to all the changes
64r.	with the apostles (in another case)—with the apostles
	like the prodigall—like good Jacob
	and lett them be as—and lett be as
64v.	and though she desended—and when she desended
65r.	noe longer then tell she—noe longer then she
	mounted upe—mounted upe againe
	reaturne againe—reaturne upe againe
66r.	converseing in earth—converseing in heaven
	with the Lord.—with the Lord and that thou hadest winges like a birde that thou mightest flee away and be at rest.
67v.	perseavest them to decay—perseavest me to decay
	unto another.— unto another tell I arive at the fullnes of the stature of Christ.
68r.	should not onely be pleaseing—should not be pleaseing
69r.	now by my writeing doune my—now of my writeing doune
	table booke so cleane—table booke so waichte
69v.	heare after.—heare after but lay them upon that skape goote Jeasus Christ that thay may be cared so away that they may neaver more be fonde.
70r.	These few—How did these few
	unfittly be so to—unfittly be compared to
	upon my harde—upon over my owne harde
70v.	love of God to thee—love of God to thy soule
71r.	then indeed it is and then it dos apeare to otherse who doe not see me in it—then as indeed it is and then it does too apeare to otherse who doe not see me through it
	inwarde sight—inwarde sight of my selfe
	showde me a false picture—showde a false picture
72v.	rekindle a new fire—rekindle a fire
73r.	to minde me how—to minde me to remember how
	layeng them by in readines had my—layeng them by had my
	I might unsouksessfully—I might have unsouksessfully
	reinflame againe my—reinflame my
	warme my heart againe—warme my heart
74r.	This may be—This meditation may be
	doe not pay—doe not at furst pay
	constant great rent—constant rent
75r.	when I had got into—when I had by geting into
	bene ther hid—bene hid
	that I might—that by composeing my minde I might

Textual Notes: Additions and Deletions 185

75v.	whilst he was doeing—whilst I was doeing
	my journy to heaven—my journy
76r.	thy great journy—thy journy
77r.	bestow upon him a more—bestow a more
	receaver in a great—receaver out of a great
	he had already distrebuted—he has all ready distrebuted
77v.	proportion that so—proportion of it that so
78r.	some of them so strongely—some of them ware so strongely
	saw it safe—saw it safe from all but
	blustering windes—blustering waves
	with being but sarvisable—with but being sarvisable
	goe my holde. I—goe my holde. But I
78v.	plouke out of—plouke them out of
	observeing the skies—observeing the weather
80r.	for it, nor ever—for them, nor ever
	pity him sofisantly for his losse of it—pity him for his losse of sight
	prefer eyes which doges—prefer that which doges
81r.	O Lord, I—O Lord, therfore I
	fire of thy love—fire of Godes love
82r.	my britest flames—my most britest flames
83r.	and all that before lived togeather are dispersed—and are all that before lived togeather dispersed
85r.	yet she is vellvet with in—but vellvet with in
85v.	finest closes—most finest closes
	must be pulded off—must be undon
86r.	color on their cheekes—color in their cheekes
	though I should find—though I find
	powre out with them penitentiall teares—powre out penitentiall teares
87r.	that when that is come—that when it is come
	Therfore make me looke—But make me looke
	but where I shall be—but ther I shall be
88r.	made me instantly—made me presently
	but as a pure blase—but a pure blase
	makes in a devoute fitt—makes in a fitt
	an even course—an even constant course
	uninterrupted sinseare obedience—uninterrupted course of sinseare obedience
89r.	that they are by Godes—that are by Godes
	bringest the bitterest cup—bringest the blakest cup
90r.	in his house to be better than—in his house better than
	But the unregenerate—The unregenerate
90v.	able to say of wisdom or religion—able to say [apparently WW's addition]

91r.	made ther a new fire—made a new fire
	making them there—making there
92r.	temptationes either to diverte—temptationes to tempte us by indeavering either to diverte
	duty to him by presently—duty to him by her presently
	converse with him, considering those—converse with him, for those
92v.	neglect quite my devotiones—neglect my devotiones
	longest and frequentest aproaches—longest aproaches
	found that any—found but any
	with thee, my God—with my God
93r.	How sone dos—How sone has
	finde first those heavenly—finde those heavenly
	doe that for me in a moment—doe that in a moment
	longest spase of time—great spase of time
94r.	But being so much a florist as not to be troubled—But being too great a florist not to be troubled
	where, when I had continued—when I had not continued
	I was doeing so—I was doeing
95r.	God has blessed—God blessed
95v.	but thinkeing it much finar [than] when I veiw'd it in the shop—and thinkeing it so much finar when I veiw'd it in the shope in the hole peece
96r.	saw the stuff in the shop in the whole—saw the stuff in the whole
	much bettar stuff—much bettar
	expectation as my desert—expectation as desert
97r.	yet it is nothing—yet is nothing
98r.	fall into sinn by—fall into sinn ether by
99r.	not so perfect—not perfectly [possibly WW's change]
100r.	sythe with a whetstone—sythe on a whetstone
	it was to use—it was to have use
101r.	other eare—other hainging eare
101v.	most humbly prostrate at—most humbly at
102r.	thinkeing himselfe to be better—thinkeing himselfe better [possibly WW's addition]
103r.	How many stikes has—How many coyelles has
103v.	mites from those—mites with those
105r.	being dronke—by his being dronke
	But, O Lord, lett this meditation be instrouktive—But O my soule lett this meditation be instrouktive to thee
	blasfeame his name—blasfeame thy name
106r.	to imbitare those—and so imbitares those
106v.	thy holy will—the will of God
108r.	this morning—this sweet morning

109r.	for her being so, informed — for her being ther informed
109v.	wold every day — and ther every day
	and learn a lesson — from this poore and learn a lesson
110r.	offer this, my all, up — offer this up
110v.	lerneing to sing like — lerneing to sing so like
	how many happy — how many too happy
111v.	I am goeing to change — I have changed
	dry have great — dry to gape have great
112r.	does not so — does not
	great neaseasetyes — great neaseasetyes and wantes
	want the modesty — want both the modesty and baichfullnes
	want of former plenty — want of plenty
113r.	I have observed — How I have observed
	when their ill neighboures — when many times their ill neighboures
113v.	let me not esteem — lett me esteem
	have an abundant — have abundant
	condition here in this their pilgrimage on earth — condition in this their pilgrimage.
114r.	against him even whilst — against him whilst
	able allso to say rivers — able to say with the sweat psalmest rivers
	how sweet — how much sweetar
115r.	goeing out and allureing — goeing out oftun and bringing
	they being often allured — being often allured
	the pleasant conversation — the searenty and pleasant conversation
115v.	disabuseing them first from — disabuseing them from
116v.	indeavering to blow up those — indeavering those
117v.	thou takest, as I charitably hope — thou takest
118r.	that I could hardly — that I thought I should hardly
119v.	with me and my actuall sines, too, as — with me as
120r.	than thay had been — than before thay had been
120v.	make me meet — make meet
	take me away — take me in to thy barne
121v.	prepared that when — prepared when
122r.	thinke them hardly worth — thinke them worth
	tear at their death — tear for their death
122v.	Mammon when thay faile — Mammon of that when thay faile
123v.	their great redeemer — their great redeemer more
124v.	too often with me in my — often with me in the
125r.	yet doe — yet lett me doe
	unknowne part of the world — unknowne world [possibly WW's addition]
	place in my prayures for acknowledging my unknown sins, for — place for my unknown sins and for

126v.	their apeareing stedfastness — their stedfastness
	for their conchanses — for their faith
127v.	now and then given — for the most part now and then given
	it ware morneing — it ware evening
	taste and relish — taste and find a relish
128r.	who before she layd it — before she layd it
	in the dust and makes — in the dust which makes
129r.	For if the possesors — If the possesors
	caution to the children — caution given to the children
	thay did not then — that thay did not then
129v.	that I be not drawn by temporalls from thee — that I doe then be carefull of being drawn from them
130r.	run freely unprest — run freely
130v.	are able to say — are able with the man after Godes own heart to say
	and, as the prophet Jeremiah phraiseth, powre — and to beg the prophet it powring out
131r.	frighted for fear of hell into atrision — frighted into atrision
	never attained contrition — never ware so able to attained contrition
132r.	how I then felte — how I felte
132v.	under a mistaken opinion — when under a mistaken opinion
135r.	so much a purer verdure — so purer a verdure
	comforted and consider — comforted to consider
135v.	thay shall rise spirituall bodyes — it shall rise a spirituall
	in a cold grave — in the cold grave
	com forth and then shine — com forth and be made glorious and shine
	kingdome of thy father — kingdome of my father
	but death in deasire — death in deasire
136r.	fruitfull aple tree — florishing aple tree
	I care not to cast — I care not yet to cast
	at last regardlesly I did so — at last I did so
	fill'd up that relation in his own family and was — fill'd up that relation and was
136v.	letting no poore — and letting no poore
	for a young son — for som young son
	was as unpleasingly regarded — was as littell regarded
137r.	for the time to come — for time to come
	then ever indeaver to wind — then ever wind
137v.	the consideration — the constraineing consideration
	be as usefull to my afectiones — be to my afectiones
	to make it blase and burn — to blase and burn
	blaze that my — blaze with more then serapheke heate that my
	mount upe to thee — mount upe to thee that when
	Upon viewing a map — Upon a map

138r.	well situated seates — well waterd seates
	who have had onely — who had onely
138v.	descry themselves before — descry before
	to others too the — to others the
	by telling me — from telling me
	orator that had onely — orator then that onely
139r.	wayes and people. — wayes and people and to take upe alone with thee alone for my fealisety. O Lord be thou unto me all in all infenettly above all and bettar then all.
	mindes me of — afterwardes mindes me of
	have appeared forward — have bene forward
	had warme affectiones — had ther affectiones
139v.	never made a show to be religious — never apeared to be religious
140r.	wash him from it — wash him from that
140v.	O Lord — as the blood of a God and make him O Lord
	which is eficatious anufe — which is anufe
141r.	murmurs, and is not able to stand under it. — murmurs at it and is not able to stand under it but is like Isacur ready to crouech under it.
	Christian courage and patience — Christian courage
	have that subjection — have that most perfect subjection
	under thine everlasting — under everlasting
142r.	they have fond — they fond
142v.	for the future make — for future time make
	that it is the fervent prayer — that the fervent prayer
	I were goeing to say — I were ready to say
	receive my spiritt. — receive my spiritt. O lett mee Jacobe like rasle with thee and not lett thee goe tell thou haste blessed me.
143r.	ones stealing by a private way — ones liveing in a private sinn
	This person — How dos this person
	in one — in a seacret sin
	steale in to hell — steale to hell
143v.	that therfore showld be wisar — and therfore showld be wisar
	which before thay likte because som — because som
	moueth at it and dearide it — moueth and dearide it
	by breakeing a wiked, profane jest, indeaver — by breakeing of a wiked, profane jest and by so doeing indeaver
	so doeing discover them selves — so doeing it make them selves
144r.	allmost before frosen hearte toucht — almost frosen hearte so toucht
	make me be often — make me often
144v.	be instrumentall som times to kindell — somtimes kindell
145r.	fragrancy there is in citron — fragrancy is in citron
	by a previous gust of heaven — by a taist (as it ware) a previous gust
	blessed land of promise — blessed heavenly Jerusalem land of promise

	lett me have a tast—doe lett me have a tast
	some larger earnest of heaven—some previous larger earnest of heaven
145v.	which may keepe some realich—which may as I keepe some taist
146v.	discoveryes made—discoveryes be made
147r.	stomake exprest, by—stomake has by
	crying has irritated—crying irritated
	whiping upon it selfe then—whiping then
	or comitting greater—or faleing in to greater
147v.	art next as a most—art next a most
	make me heare the rod and consider who—heare the rod and who
148r.	if before they drew their curtain God—if God
	that of many candells appear—that apeare of many candells
148v.	not hid from them that are at preasent—not at that time hid from them that are at for that preasent
	night the other is kepte—night is kepte
149r.	with which I may—which I may
	lett me find, too,—lett me too find
149v.	bird being tyed—bird is by being tyed
	yet by that is kept—yet he is by that kept
	as many are—as many are if discharged
	Gideones one bastard son—Gideones bastard son
	coruption chearished will—coruption will
	Christ Jeasuses sake.—Christ Jeasuses sake but thou whose prerogative it is to soubdew eniquitise sobdew all mine
150r.	warbeling out hur takeing notes—ther warbeling out hur prite takeing notes
	inticeing bait she was—inticeing snare she was
	we are happy—we are pleasantly happy
150v.	as I may neaver more by him be caught—as neaver more to be led captife by him
151r.	Every place is enricht—Every wher is enricht
	This may put me in mind of—This may be mindfull of
151v.	call them thy jewelles—call thy jewelles
	live with them for ever—live with them heare and for ever
152r.	This may put me in mind—This may be mindfull
152v.	neaver make them to doe so—neaver make them yeald to doe so
	Saviour did, who in the days of his fleach offard—Saviour did offar
154r.	affecting thoughtes—affecting sad thoughtes
	wives (or mothers)—wives
	husbandes or children—husbandes
155r.	flood of teares—flood of penitent teares
155v.	Upon a doctors—Upon seeing a doctors

Textual Notes: Additions and Deletions

156r. many sad sighes—many sad complaintes
       sick persone mourne and complaine—sick persone complaine
156v. send what ones thou seest fitt—send what smarting ones thou seest fitt
       but save our soules
157r. threatenest (thy people) that—threatenest that
       lett me not so strongly—lett me so strongly
       heard the rod and him who—heard the rod and who
157v. too much contented with out doeing so where as—too much contented with that where as
       make me now to have my soule prosper—make me now to grow in grace and to thee prosper
158r. this garden—this fine garden
       breake over in to though—breake over though
       thy designed inheritance—thy inheritance
159r. Upon the opinion—Upon the receaved opinion
       that digg up—that so digg up
159v. life time till my death, but open my eyes—life time but open now my eyes
160r. that there is still—that it is not lost for there is still
       this darke, cloudie day—this darke day
161r. by them derided and the practicers—by them laught at and skorned and the practicers
161v. with the most to follow—with the streame to follow
       though with much—with much
       mankindes temptationes—mankindes hapynes
       rather than to offend—than to offend
162r. made on me—made upon me
       in owneing it, that—in owneing that
163r. secret drawer of it consealed—secret and undescovered drawer of it bene consealed
       the hid treasure, but it was fond—the consealed treasure but was fond
       canest find skairse any—canest not find any
163v. And, oh Lord—Oh Lord
164r. so changed faln on the ground—so changed lye faln to the ground
       ones fell in my sight—ones that still ware left on fell in my sight
164v. whiteness of the milke represented in their skins—whiteness of the milke in their skins
166r. dead leaves among which I walkd this fall—dead leaves which I wold walk this fall amongest
       amongest dead persones, though—amongest dead persones that we have converst with though
       are, too, the less able—are the less able
       alive, haveing a vegetive life, made it—alive made it
       out of his, not—out of his sight not

166v.	love best the soules—love the soules
	have out of them taken their flight—have from them taken their everlasting flight
	and from being—and being
	live for ever hapy—live comfortably for ever
	my Lady Lakes—my old Lady Lakes
167r.	and that great wealth—and great wealth
	long, diligent—long and diligent
167v.	found that great sum of gold—that very great sum of gold
	durst trust even—durst not trust even
	very much richer—very richer
	little of worth in them—little in them
168r.	that though thou—that thou
	thay are worthy—thay are by me worthy
169r.	deathes of many—seaverall deathes of many
	by all their beholdars been taken—bene by all their beholdars taken
	Gods withholding from them at that time his—Gods holding from them his
169v.	best not to judge—best not so much to judge
170r.	his poore saints—his poore saintefide saints
170v.	sentance on me, come—sentance, come
	Upon my haveing but—Upon haveing but
171r.	see more out of them—see out of them
	God was pleased so to open—God was pleased to open
	see those things—see clearelyur those things
171v.	I now have—I now have got
	what I see—what I yett see
172r.	inticements draw thee—inticements to thee draw
	worke by which thay may smutch—worke which may smutch
	make me a companion—make a companion
	to make my way—make me make my way
172v.	smelling spice—smelling much spice
173v.	hopping from one bough—hopping from plase
174r.	pretious, being—pretious things being
175r.	may be nesisary to mind me of the great—may be usefull to mind me of lookeing of the great
	now be so diligent—now be diligent
175v.	that which will make—that will make
	make there any long stay—make any long stay
176r.	a long stay—a long stay with hur
	exprest by much indeareing—exprest by soe indeareing
	ware so after my reaturne—ware after my reaturne
	so thought onely to have had—so onely to have

176v.	unvalewable kindness I have had from—indearering kindness I have from
	to stoope so beneath thy greatness as to converse—to stoope beneath thy greatness and to converse
177r.	wold at first sight have—wold have at first sight
	the wiked world—the world
177v.	to feare there—to thinke there
	beleeve himself to be the onely persone alone that was left—beleeve himself the onely persone that was left alone
178r.	water and did so—water which did so
	that soule that is in earnest in its pershutes after God will—that soule that has tasted how gratious God is will
178v.	Upon this passage in the life of Alexander the Great that hee was troubled because—Upon a pasage in the life of great Alexander that was troubled because
179r.	for want of it—for want of so inconsiderable a thing
179v.	pleased to give me with—pleased to give with
	pleased often to make me call—pleased to cale
180r.	their home did plainely—their hom at Lees did plainely
	be at it—be at home
	given a prospect—given them a prospect
	running in the wayes—running the wayes
181r.	and pharesaiecaly to justifye—and to justifye
	not finished my journey—not don my journey
181v.	and by my own coruptions been detained—and my own coruptions detained
182r.	as I have observed—I have observed
	that once lived with them—that lived long with them
182v.	thou waste pleased—thou hast bene pleased
183r.	hast allready attained to—hast allready attained
	one degree of it—one degree of grace
183v.	big and grown man—big and full grown man
184r.	those first motions and actions—those actions
	so do contribute—so contribute
	care of the first inticements—care of my first inticements
185r.	and excites us to admire—and to admire
185v.	doe, too, with adoration—doe with adoration
186r.	never to stagger—never more to stagger
	really and firmly to rely upon—to really firmly upon them
	knowing that thay are in thee, yea and amen—knowing that thay are, yea and amen
186r.-v.	sweetly gine [join]—sweetly acompeny one another
186v.	they by their good—they may by their good
	fellow Jews—fellow Christians

187r.	setting on others to reaturn glory—setting others of reaturneing glory
	many birdes—many pretty birdes
	Which observation may—Which may
	For though these birds that by their not being—For these birds that by not being
187v.	and at last—yet at last
	still singing quiet and safe—still quiet and safe
	though company is by most—though liberty is by most
	in incountering with these temptations which are—in these temptations are
	to be mett with in—to be mett in
188r.	who art sofisiant [self-sufficient] and all sufficient—who art all sofisiant and selfe sufficient
	meditation to caution thee against—meditation against
188v.	nor rough stormes—and wher rough stormes
190r.	brought to my sad rememberance—brought againe to my rememberance
	my only son, whom I had—my only son which I had
192r.	makes them exchange—makes them to gaine them exchange
	who, too, often prefer—who often prefer
	which Christ has purchased—which he has purchased
193r-v.	dare to disesteme—dare to dispise or to disesteme
194r.	sensible a trouble—sensible impreesions
	I made him of it would—I made him would
195r.	in this kind is so—in this kind in thy own opinion is so
195v.	then lett the cry—lett the cry
196v.	to teach him his catekism—to heare him his catekism
	which made him—which made him againe
	asked me this question—asked this question
	had done thondering yet—had yet done thondering
197r.	hast inconsiderately by som—hast inconsiderately bene by inconsiderable som
197v.	showld by laying his—showld by his laying his
	I have departed—I have againe departed
198r.	so, too, from thee—so from thee
	and to thee—and thee
199r.	thou dost practise—thou practist
200v.	many times has made thee—many times makes thee
200v-201r.	that thou wouldst—that it may
201r.	assist me in my cure—assist my cure
	give me the great blessing—give the great blessing
	wouldst now be pleased—wouldst be pleased
201v.	unto thee who by faith—unto thee by faith
202v.	flower, which—flower who

Textual Notes: Additions and Deletions

203r.	often when I have — often I have
203v.	have had a soden good thought cast in to my mind — have a soden good thought cast in to mind
	in the service — from the service
204r.	give it a speedy one — give it a speedy enterance
205r.	sugar; in it which — sugar in which
205v.	tryalles of my life when — tryalles of my life which
206r.	O Lord — But O Lord
	my tryalles — my trobles
207r.	its desired liberty — the desired liberty it had lost
207v.	sightes and places makes — places makes
209r.	and make them experimentally able — and experimentally able
210r.	onely with her mouth — with her mouth
	to blaze — to a most glorious blaze
	what worke tis possible — what tis possible
211r.	opium by which — opiam by for want of which
212r.	how often persones — how often I have observed persones
	thay are so filled — thay are so thay
212v.	knaukte so loude — knaukte loude
214r.	make thee reflect — make thee with detestation reflect
	God, who has so — God, whose bounty has so
215r.	an acceptable gifte — thy acceptable gifte
216r.	repeating it, has so irritated — repeating it againe has so irritated
	doeing ill — doeing ill before
	addresses at the throne — addresses to the throne
216v.	so often on my selfe — so often to my selfe
217r.	finding him to be so — finding him so
217v.	be a quieting consideration — be the onely quieting consideration
	exsersise me with — exsersise me under
218r.	These ugly, discoloured leaves — These yelow ugly discoloured leaves
218v.	falling on the ground — falling to the ground
	by death in to it — by death in to the grond
	sett home that — sett home to me that
219v.	give more cleare — give me more cleare
220r.	rejoyce in a storme — rejoyce even in a storme
	nor any thing — nor thing
	look beyond it — look upon it
	strength to stand under it — strength to with stand it
221r.	deasigned inheritance, and so — deasigned inheritance heare and so
222r.	som diligense has — som diligense and
	but he has also lost his — but allso forfetud his
	Which may be usefull — may be usefull

222v.	some of my youeth—my youeth
	of another to my selfe—of another world to me
223v.	stand, though thay—stand ferme though thay
224r.	this meditation—this ocasionall meditation
	young professors—young Christianes
224v.	make me rather suffer—make me with Luther rather suffer
225r.	perceive hardly what—perceive nothing that
	I had finished my morneing prayur—I had my morneing prayur
226r.	yet I have come away—and yet have come away
227r.	more choyse provisiones—choyse provisiones
	many temporall benefittes—many benefittes
227v.	wishes, and a beleeveing—wishes, beleeveing
230r.	that so I might—that I might
	mindes me of Zakeaus—mindes of Zakeaus
230v.	goe seekeing—goe as Mary did seekeing
	clearer and more unclouded—clearer and unclouded
231r.	wound by grief made—wound was by grief made
	made the persone shed—made them shed
	may heare after make—may againe make
231v.	disquieting pationes—disquieting grifes
	the will of thee, my God—the will of God
	neaver be a repineing—neaver more be a repineing
232r.	so many strong throwes—so strong throwes
	sone after forgett all—forgett all
233r.	puttes me next upon—puttes me upon
	grant I may try—I may harkene and try
	spirituall birth—new birth
	my being so—my being borne againe
234r.	consider it by who—consider by who
234v.	time that is yet lent—time is yet lent [WW's addition]
237v.	haveing had a preavious gust—haveing a preavious gust
238r.	value an estate—value a lease
	to end with our lives—to indure unto eternety
	when my life does—when my life does end so to me
239r.	being full of that—being againe full of that
	taken notice, too, that—taken notice that
239v.	that the durt—that all the durt
	than I should do if—than I should if
240r.	come near me—come near
241r.	addresses at the throne—addresses to the throne
	in a more than usuall—for a more than usuall
	ring himselfe the bell—ring the bell
242r.	but also the presence of thee—but the presence of thee

Textual Notes: Additions and Deletions

243r.	when he pleases—when he will
243v.	receiving there with joy—receiving with joy
244r.	waiting for some of the broken meat which is—waiting tell some of the broken meat is
	Triumphant above that of the—Triumphant and that of the
	are every day feasted—and are every day feasted
244v.	the porch of glory—the very porch of glory
245v.	better'd under thy correcting hand—better'd by thy correcting hand
246r.	sanctifying them to me—sanctifying it to me
	would have but littell dust been—would have bene but littell dust
	which thou, my heavenly father, givest me—which my heavenly father hast given me
247r.	very happy—very happy persones
247v.	which penitentiall teares—which teares
249r.	looked upon—looked out upon
	noe windes to make it rough—noe roufe windes to make it rough
251v.	true evangelical one—true evangelical repentance
	saft with out but yet with in—saft but yet with in
252r.	adorenieng cover—adorenieng carputt
252v.	but make me look to the inward and spirituall performance of them—but to the inward and spirituall part of them
254r.	corected him for it—corected him for
	ware the beholderes of in the strete—ware beholderes in the strete
254v.	which ought to be—that ought to have
	imployde in learneing—employde in learneing ther
255r.	prevent the mischife—prevent mischife
	care of their not afterwards falling—care of their afterwords falling
256v.	love putt out of my heart by—love putt out by
258r.	thay have faithfully by them bene preserved—thay have bene faithfully preserved
259r.	crouech under my burthen—to crouech under my burthen
260v.	come and awaken me out of sleepe—goe and awaken him out of my sleepe
	unequall in my devotiones—unequall in devotiones
	thou seest me—thou againe seest me
261r.	least hur not doeing so—least hur doeing so
	prove to thee, my soule—prove to my soule
261r.-v.	be watchfull that I do not loose my stomack—be watchfull against the forbearing to have a stomack
261v.	make me so constant—make so freaquent
262r.	starve my soule—starveing of my soule
262v.	creator with it, he—creator with he
263r.	destrouktion with out repentance, it being—destrouktion, it being

263r.-v.	send the fire from heaven—send fire from heaven
264r.	it has confined—it is confined
264v.	that which is the monument—that is the monument
	sickness of the fish—sickness of a fish
265r.	And it is in—And is in
266r.	and that the silke—because the silke
266v.	night of death—night of death by me
269v.	resolved to try to concure—resolved to concure
270r.	canot heare—canot hardely heare
	censure upon of this boyes behaviour may—censure upon of this boyes may
	I have then in—I have in
270v.	my own advantage—my own good advantage
271v.	out of my own mouth—out of my mouth
	transactiones with creatures—transactiones with men

Biblical Citations

Old Testament

Genesis
3:7	171n606
3:19	56n75, 147n491
5:1–32	130n417
5:24	21n58
13:13	136n445
18:20	136n445
19:1–29	136n445
23:4	120n376
23:19	120n376
24:63	21n58, 22n71
30:27	112n329
32:10	82n186
32:24	113n337
32:26	106n301
39:5	112n329
41:9	48n34, 66n120, 174n616
43:34	47n30
44:4	136n442
44:12	118n366
49:14	141n465, 168n592

Exodus
7–10	69n132
23:2	117n362

Leviticus
6:13	47n33, 167n590

Numbers
6:25	117n359, 148n496
11:33	58n80
13:23	79n175, 108n307
25:7–14	58n81

Deuteronomy
6:11–14	98n259
31:17–18	148n499
32:10	67n126
32:49–52	62n99
33:27	55n70, 105n295
34:1–8	62n99

Joshua
24:13	138n454

Judges
8:31	111n324
9:5	111n324
9:53–54	111n324

1 Samuel
1:10–11	105n297
1:10–18	152n517
1:15	105n297
1:18	105n297
2:1–10	105n297
3:18	162n574
5:2–5	159n556
16:7	121n379
25:21	174n620

2 Samuel
3:39	159n555
19:22	159n555
22:29	131n426

1 Kings
12:11	162n571
16:8–20	58n81
19:18	126n401
21:27–29	165n582

2 Kings
2:11	84n193, 145n477
4:32–37	50n47
9:30	74n148

1 Chronicles
2:16	159n555
21:26	43n10
28:9	166n586

2 Chronicles

6:30	121n380
7:1	43n10
10:11	162n571

Job

1:20	84n192
4:19	42n6, 60n91, 74n151, 96n248, 119n372, 147n492, 157n546, 160n563
7:21	154n528
9:20	174n622
14:14	57n76
15:6	174n622
18:14	93n231
19:28	122n386
21:26	154n528
24:20	42n7, 147n492, 154n528
29:15	179n652
34:15	130n417
42:5	103n282

Psalms

4:4	138n450
4:6	46n22, 46n25
6:6	88n209
9:9	148n497
13:3	97n252, 116n357
16:3	87n204
16:11	67n124, 71n140, 79n178, 92n227, 97n256, 152n519
17:7	152n519
17:8	54n68
17:15	101n276
18:2	134n433
18:35	69n130
19:1	110nn320–321, 131n427
19:11	178n648
19:12	95n242
19:13	55n72
22:14	63n109, 114n343, 136n443
23:6	174n623
26:2	118n368
26:4	87n202
27:9	148n499
27:11	50n49
28:1	134n433
29:2	75n159, 178n643
31:2–3	134n433
34:3	132n429
34:8	76n163, 89n214, 89n216, 103n285
36:7	54n68
36:8	67n124, 108n309
36:9	44n14, 53n56, 53n60
38:6	65n114
39:3	42n8, 170n604
39:13	130 n 421
44:3	76n165
44:21	166n586
45:13	73n144, 172n609
46:1	148nn497–498
48:13	116n354
50:23	43n12
51:1–2	63n107
51:2	137n446
51:6	54n63, 130n425
51:7	63n103
55:1	148n499
55:6	60n92, 61n93
55:14	49n45
57:1	54n68
57:7	124n390
59:16	148n497
61:4	54n68
62:2	134n433
63:6	22n71
63:7	54n68
63:8	169n594, 174n619
64:7	92n228
71:3	134n433
71:18	147n493
73:22	47n28, 127n404
73:27	69n130
84:6	46n21
84:10	75n161, 126n399
89:15	46n22, 46n25, 79n172, 108n314
89:48	130n418
90:8	46n25
91:4	54n68
92:15	134n433
94:19	148n500
103:1	43n13, 96n247, 122n385
104:29	130n417
106:5	119n369

Biblical Citations

108:1	124n390	2:9	148n495
112:4	131n426	3:1	48n38
116:12	138n453, 145n478	3:4	154n533
119:18	116n357	4:12	53n60, 116n353
119:32	128n406	5:3	48n35
119:68	179n653	5:16	155n536
119:71	147n490	Isaiah	
119:117	69n130	1:18	63n103, 136n444, 174n621
119:136	51n51, 89n212, 99n263, 114n343	1:25	42n5
		2:22	93n230
119:164	152n518	3:9	136n445
128:3	156n543	5:20	70n136
139:17–18	124n391	6:2	154n534
141:2	106n299	6:6–7	90n218
142:5	100n266	17:10	133n433
146:4	93n229	28:15	56n74
148	132n430	32:8	176n629
Proverbs		40:4	82n184
3:9	139n456	40:31	128n409
3:16	152n519	48:10	115n350, 162n572
3:17	76n164, 89n215, 178n641	50:10	46n26
3:34	107n302	51:20	146n486
11:25	94n236, 175n626	53:2	154n535
11:31	150n506	53:5	49n42
12:26	75n155, 112n331	55:8–9	146n482
13:13	178n648	56:7	75n160
14:9	163n576	58:9	148n500
14:27	44n14, 53n56, 53n60	58:11	177n636
16:31	74n150	64:6	119n373
17:3	162n572	Jeremiah	
20:22	150n506	2:13	138n449
20:27	156n540	6:14	100n267
22:6	112n332	8:11	100n267
29:17	167n588	9:1	63n109, 99n264, 114n343
30:28	176n633	11:20	118n368
31:21–22	172n611	17:10	118n368
31:26	19n52	17:13	44n14, 53n56, 53n60
31:30	119n371	20:9	170n604
Ecclesiastes		23:14	136n445
1:8	143n469	31:12	78n171, 92n224, 177n636
1:14	143n469	33:11	151n515
2:17	143n469	50:20	95n244
5:10	171n608	Lamentations	
12:1	177n637	3:19	83n191, 141n464
12:7	130n417	3:25	178n647
Song of Solomon		3:29	109n318
2:4	76n162	3:33	146n489, 162n570

Ezekiel
   11:19   49n40
   16:49–50 136n445
   36:26   49n40
Daniel
   3:19   65n112, 90n217
   4:30   98n260
   4:31   98n261
Hosea
   4:14   115n348
   6:4   74n153
   7:9   119n374
   11:4   60n88, 174n618
   13:3   169n598
Joel
   3:18   44n14, 53n56, 53n60
   3:18–21 80n179, 104n290, 122n387
Jonah
   1:6   169n599
Micah
   6:9   109n317, 115n349, 162n569
Zechariah
   3:2   178n645
   9:14   92n228
   12:10   58n84
   13:1   53n60, 80n179
Malachi
   3:1   46n27
   3:17   103n284, 112n330, 122n388
   4:2   46nn23–24, 78n170,
               88n210, 108n312, 117n358,
               140n460, 148 n494, 157n550

New Testament

Matthew
   3:3   67n123
   3:12   126n400
   3:16   152n516
   3:17   122n384
   5:4   88n210, 163n578
   5:5   164n580
   5:16   75n157, 92n223, 121n382,
               179n651
   6:27   29, 115n352
   7:3   55n71, 129n410
   7:13–14   67n123
   7:14   108n313, 117n363,
               129n414
   7:17–20 121n381
   7:21   177n638
   7:24–27 134n433
   9:29   103n284
   10:15   136n445
   10:37   127n402
   11:12   113n335, 128n407
   11:24   136n445
   11:30   178n642
   12:30   54n66
   13:23   45n19
   13:43   101n275, 119n375
   13:45–46 135nn437–438
   13:52   87n203
   15:27   108n311, 161n566
   16:18   133n433
   16:24   105n293
   17:4   59n86
   17:5   122n384
   18:12–14 65n113
   18:22   146n483
   19:6   157n545
   20:6   125n394
   23:27   53n62, 73n143, 166n584
   23:37   54n69
   25:1–13 53n57
   25:14–30 94n237
   25:21   125n396
   25:33–34 152n519
   25:34   122n389
   25:34–36 176n632
   25:36, 38, 40 172n613
   25:41   150n510
   26:28   105n291
   26:36   42n9
   26:40   169n595
   26:75   51n51
   27:32   105n295
Mark
   1:3   67n123
   1:11   122n384
   6:11   136n445
   7:28   108n311, 161n566

Biblical Citations

8:34	105n293	20:36	101n272, 153n526
8:38	107n303, 118n364	21:19	146n487, 155n537, 164n580
9:5	59n86	22:62	51n51
14:72	51n51	23:26	105n295
15:21	105n295	23:31	130n420
16:9	48n37, 117n360, 154n532	23:39–43	177n640

Luke
		24:32	49n46
1:19	49n41	John	
1:37	114n340	1:16	53n59, 53n61
2:13–14	114n345	3:3, 7	156n542
2:19	21n58, 44n15	4:10–14	44n14, 53n56, 53n60
2:35	136n440	4:24	113n334
3:4	67n123	4:38	138n455
3:5	82n184	5:35	179n650
3:22	122n384, 152n516	8:12	131n426
6:46–49	134n433	9:4	125n395
7:25	172n610	10:27–28	69n131
7:38	99n265	11:1–2	60n90
8:1	49n41	11:11	169n597
9:23	105n293	11:12	169n596
9:26	107n303, 118n364	11:35	113n336
9:33	59n86	12:35	46n26
10:12	136n445	12:46	131n426
10:34	141n466	14:2	128n408
10:38–42	60n90, 137n448	14:26	152n520
12:19	144n476	14:27	141n467, 153n521
13:7	102n281, 178n649	15:5	51n52
13:11	47n29	16:21	155n539, 156n541
13:27	150n510	18:1	22n71
13:34	54n69	18:11	41n3, 75n156, 105n294, 141n463, 162n573
14:14	150n506	20:11	66n118
14:26	127n402	20:11–18	48n37, 117n360, 154n532
15:4–6	65n113	Acts	
15:7	114n344	2:42	94n239
15:11–32	59n87	3:19	63n107
15:24	114n342	7:59	106n301
16:6	95n241	9:31	152n520
16:9	94n238	21:13	96n246
16:11	94n238	24:1–27	141n461
16:19–31	88n207, 102n280	26:28	69–70n133
16:21	108n311, 161n566	Romans	
17:10	66n121	3:2	98n258
17:15	144n473	5:9	105n291
17:17–18	138n452	5:10	109n315
18:10–14	81n182, 129n410	5:12	93n234
18:22	175n627	5:21	93n234
19:4	154n531		

6:7	93n232	5:22	77n168
6:14	111n325	5:31	157n545
8:15	65n114	6:10	74n149
8:27	166n586	Philippians	
8:28	146n488	1:23	97n253, 154n529
8:31	54n66	2:12	157n547
11:2–4	126n401	3:20	85n198
12:1	49n43, 60n89, 76n166, 86n201, 174n624	Colossians	
		1:10	83n188, 102n279
12:21	136n441	1:12	92n225
13:14	73n145	1:14	105n291
15:16	44n16	1:20	109n315
1 Corinthians		2:3	53n58
1:2	44n16	2:14	95n245
2:9	79n174	3:2	111n326
5:7	54n64	3:3–4	97n251
7:30	71n139	3:12	164n580
10:4	133n433	3:18	77n168
14:25	75n155	1 Thessalonians	
15:44	101n273	4:13–14	101n271
15:53–54	134n433	4:14	97n250, 101n274, 114n339, 153n527
2 Corinthians			
2:16	45n20	4:17	79n177, 92n226, 97n255
4:6	79n172, 108n314, 153n522	5:6	169n595
4:18	62n100, 84n194, 98n257, 158n553	1 Timothy	
		1:15	139n458
5:18	109n315	3:7	55n70, 57n78, 111n328, 129n415
6:14	49n44		
9:6	176n628	5:5	16
Galatians		5:6	117n361
3:10	49n39	6:11	164n580
4:26	129n411	6:17	142n468
6:9	150n507	6:18–19	139n457
6:10	176n630	2 Timothy	
6:12	151n512	2:26	55n70, 57n78, 111n328, 129n415
Ephesians			
1:7	105n291	3:10	164n580
1:14	149n502, 158n551	3:12	151n513
1:18	70n135, 116n356	3:16	98n258
2:2	66n121	4:7	91n219, 108n310, 129n413
2:8	130n424	Titus	
4:7	130n424	2:5	77n168
4:13	61n96	2:11	130n424
4:18	70n135	3:7	130n424
4:23	75n158, 120n377, 122n383, 176n634	Hebrews	
		4:13	166n586

4:16	130n424, 145n481, 159n557	5:8	54n65
6:12	164n580	5:12	122n383, 130n424
6:17	131n428	2 Peter	
9:14	63n106	1:6	164n580
9:27	130n418	1:17	122n384
10:29	58n84	2:6–8	136n445
10:36	164n580	3:8	75n161
11:10	62n101, 157n549	1 John	
11:25	72n141, 151n514, 173n615	1:7	80n179, 92n222, 100n269, 105n291
12:22	103n283		
12:23	79n176, 85n196	5:1	176n631
13:15	151n515	Jude 1:7–8	136n445
James		Revelation	
1:4	164n580	1:5	80n179, 85n197, 92n222, 100n269, 105n291
1:22	45n17		
2:5	88n208	2:11	101n278
4:6	82n183	2:23	118n368
4:8	125n397, 160n561	5:5	54n67
4:9	163n577	7:10	63n103
5:11	84n192	7:11	159n559
5:16	106n300	7:14	63n104
1 Peter		7:17	44n14, 53n56, 53n60
1:4	149n504	13:8	97n254
1:5	58n82	14:12	164n580
1:19	63n104	17:8	97n254
1:23	156n542	19:1	114n345
2:3	76n163, 89n214, 89n216, 103n285	19:7	108n308
		19:9	108n308, 152n520, 161n565
2:25	138n451	20:6	101n278, 114n341
3:1	77n168	20:12	97n254
3:4	59n85, 73n146, 172n612	20:15	97n254
5:4	150n511, 153n525	21:23	84n195
5:5	59n85, 82n183, 82n185	22:11	178n646

Index

Abbot, George
 Brief Notes Upon the whole Book of Psalms, 88n207
 The Whole Booke of Iob Paraphrased, 84n192
Adam, Melchior, *The Life and Death of Dr Martin Lvther*, 106n298
Adams, Thomas, *The Main Principles of Christian Religion*, 60n88
Aesop's fables, 43n11
Agrippa, Marcus Julius, 69, 69n133
Aikin, Arthur, *The Natural History of the Year*, 89n213
Alexander the Great, 127, 127n403, 154
Ambrose, Isaac, *Media: the Middle Things*, 2n6, 5n14, 21n60, 22n67, 22n71, 127n402
Andrewes, George, 36
Apothecaries' Garden, 78n169
Apsley, William, 7
Aristotle, 93n231
Augustine, *Confessions*, 44n14, 178, 178n644
Austen, Katherine, 2n3, 4n11, 28n88
Babylon, 98, 98n260
Ball, John, *A Treatise of Divine Meditation*, 3n6, 22n67
Barham, Francis Foster, 36
 Memoir of Lady Warwick: Also Her Diary, 36n101
Barrington, Anne (née Rich), 19n50, 26, 80, 80n180. *See also* Anne Rich
Barrington, Dorothy, 80n180
Barrington, John 80n180

Barrington, Thomas 80n180
Barrow, Isaac, "Sermon VI. Of the Duty of Prayer", 60n92, 113n335
Baxter, Richard, 11, 18, 20
 A Call to the Unconverted, 58–59n84
 Certain Disputations Of Right to Sacraments, 109n315
 A Christian Directory, 2n6, 18nn47–48, 22n69, 45n18, 58–59n84, 82n186, 88n207, 93n231, 103n284
 The Crucifying of the World, by the Cross of Christ, 134n433
 The Duty of Heavenly Meditation, 33n92
 The Life of Faith, 82–83n187
 A Paraphrase on the New Testament, 60n90, 99n265
 Reliquiæ Baxterianæ, 41n2
 The Saints Everlasting Rest, 2n6, 11, 11n36, 20, 21, 21n62, 21n65, 22, 22n69, 22nn71–72, 23, 23n73, 66n121, 67n123, 79n175, 85n197, 128n407, 130n424
Bayly, Lewis, *The Practice of Piety*, 97n253
Beadle, John, 5,
 The Journal or Diary of a Thankful Christian, 5, 5nn14–16, 6n19, 9n31, 10, 10n32, 16, 16n44
Berkeley, Elizabeth (née Massingberd), 71n137
Berkeley, George, first Earl of Berkeley, 71n137
 Historical Applications and Occasional Meditations upon Several Subjects, 71n137, 82n186, 125n398

Berkeley, Mary, 71n137
Biblical figures
  Abimelech, 111n324
  Abraham, 120, 120n376
  Adam, 109n315, 130n417, 171, 171n606
  Ahab, 165, 165n582
  Anna, 16
  Baal, 58n81, 126, 165n582
  Benjamin, 47, 118
  Christ [or Jesus], 22, 59n86, 60n90, 66n118, 99n265, 137, 152n516, 154, 169n595
  Cozbi, 58, 58n81
  Dagon, 159, 159n556
  David, 21n58, 22, 33, 42, 43n10, 49, 51, 127, 132, 159n555
  Dives, 88, 88n207, 102n280
  Elah, 58n81
  Elijah, 33, 84, 126, 144–45, 165n582
  Elisha 50, 50n47
  Enoch, 21n58
  Eve, 109n315
  Felix, Marcus Antonius, 140–41, 140n61
  Festus, Porcius, 69n133
  Gideon, 111, 111n324
  Good Samaritan, 32, 141
  Hannah, 33, 105, 105n297, 152
  Isaac, 21n58, 22
  Issachar, 141, 141n465, 168
  Jacob, 23, 59n7, 82n186, 106n301, 112, 113, 113n337, 141n465
  James, 59n86
  Jezebel, 74, 165n582
  Job, 56, 84n192, 93n231
  John, 59n86
  John the Baptist, 179
  Jonah, 169
  Joseph, 112, 136
  Joshua, 21n58
  Jotham, 111n324
  Judith, 16
  Laban, 112
  Lazarus, 60n90, 169
  Leah, 141n65
  Martha, 60, 60n90, 99n265, 137
  Mary Magdalene, 48, 66, 66n118, 99n265, 117, 154
  Mary (mother of Christ), 21n58, 44, 136n440
  Mary (sister of Martha), 60, 60n90, 99n265, 37
  Mary (washed Christ's feet), 99, 99n265
  Moses, 31, 32, 62, 62n99, 128
  Naboth, 165n582
  Naomi, 16
  Nebuchadnezzar, 98, 98n260
  Paul, 16, 69–70n133, 96n246, 97n253, 140–41n461
  Peter, 51, 59n86, 133n433, 169n595
  Pharaoh, 69, 69n132
  Pharaoh's butler, 48, 66, 73–74
  Pharisee, 31
  Phinehas, 58n81
  Potiphar, 112
  Prodigal, 59
  Salu, 58n81
  Sarah, 120, 120n376
  Simeon, 136n440
  Simon of Cyrene, 32, 105n295
  Solomon, 21n58, 43n10, 119, 119n371, 143
  Stephen, 106n301
  Zaccheus, 154, 154n531
  Zeruiah, sons of
    Joab, Abishai, and Asahel, 159, 159n555
  Zimri, 58, 58n81
Blackwood, Christopher, *A Treatise Concerning Repentance*, 17n45, 30n91, 98–99n262, 99n265, 165n582
Bolton, Edmund, *Nero Cæsar, or Monarchie Depraued*, 104n289
Book of Common Prayer, 42n6, 49nn43–44, 62n100, 69n130, 76n163, 79n177, 92n228, 94n240, 153n521, 159n558
Book of Life, 11, 32, 97
Booty, John, 20n54
Boteler, Francis (Rich's relation), 17
Bourn, Samuel, *The Believer's Hope of the Transforming Vision of Christ*, 170n603
Boyle, Catherine, Countess of Cork (née Fenton, Rich's mother and second wife of first Earl of Cork), 6, 7n24
Boyle, Joan (née Naylor, Rich's grandmother), 7

Index

Boyle, Margaret, Lady Broghill, Countess of Orrery (née Howard, Rich's sister-in-law), 26, 118, 118n365
Boyle, Richard, first Earl of Burlington and second Earl of Cork (Rich's brother), 12n39
Boyle, Richard, first Earl of Cork (Rich's father), 6, 6n20, 7, 7nn23–24, 8, 8n28
  "True Remembrances", 6n20, 7, 8, 8nn25–26, 8n28
Boyle, Robert (Rich's brother), 2, 13n40, 20, 35
  An Account of Philaretus, 7n24
  The Aretology, 104n289, 111n324
  "Discourse", 3, 3n7, 22n70, 23, 23nn74–77, 23n79, 24, 24n81, 33nn92–93, 34n95
  Occasional Reflections upon Several Svbiects, 20, 25, 25n82, 52n55, 58n83, 62n97, 68n127, 135n439, 172n614
  "Preface", 20, 20nn55–56
Boyle, Roger, Lord Broghill and first Earl of Orrery (Rich's brother), 118n365
Boyle, Roger, Lord Broghill (first Earl of Orrery's son), 118n365
Boyle, Roger (Rich's grandfather), 7
Brentwood, Essex, 67n125
Bridge, William, *Christ and the Covenant*, 21n57
Browne, Thomas, *Pseudodoxia Epidemica*, 116n355
Burnet, Gilbert, 11, 21n63
Bury, Edward, *The Husbandmans Companion*, 3, 21n58, 23n76, 23n78, 26n83, 45n18, 68n127, 91n220, 132n431
Caesar, Julius, 154
Calamy, Edmund
  The Art of Divine Meditation, 2n6, 21n57, 22n67, 22n72
  An Exact Collection of Farewel Sermons, 56n73, 87n205
Calvin, Jean, *The Psalmes of Dauid and others*, 46n21
Canaan, 62n99, 98, 120n376
  heavenly, 31, 62, 62n99, 82

Canny, Nicholas, 7nn21–22
Carey, Mary, "Lady Carey's Meditations, & Poetry", 2n3
Catherine of Braganza (Charles II's wife), 12, 110n319
Cecil, Charles, Viscount Cranborne, 156n544
Cecil, Diana, Lady Cranborne (née Maxwell), 156, 156n544
Cecil, James, third Earl of Salisbury, 156n544
Cecil, Margaret (née Manners), 156n544
Certaine Sermons or Homilies Appointed to be Read in Churches In the Time of Queen Elizabeth I, 41n2
Charity, 18, 29, 67–68, 87, 90n218, 102, 107, 172, 172n613, 175–76. *See also* Mary Rich
Charles II, King of England, 12, 71n138
Charleton, Walter, *Physiologia Epicuro-Gassendo-Charltoniana*, 163n575
Chelsea garden, 16, 78, 78n169
Chelsea, Middlesex, 12, 26, 27, 31, 67, 67n125, 68–69, 68n127, 71n137, 164
Child or children of God, 26–27, 45–46, 55, 75–76, 97, 98–99, 101, 104, 153
Christ, 69, 69n129, 96, 96n246, 103n284, 109n315, 133n433, 152n519
  sleep in Jesus, 97n250, 101, 114, 153
  See also biblical figures
Christian conference, 17–18, 18n47, 29
Chrysostom, John, Saint, 127, 127n402
Church Militant, 161
Church Triumphant, 24, 103n284, 114, 161
Citron water, 107–8, 108n306
Clarendon House, 12
Clarke, Elizabeth, 4n12
Clarke, Samuel
  The Life & Death of Alexander the Great, 127n403
  The Lives of Thirty-Two English Divines, 87n205
Cleyton, Anne, 7
Cleyton, Randall, 7
Cockburn, John, *Fifteen Sermons*, 134–35n436

Coleman, Ann, 149n505
Coleman, Tom (Riches' servant), 34, 149, 149n505
Collins, An, *Divine Songs and Meditacions*, 2n3
Communion of saints, 49, 49n44
Company
  undesirable or harmful, 29–30, 50–51, 82–83, 86, 104, 107, 123, 126, 163
  worldly, 44, 47
Consumption, 26, 61, 61n94
Conversation and discourse of virtuous, saintly, 11, 17–18, 20, 21, 29–30, 50, 50–51, 64, 70, 76, 86–87, 89, 103–4, 123, 125, 135, 143, 179
Conversing or communion with God, 51, 61, 66, 76–77, 83, 85, 125, 154–55
Cords of God, 59–60, 60n88
  love, 60n88, 65, 174
  mercy, 59–60
Cox, John, 35
Cox, Margaret (née Walker), 35
Cranborne, Lady Diana, *see* Diana Cecil
Crawford, Patricia, 1n2
Crimson sin, 63, 136, 136n444, 174
Croker, Thomas Crofton, 36, 36n100
  Autobiography of Mary Countess of Warwick, 35n97, 36n102, 36–37
Cromwell, Oliver, 133n432
Culpeper, Nicholas, *Two Treatises: The First of Blood-letting*, 114n346
Cup of heavenly father, 32, 41, 41n3, 75, 105, 141, 162
Curtius Rufus, Quintus, *The Life and Death of Alexander the Great*, 127n403
Davy, Sarah, *Heaven Realiz'd*, 2n3
Death
  bad, 56, 177
  good, 32, 56–57, 92, 97
  measure of life, 122
  See also Mary Rich
Death of regenerate and pious, 56–57, 121–22
  young children, 90
Delaval, Elizabeth, *The Meditations*, 2n3, 4n11, 28, 28n88, 113n338

Deliberate meditation, 22, 24. *See also* meditation
Derision, laughter, scorn, 30, 55, 75–76, 86, 104, 106–7, 117–18, 163, 170
Devil, 30, 69, 89, 111, 115, 116, 142, 143, 151, 166, 166n585. *See also* Satan
Digby, Kenelm, *Choice and Experimented Receipts in Physick and Chirurgery*, 112–13n333
Disciples
  Christian, 31, 150–51
  evangelical, 30
  experienced, 103–4
  young, 177, 179
Discourse
  beneficial for self and others, 30, 33, 70n134, 71n137, 76, 86, 107, 135, 143, 179
  See also Christian conference
Dissolve with Christ, 15, 97, 97n253, 101, 101n277, 130, 154
Divine gusto, 66, 83, 107–8, 170
Douay-Rheims Bible, 97n253
Durdans (Durdens), Epsom, Surrey, 71, 71n137
E., T. (Edgar, Thomas[?]), *The Lawes Resolvtions of Womens Rights*, 16, 16n43
Educating young, 112, 137, 142, 161
Edwards, John
  A Brief View of the Mistakes about Happiness, 119n371
  The Doctrin [sic] of Faith and Justification, 103n286
Egerton, Elizabeth, Countess of Bridgewater, 4n11
  "Devotional Pieces", 1n2, 2n3, 4n11
Eliza's Babes: or The Virgin's Offering, 2n3
Epicurism, 75
Epicvrvs's Morals, 93n231
Epping, Essex, 133n432
Epsom, Surrey, 13, 71n137
Evangelical
  repentance, *see* repentance
  sorrow, *see* sorrow
  work, 132

Evelyn, John, 71n138
  The Diary, 71nn137–38, 110n319
  Sylva, Or a Discourse of Forest-trees, 100n270
Everard, Frances, 17
Everard, John, *The Gospel-Treasury Opened*, 88n211, 133n433
Everard, Richard, 17
Everard, Richard (Richard Everard's son), 17
Experimentally, 31, 88, 88n211, 103, 141, 142–43, 178, 179
  experimental divinity, 103, 103n287
Eye of faith, 103, 103n284, 108n314, 111, 117, 128, 149, 150
  prospective glass of faith, 31, 62, 62n97, 67n99, 108n314, 128
  spectacles of faith, 108
Ezell, Margaret, 4n11
Featley, John, *A Fountaine of Teares*, 113n337
Fell Smith, Charlotte, 5n16, 5–6n18, 9n29, 17n46, 35n97, 78n169, 133n432, 149n505, 154n530
Fenton, Geoffrey, 7
Finch, Anne (née Hatton), 85n199
Finch, Daniel, 85n199
Finch, Elizabeth (née Harvey, Essex Rich's mother-in-law), 17–18, 85n199
Finch, Essex (née Rich), 19n50, 85n199, 106n298, 155n538. *See also* Essex Rich
Finch, Heneage, 85n199
Fine, 65, 65n116
Fire of devotion, 42, 49–50, 143
Flavel, John
  Husbandry Spiritualized, 3, 43n11, 161n568, 172n614
  The Method of Grace, 41n2
  The Touchstone of Sincerity, 130n424
  Two Treatises: The first of Fear, 93n231
Fountain
  of Judah and Jerusalem, 26, 80, 80n179, 104, 122
  of life, 44n14, 53n56, 53n60, 138
  of mercy, 44, 53
  sealed, 53, 53n60
Franklin, Richard, 80n180

Fuller, Francis, *A Treatise of Faith and Repentance*, 17n45
Fuller, Thomas
  Good Thoughts in Bad Times, 109n316
  Good Thoughts in Bad Times. Together with Good Thoughts in Worse Times, 50n48, 166n587
  The Holy State, 111n324
Garden of Babylon, 98n260, 127, 127n403
Gauden, John, *The Whole Duty of a Communicant*, 100n268
Gearing, William, *The Mount of Holy Meditation*, 3n6, 21n57, 22n67, 45n18
Geneva Bible, 84n192
Gifford, George, 18, 33, 93n235, 171n607
God's shining countenance, 26, 46, 76, 78, 78–79, 89, 97, 108, 110, 148
Gomorrah, 136n445
Gouge, Thomas
  Christian Directions, 22n67
  God's Call to England, 60n88
  A Word to Sinners, And a Word to Saints, 71n140
Gouge, William, *A Learned and Very Useful Commentary on the Whole Epistle to the Hebrewes*, 88n207
Grace
  converting, 10, 75
  free, 31, 43, 53, 154
  grow in, 68, 92, 115, 131
  promise of, 131
  sincere, 130, 130n424
  spirit, 58, 58n84
  supporting, 75
  true, 130n424
  unmerited, 31, 154
Gray, Andrew, *The Mystery of Faith Opened up*, 87n205
Greatrakes, Valentine, 13n40
Grey, Cecilia (née Wentworth), 133n432
Grey, Ford, 133n432
Grey, Ralph, 133n432
Grey, William, first Baron Grey of Warke, 133, 133n432
Gurdon, Anne (née Woodrooffe, William's daughter), 36, 36n102

Hale, Matthew, Lord Chief Justice, 17
Halkett, Anne, 2n3, 4n11
Hall, Joseph, 2, 3, 4n11, 20, 23
  The Art of Divine Meditation, 2, 2n5, 20, 21, 21nn58–59, 21–22, 22n66, 22n68, 22n71, 23, 23n75, 60n90
  Occasional Meditations, 2, 3, 20, 26n83, 27, 27nn84–85, 28, 28n87, 29, 29nn89–90, 52n55, 58n83, 67–68n127, 70n134, 74n154, 81n181, 91n220, 107n304, 109n316, 113n338, 115n351
Hall, Thomas, *A Practical and Polemical Commentary*, 46n21
Hamilton, James (Claneboye's son and Rich's suitor), 7
Hamilton, James, first Viscount Claneboye, 7
Hamilton, Jane (née Philipps), 7
Hartlib, Samuel, *The Reformed Commonwealth of Bees*, 71n138
Hartman, George, *The Family Physitian*, 108n306
Health
  physical, 96, 139
  spiritual, 139
Heavenly
  crown, 26, 31, 150, 153, 154
  father, 29, 41, 55, 59, 75, 79, 104, 105, 109, 162, 174
  Jerusalem, 31, 79, 84–85, 91, 103, 109, 116, 129
  mindedness, 33, 33n92, 92
  See also Canaan
Heliodorus, bishop of Antinum, 127n402
Hell, 19, 31, 95, 99, 106, 157, 163, 165, 170, 170n603
Henchman, Henfrey, bishop of London, 11
Herbert, Charles, 149n501
Herbert, George, 69n130, 82n186
Herringham, William, 36, 36n102
Hildersam, Arthur, *CLII Lectvres Vpon Psalme LI*, 84n192
Hill, Thomas, *The Spring of Strengthning Grace In the Rock of Ages*, 133–34n433
Holbech, Martin, 11

Holy Cross Church, Felsted, Essex, 19
Holy Ghost, 21, 90n218, 98–99n262, 103, 151, 152, 152n516
House of Clay, 42, 60, 74, 96, 119, 147, 157, 160
Howard, Elizabeth (née Home), 118n365
Howard, Theophilus, second Earl of Suffolk, 118n365
Hyde, Anne, Duchess of York, 12, 12n39
Hyde, Edward, first Earl of Clarendon, 12, 12n39
  The History of the Rebellion, 9n30, 12n37
Hyde, Henrietta (née Boyle; Rich's niece, daughter of the first Earl of Burlington), 12n39
Hyde, Laurence, 12n39
Hypocrisy, 53, 54, 166
Jackson, Arthur, *Annotations Upon The five Books, immediately following the Historicall Part of the Old Testament*, 84n192
Jacob's ladder, 23–24
Janeway, John, 11
Jerome, Saint, 127n402
Jerusalem, 96n246
  See also fountain of, heavenly
Jones, Katherine, Viscountess Ranelagh (née Boyle, Rich's sister), 10, 12, 35, 50, 50n50
Jordan, 31, 62, 62n99, 79
Journey to heaven, 31, 46n21, 50, 55, 66, 66n122, 67, 82, 91, 108, 109, 128, 129, 150, 157, 177
Judah
  sins of, 95
  tribe or house of, 54, 104
  See also fountain of
Ken, Thomas, *The Works*, 90n218
King of Terrors, 93, 93n231, 130
Kingdom by storm or violence, 113, 113n335, 128, 128n407, 144
L'Estrange, Roger, *Fables, of Aesop*, 43n11
Lake, Arthur, 120n378
Lake, Frances (née Cheke), 120n378
Lake, Lancelot, 120–21, 121n378

Index

Lake, Lettice (née Rich, Charles Rich's aunt), 120n378
Lake, Mary (née Rider), 34, 120, 120n378
Lake, Thomas, 120n378
Land of promise, 31, 62n99, 79, 79n175, 108
Last Judgment, 19, 22, 24
Lead, Jane, *The Revelation of Revelations*, 90n218
Leake, Frances, Countess of Scarsdale (née Rich, Charles Rich's sister), 19n50
Legal repentance, *see* repentance
Leighs, Essex, 9, 10, 11, 17, 19, 31, 33, 34, 67n125, 110n319, 157, 157n548, 165n581
Leighs estate [Priory], 8–9, 8n29, 11, 12, 20, 66, 144
  heirs of, 11, 19n50, 34, 148n501
  parliament aid, 17, 17n46
Leighton, Robert, *A Practical Commentary upon the First Epistle General of St. Peter*, 18n47
Lesly, John, *An Epithrene*, 165n582
Lewalski, Barbara K., 1n2, 20n54
Life estate or tenancy, 148–49, 149n502, 158, 158n552
Lincoln's Inn Field residence, 12
Lowther, An (née Parsons), 6n20
Lucas, Richard, 70n134
Luther, Martin, 106, 106n298
Lyttelton, Charles, 13
Maddison, R. E. W., 7n23
Marriage of lamb, 108, 152, 161
Martz, Louis L., 20n54
Mascuch, Michael, 5n14
Mason, John, *The Midnight-cry*, 53n57
Mather, Cotton, *Small Offers Towards the Service of the Tabernacle in the Wilderness*, 135n436
Maxwell, Elizabeth (née Besyne), 156n544
Maxwell, James, Earl of Dirletoun, 156n544
McChartie, Charles, 6n20
Meditation, 20–24
  elevating, 22, 22n70, 60, 60n92, 85n197, 102, 178
  heavenly, 85n197, 102, 125

  refreshing hours, 17, 44, 51, 161
  rekindling devotion and affections, 42–43, 44, 47, 51, 65, 77, 85n197, 90, 102, 161, 178
  See also deliberate, occasional, and Mary Rich
Melanchthon, Philipp, 106n298
Mendelson, Sara Heller, 1n2, 5–6n18, 6n20, 10n34, 35n97
Milton, John, *Paradise Lost*, 69n129
Montagu, Anne (née Rich, Charles Rich's sister and mother of Robert Montagu), 12, 12n38, 19n50, 148n501
Montagu, Anne (née Yelverton), 149n501
Montagu, Charles, Duke of Manchester, 149n501
Montagu, Edward, second Earl of Manchester, 12, 148n501
Montagu, Robert, third Earl of Manchester, 19n50, 34, 148–49, 149n501
Montagu, William, 149n501
Morant, Philip, *The History and Antiquities Of the County of Essex*, 8–9n29, 19n50, 133n432, 149n501
Mordaunt, Elizabeth, Countess of, 17n45
Mount Nebo, 31, 32, 62, 62n99, 128
Nero Claudius Caesar, 104n289
New Jerusalem, 62n99, 79n175
Occasional meditation, 1–3, 20, 22–24. *See also* meditation
Ophir, 118, 118n367
Opium, 32, 143, 143n471, 146
Orange water, 112–13, 113n333
Ordinance, 47, 47n31, 48, 52, 63, 75, 95, 160, 169, 169–70, 176–77
Owen, Charles, *Hymns Sacred to the Lord's-Table*, 161n568
Painted sepulcher, 53, 73, 166
Palgrave, Mary E., 35n97
Park stand at Leighs, 87n206, 154, 154n530
Patience, 14, 28, 32–33, 42, 75, 84, 84n192, 93, 101, 105, 124, 145, 146–47, 155, 164, 164n580, 168
  fortitude, 29, 32, 75, 146
Patrick, Simon, 11

Penitential tears, 30, 65, 66, 69, 74, 88, 89, 99, 163
Godly sorrow, 49, 51, 88, 99
Peppercorns, 145, 145n479
Pepys, Samuel, *Diary*, 68n127, 71n138
Perkins, William, *Two Treatises. The first, Of the Nature and Practice of Repentance*, 30n91
Pharisaical, 30, 81–82, 128–29
Physical beauty and aging, 32–33, 73–74, 119, 147
Physician of souls, 41, 41n2, 61, 115
  spiritual, 100, 139, 170
Pilgrimage, 31, 88, 108
Pious or excellent Christian, 32, 56, 70, 75, 76, 81, 92, 121, 126–27, 128
Pisgah, 62n99
Plague, 28–29, 112n333, 113–14, 114n338
Playford, John, *An Introduction to the Skill of Musick*, 163n575
Pliny the Elder, *The Historie of the World*, 104n289
Plutarch, *Plutarch's Lives of the Noble Grecians and Romanes*, 127n403
Porter, Roy and Dorothy, 143n471
Praise, 33, 43–44, 85, 132, 138–39, 140, 145, 151, 152, 160, 178
Preston, John, 87n205
Professors of religion or faith, 30, 32, 151
  formal, 166, 176
  proud, 176
  young, 150–51
Psalmist, 33, 47, 152
  man after God's heart, 86–87, 124, 131, 146–47
  See also David
The Psalter of David, 92n228
The Queens Closet Opened, 108n306
A Queens Delight, 108n306
Ranew, Nathanael, 20, 35
  Solitude Improved by Divine Meditation, 3n10, 20–21, 21nn57–58, 21n60, 22, 22nn70–71, 23n73, 23n76, 24, 24n80, 97n253

Ranew, Nathanael (Ranew's son), 35, 175, 175n625
Ranger, Terence O., 7nn21–22
Regenerate, 75, 101, 156, 163
Repentance
  deathbed, 177
  evangelical and legal, 30, 30n91, 33, 98–99, 99n262, 164–65, 165n581
Reputation, 55–56
Retirement, 12, 42, 50–51, 82–83, 105, 132–33, 154. *See also* solitude
Reversion, 149, 149n502
Reynolds, Edward, *True Gain, Opened in a Sermon*, 135n436
Reynolds, Lancelot, 27
  Spiritvall Intervals, Or The Soules Exercise, 3, 27, 27n85, 57n77, 70n134, 81n181
Rich, Anne (née Cavendish, wife of Rich's son), 12
Rich, Anne (née Montagu, wife of fifth Earl of Warwick), 12n38
Rich, Anne (Rich's niece), 11, 85n199. *See also* Anne Barrington
Rich, Charles, fourth Earl of Warwick (Rich's husband), 8, 9, 13, 24–25, 134
  death, 15–16, 28, 32, 157
  will, 17, 19n50
  anniversary commemoration, 16
  death of son, 12–13
  ill temper and bitterness, 14, 14n41, 15, 28, 136, 136n440
  illness, 13, 13n40, 14–15, 15n42, 16
  gout, 13, 71n137
  inherits title, 11
  marriage, 8, 8n27
  marriage portion, 8, 8n28
  parliamentary and state service, 12, 12n37
Rich, Charles (Rich's son), 130
  birth, 9
  death, 12–13, 24–25, 32, 130, 130n419, 134
  anniversary commemoration, 13, 134n434
  illness, 9–10, 12

Rich, Eleanor (née Wortley, third wife of second Earl of Warwick), 5, 9
Rich, Elizabeth (Rich's daughter), 9
Rich, Essex (Rich's niece), 11, 17, 26, 85, 85n199, 107n305. *See also* Essex Finch
Rich, Hatton (Charles Rich's brother), 14
Rich, Henry, first Earl of Holland, 19n50
Rich, Mary, Countess of Warwick, 4n11, 5n16, 7n24, 20, 21, 85n197, 85n200, 106n298, 110n319, 119n371, 127n403, 137n447, 154n530, 155n538
  birth, 6, 6n20
  charity, 18, 19, 24, 94n236. *See also* charity
  Countess of Warwick, 11
  daughter Elizabeth's death, 9
  death and burial, 19
    contemplation of her death, 18–19, 24, 26, 57, 92, 93, 95, 96, 116, 129–30, 134, 153–54, 156–57
  early years of vanity, 9, 16–17, 178
  executrix, 17, 17n46
  failure to have another child, 13
  father Richard Boyle, relation with, 6, 7–8
  godparent, 133n432, 155n538
  guardian of nieces, 11, 80n180
  husband Charles
    concern for his soul, 14–15
    death, 15–16, 28, 28n86, 157
    commemoration, 16
    disputes with, 14–15
    illness, 13–15
    passionate and ill temper, 14–15, 136, 136n440
  illness, 41–42, 96, 96n249, 99–100
  marriage, 8, 8n27
    marriage portion, 8, 8n28
    married life at Leighs and London, 8–9
  melancholy, 15
  mother's death, 7n24
  religious conversion, 9–10
    and affiliation, 10–11, 11n34
  Self-reproach and abasement, 16, 18, 27, 63, 91–92, 104–5, 115, 122, 125, 128–29, 136n445, 145–46, 174
  son Charles
    birth and illness, 9–10
    death, 12–13, 13, 134
    anniversary commemoration, 13, 24–25, 134n434
  "Diary", 5, 6, 9, 11, 12, 13, 14, 15, 16, 17, 17n46, 18, 19, 24, 25–26, 27, 28, 28n86, 33, 35n97, 36n98, 41n3, 44n14, 46n21, 58n83, 60n88, 60n90, 62n99, 62–63n102, 66n119, 66n122, 67n123, 67n125, 70n134, 71n137, 78n171, 80n179, 82n186, 83n189, 88n211, 91n221, 93n231, 93n235, 96n249, 99n265, 102n281, 103n284, 105–6n297, 106n298, 113n335, 118n365, 119n370, 126n399, 128n407, 133n432, 134n433, 136n440, 136n445, 141n465, 148n501, 149n505, 154nn530–531, 155n538, 157n548, 161n568, 165nn581–582, 167n589, 171n607
  Meditations
    birthday, 19
    excerpted, 36n98
    influenced by, 20
    on husband, 27–28, 136–37
    on son, 24–25, 134
    practice, 3–4, 23, 25–29, 33–34
    rereading, 4, 19, 33, 37
    writing, 23, 119n370
  "A most pious Letter", 125n398
  "Rules for holy living", 71n137, 82n186
  "Some Specialties In the life of M Warwicke", 5, 5n13, 6, 6n20, 7–13, 80n180, 85n199
Rich, Mary (Rich's niece), 11, 17, 85n199, 107n305. *See also* Mary St John
Rich, Richard, first Baron, 8
Rich, Robert, second Earl of Holland and fifth Earl of Warwick, 12n38, 19n50
Rich, Robert, second Earl of Warwick (Rich's father-in-law), 5, 8, 8n27, 8–9, 9n30, 10, 11, 20, 68n127, 133n432, 148n501
Rich, Robert, third Earl of Warwick (Rich's brother-in-law), 11, 80n180, 85n199

Rich, Susan (née Halliday, second wife of second Earl of Warwick), 8, 9
River Ter, 9n29, 10
Roberts, Francis, *The True Way to the Tree of Life*, 53n57
Robartes, John, first Earl of Radnor, 35n97, 68n127, 133n432
Robartes, Letitia Isabella (née Smith, Charles Rich's cousin), 26, 68n127
Robartes, Lucy (née Rich, Charles Rich's sister), 19n50
Rock of Ages, 133–34, 134n433
Rogers, Richard
 The Practice of Christianitie, 2n6, 22n67, 22n71
 Seaven Treatises, 22n70
Rutherford, Samuel
 Christ Dying and Drawing Sinners to Himselfe, 152n519
 Joshua Redivivus, 161n568
Salmon, William, *The Family-Dictionary; Or, Houshold Companion*, 108n306, 112n333
Satan, 54, 58, 111
 grand or great enemy, 55, 57, 66, 76, 110, 117, 124, 129, 140
 See also devil
Satanic snares, 55, 55n70, 57, 57n78, 58, 111, 116, 129
Savior, 49, 77, 96, 99, 100, 113, 122, 127, 136
Scarifying, 114, 114n346
Scoular, Kitty W., 74n154
Shakespeare, William, *Henry IV, Part Two*, 153, 153n523
Sheffield, Edmund, second Duke of Buckingham and Normanby, 19n50, 149n501
Sheldon, Gilbert, Archbishop of Canterbury, 11
Shepard, Thomas, *The Parable of the Ten Virgins Opened & Applied*, 46n21
Sibbes, Richard, *Divine Meditations and Holy Contemplations*, 21, 21n61
Sloane, Hans, 78n169

Smallpox, 12
Smith, George, *A Compleat Body of Distilling*, 107–8n306
Smith, Isabella (née Rich, Charles Rich's aunt), 68n127
Smith, John, 68n127
Smythe, Mary, 6n20
Sodom, 91, 136, 136n445
Solitude, 12, 16, 19, 24, 42, 66, 76, 83, 125. *See also* retirement
Sorrow
 godly, 49, 51, 88
 legal and evangelical, 98–99, 98n262, 165
 See also repentance
The Spiritual Bee, 163n575
Spiritual sloth, 17, 139
Spurr, John, 10–11n35
Spurstowe, William, 34
 The Spiritual Chymist, 34, 34n94, 52n55, 58n83, 144n472, 145n479
St John, Mary (née Rich), 18, 19n50. *See also* Mary Rich (Rich's niece)
St Nicholas Church, Shepperton, Middlesex, 8, 8n27
Stalbridge House, Dorset, 7, 7n23
Stillingfleet, Edward, 11
Stone, Lawrence, 10n33
Stony heart, 24, 48–49, 49, 64
 frozen, 29, 48–49, 49, 107, 143
 hard, 63, 64, 69, 99, 139
Straight and narrow gate, 31, 67, 67n123, 129n414
Straight path, 67, 67n123, 108, 157
 and holy, 94, 103, 117, 179
Sun of righteousness, 32, 46, 78, 88, 108, 117, 140, 147–48, 157
Surety, 95, 95n243
Swan, John, *Specvlvm Mundi*, 163n575
Swinnock, George, *The Christian-Mans Calling*, 3n6, 33n92, 62n99, 154n531
Tarentism, 162–63, 163n575
Taylor, Jeremy
 "Of Meditation", 21, 21n64
 The Rule and Exercises of Holy Living, 60n88

Taylor, Thomas
  Meditations From The Creatures, 2n6, 23n76
  The Practice of Repentance, 99n262
Tears and weeping, 24, 27, 28, 51, 63, 63n109, 113, 114, 114n343, 136. See also penitential tears, sorrow
Tenants at will, 160, 160n562
Thames River, 26, 31, 164
Theopneustos, 98n258
Thornton, Alice, *The Autobiography*, 2n3
Tilley, Morris Palmer, 57n79, 64n110
Tillotson, John, "Sermon LVII", 111n323
Tonbridge, Kent, 13
Toplady, Augustus Montague, 133n433
Traherne, Philip, *The Soul's Communion With her Savior*, 87n205
Travitsky, Betty, 1n2
Tumsole, 139–40, 140n459
Unmerited goodness, 136
  love, 65, 102, 141
  mercy, 43, 63, 96, 98
  See also grace
Unregenerate, 29, 30, 65, 75, 76, 81–82, 88, 89, 126, 154, 156, 163
Ussher, James, 21, 21n63
  A Method for Meditation, 21, 21n63, 22n71
Valley of tears, 26, 45–46, 46n21, 62, 108, 141, 161
Vanity, 5, 9, 12, 16–17, 19, 58n83, 64, 119, 119n371, 142–43, 178
Walk with God, 21, 31, 49, 49n45, 83, 178
Walker, Anthony, 10, 14, 19, 35, 175n625
  Eureka, Eureka, 1n1, 2, 2n4, 5, 5n17, 10, 10n34, 10–11n35, 18, 18n49, 19nn50–51, 19n53, 36n101, 82n186, 85n200, 94n236, 125n398, 160n564, 164n579, 165n583, 166n587, 167n589, 168n591, 168n593, 170n602, 171n605, 175n625
  Leez Lachrymans, 14, 14n41
Warwick House, 14, 19n50, 157n548
Watson, Thomas
  A Body of Practical Divinity, 87n205, 93n231, 170n603

A Christian On the Mount, 2–3n6, 22n67, 45n18
The Doctrine of Repentance, 30n91
The Duty of Self-denial Briefly Opened and Urged, 127n402
The Godly Mans Picture, 166n585
Heaven Taken by Storm, 129n412
A Pastors Love Expressed to a Loving People, 56n73
Wentworth, John, 133n432
White Hart Inn, 67n125
White, Thomas, *A Method and Instructions for the Art of Divine Meditation*, 22n72, 23, 23n76, 23n78
Whitehall Banqueting House, 12
Wilcox, Helen, 4n12
Wilderness retreat, 10, 12, 16, 24, 24–25, 27, 59, 66–67, 67n119, 87n206, 134, 172
Wilkins, John, 71n138
Wilkinson, Henry, 11, 33, 165nn581–582
Willis, Thomas, *An Essay of the Pathology of the Brain and Nervous Stock*, 163n575
Wilmot, John, second Earl of Rochester, 170n603
Wilson, Thomas, *A Complete Christian Dictionary*, 44n16, 47n31, 116n353
Wings of affection, 102
  devotion, 60–61, 60n92
  meditation, 22n70, 60n92
  protection or healing, 46, 54, 78, 147–48
Woodrooffe, Anne (William's mother), 19, 19n52, 35n96
"A Copy of what my good Mother wrote upon ye Death of Lady Warwick", 19, 19n52, 35n96
Woodrooffe, John (William's son), 36n102
Woodrooffe, Nathaniel George, 36, 36n100
Woodrooffe, Thomas (Riches' chaplain and William's father), 11, 19n52, 35, 35n97
Woodrooffe, Thomas (William's brother), 35, 35n97
Woodrooffe, Thomas (William's grandson and Gurdon's executor), 36, 36n102

Woodrooffe, William, 15n42, 19n52, 35, 35n97, 35–36, 36n99, 36n102, 37, 39, 41n1, 50n50, 66n122, 70n134, 76n164, 80n180, 87n206, 89n213, 93n233, 124n392, 127n402, 144n475, 145n480, 146n485, 149n504, 150n508, 169n600, 185, 186, 187, 196

Woolley, Hannah, *The Accomplisht Ladys Delight*, 113n333

Works (good), 11, 31, 32, 49, 75, 86, 92, 93, 94n240, 101–2, 107, 121, 139, 179

Worthington, John, *The Great Duty of Self-Resignation to the Divine Will*, 84n192

Wray, Ramona, 6n18

Youghal, Ireland, 6, 6n20